Object-Oriented
Information Engineering

Object-Oriented Information Engineering

Analysis, Design, and
Implementation

Stephen Montgomery

AP PROFESSIONAL
A Division of Harcourt Brace & Company

Boston   San Diego   New York
London   Sydney   Tokyo   Toronto

AP PROFESSIONAL
955 Massachusetts Avenue, Cambridge, MA 02139

An imprint of ACADEMIC PRESS, INC.
A Division of HARCOURT BRACE & COMPANY

United Kingdom Edition published by
ACADEMIC PRESS LIMITED
24–28 Oval Road, London NW1 7DX

Library of Congress Cataloging-in-Publication Data

Montgomery, Stephen.
  Object-oriented information engineering: analysis, design, and
implementation / Stephen Montgomery.
        p.   cm.
  Includes bibliographical references and index.
  ISBN 0-12-505040-2 (alk. paper)
  1. Object-oriented databases. 2. Systems engineering. I. Title.
QA76.9.D3M649   1994
658.4'038'0285421—dc20   93-43044
                                                    CIP

Printed in the United States of America
94 95 96 97 98 ML 9 8 7 6 5 4 3 2 1

Contents

14 Redesigning Existing Systems for the Future 183

15 Programming Languages 213

Preface

Object orientation is becoming very important to application developers now that major vendors such as IBM, Apple, Hewlett-Packard, Microsoft, Borland and others are becoming heavily involved with object-oriented technologies. Structured analysis and design techniques are well established for building traditional systems, but object-oriented development still has few good techniques.

The two seemingly separate worlds of traditional development and object-oriented development need not be separated at all. Many techniques appearing in object-oriented literature have close parallels in more traditional structured techniques, which themselves are new to many developers. This book shows the reader how to integrate the two into a basic framework for developing advanced information systems.

In the first two chapters, the reader is exposed to the basic concepts of information engineering and object orientation. From the third chapter on, an integrated view of the two approaches is presented. Although information engineering is the foundation for business planning and analysis, the emphasis on object orientation in analysis and design has become the primary approach in implementation.

A strong emphasis is placed on analysis in this book. I feel that this is the development phase where the transition to object orientation can best be introduced to development projects. Design can proceed in a traditional fashion, but I discourage this because I present an object-oriented design approach.

Many readers will still need to design and implement systems in an information engineering environment, but I assume that this approach is somewhat understood. Object orientation is lacking in current development approaches, and information engineering is no exception. The later chapters address the need for extending existing approaches with object orientation and give many examples of how this extension can be accomplished.

The last portion of the book deals with the choices that must be made when it comes to implementing an object-oriented design. Object-oriented languages and database management systems are not required in order to implement a design successfully, but they can greatly ease the burden of doing so. I present the most likely program and database development options as a guide to build object-oriented systems or to migrate existing systems to more object-oriented ones.

1

What Is Information Engineering?

1.1 OVERVIEW OF INFORMATION ENGINEERING

The term "information engineering" was coined by Clive Finkelstein in the early 1980s and popularized by James Martin in the mid- and late-1980s. The term refers to an integrated set of methodologies for creating and operating information systems. Information engineering relies upon fully normalized data models of information in a business enterprise. Such models are maintained in an automated system that uses workstation tools to build business applications that use enterprise data. The modeling tools support enterprise planning, business analysis, business and technical design and building and maintaining the resulting information systems. A major objective of the information engineering approach to system development is avoidance of common development and maintenance problems.

Enterprise-Wide Approach

One concept that separates information engineering from many other system development approaches is the application of structured development techniques to an entire business enterprise, not just a single development project or group of projects. The enterprise focus creates integrated data and process models that form the basis of separate systems developed together into a common architecture or framework.

Engineering Approach

Information engineering can also be contrasted with software engineering. Software engineering focuses on structured techniques for specifying, designing and constructing application programs. Information engineering, on the other hand, focuses on information that is stored and maintained by various application programs. It also is concerned with structured analysis and programming, but embraces development using nonprocedural languages, specification languages, application generators and computer-assisted design (CAD) in order to minimize development effort.

Data Sharing

Data concepts, rather than programming ones, form the basic premise of information engineering. Data are stored and maintained by processes that create, modify and delete the data. All data in an enterprise should be captured and recorded with controls on data accuracy and format. Data are seen as central to information system development because data may be used in several information systems concurrently, stored in different ways, distributed and often updated and modified by way of network links and nodes.

   Another basic premise of information engineering is that data types do not change often. Entity types do not usually change, but new types may occasionally be added. Attributes that describe entity types do not often change, either. The instances of entity types and the values of the corresponding attributes will change often but the basic structure of the data model does not change.

Automated Tools

One development that makes information engineering feasible is the creation of advanced development tools for business systems planning, analysis, design and construction. In order to build elaborate, extensive networks of integrated information systems, we need automated support in order to handle the complexity and speed up routine tasks. We not only can change the way that systems are generated but also handle many more types and numbers of systems. Organizations must automate not only the management of business information but the automation of the development of these systems.

Structured development techniques have been with us since the 1970s. Comprehensive tools for computer-assisted software engineering (CASE) are now widely available that support structured development techniques. Development as described in this book would not be possible without such automated support. This support allows the development of engineered systems based on comprehensive strategic information planning.

1.2 THE PHASES OF INFORMATION ENGINEERING

Today several versions of Clive Finkelstein's and of James Martin's concepts of information engineering exist. Finkelstein[1] describes three broad stages of information engineering:

Analysis Phase
  1. Project Scope Stage
  2. Strategic Modeling Stage
  3. Tactical Modeling Stage
  4. Operations Modeling Stage
Design Phase
  1. Strategic Design
  2. Tactical Design
  3. Operational Design
Generation Phase
  1. Implementation Strategies
  2. Systems Generation

Martin, on the other hand, discusses four broad phases of information engineering:[2]

Planning Phase

Analysis Phase

Design Phase

Construction Phase

In practice the analysis phase and design phase are subdivided into two or more stages.

Finkelstein's Information Engineering Approach

Analysis Phase

The analysis phase progressively defines data and information derived from the data required at the strategic and at the tactical management levels of an organization. It is subdivided into four stages:

1. Project Scope
2. Strategic Modeling
3. Tactical Modeling
4. Operations Modeling

Project scope stage   This prepares a team for a formal information engineering study and identifies a project area for the study. Management support and sponsorship are lined up and experienced system users made available to the project team. The system users are needed to provide vital knowledge about relevant data and expert business rules. Project plans are established, along with tasks, milestones and funding. Available documentation is identified and project personnel trained in strategic and tactical modeling.

Strategic modeling stage   This consists of strategic modeling, strategic objectives modeling and strategic refinement.

Strategic modeling sets strategic directions with management responsible for the project area. It analyzes strategic statements and directions set for the future. Broad strategic data of interest to management are identified along with operation parts of the organization that generate tactical data on which strategic data are based.

Strategic objectives modeling reviews goals and objectives, policies and concerns and issues. It determines performance criteria for performance monitoring and identifies strategic data for measurement of performance criteria. Finally, it establishes performance ranges and controls for decision early warning.

Strategic refinement progressively refines strategic data using a formal approach, identifies standard terminology and expert rules at the strategic level and produces strategic data models that represent a strategic blueprint for management and a basis for applying tactical modeling.

Tactical modeling stage   This consists of tactical modeling, tactical objectives modeling and tactical refinement. Tactical modeling:

- identifies the tactical environment with middle and operational management,
- expands strategic data models based on detailed analysis of markets, products, services and channels in key functional areas of the project area and
- identifies detailed tactical data of interest to middle and operational management and data used to derive strategic data of interest to top management.

Tactical objectives modeling:

- examines management objectives at various levels in the project area,
- progressively refines objectives, strategies and tactics,
- further refines strategies for later detailed definition of expert rules,
- identifies data necessary to manage achievement of objectives and
- identifies exception reports and decision triggers at the tactical level.

Tactical refinement:

- progressively refines tactical data using a formal approach applied against each functional area separately,
- establishes standard terminology and expert rules at the tactical level and
- produces tactical data models, which form a detailed blueprint of the organization.

Operations modeling stage This consists of current systems modeling, operational objectives modeling and operational refinement. Current system modeling:

- is optionally used with tactical modeling for current manual or automated systems or packages needed for the future and
- formally cross-checks data presently used in existing source documents, reports, inquiries, ledgers and computer files against tactical data models.

Operational objectives modeling:

- examines operational objectives in the project area,
- identifies data necessary to manage achievement of objectives and

- identifies exception reports and decision triggers and the operational level.

Operational refinement:

- progressively refines operational data for each functional area separately,
- establishes standard terminology and expert rules at the operational level and
- produces operational data models for day-to-day operation of the organization.

Design Phase

The design phase uses an expert design dictionary to automate development. It is comprised of strategic design, tactical design and operational design.

Strategic design This places strategic data identified in the analysis phase and enters them into an expert design dictionary. This dictionary fully automates the development process, checking for consistency and completeness of definitions. It identifies strategic data common across several data models when these exist and automatically combines common data into an integrated strategic model.

Tactical and operational design This incorporate tactical models, tactical objectives models and tactical refinements, created in functional areas during analysis, into the design dictionary. These data, perhaps extended to operational data in the operations modeling stage, are checked for consistency and completeness. Tactical and operational data models for each functional area are analyzed and common data are combined into integrated tactical and operational models.

Generation Phase

After strategic, tactical and operational designs have been completed, integrated data models are fed into system generator tools to implement the design blueprints. Generation defines implementation strategies for each part of the integrated strategic and tactical models and determines:

- hardware
- software

- communication facilities
- physical systems design
- development of systems

Data, reports and systems implementation details are described in physical terms.

Martin's Information Engineering Approach

Planning Phase

Planning refers to strategic planning for data, activities and technology, based on the strategic planning of an organization. During this phase, top management must work together with information systems executives to development an overall strategic vision that views how future technology could affect the organization, its products or services and its goals and objectives.

Analysis Phase

Analysis builds conceptual models that describe the fundamental data required to operate an organization, activities that use these data and the technologies used to store, maintain and manipulate the data. The focus during this phase is on what needs to be done, not how these requirements are to be met by systems. A migration plan will be developed to depict how the organization will evolve from existing applications to a fully engineered, integrated systems environment.

Design Phase

This phase develops detailed designs for data, systems that interact with data and hardware and software technologies that are to be used. Here is where the ways that the system requirements, which were defined during analysis, are defined in detailed business terms. Design is not concerned with the implementation details of the systems to be generated, except for the user interfaces.

Construction Phase

Construction is concerned with activities related to the building of physical databases and application program systems that access these databases using specific hardware and software tools. This phase defines the files, database systems, program structures, technical designs and other implementation details.

1.3   OBJECT-ORIENTED INFORMATION ENGINEERING

With an object-oriented modeling and developing environment, information engineering models change to models of objects. The basic philosophy and approach of information engineering remain the same. Enterprise systems are still viewed as ones that share data, are enterprise-wide (not application-wide), are end-user oriented and make heavy use of CASE tools and methods.

To create complex collections of integrated information systems, models of an enterprise must still be constructed. Now, however, the focus here is on identifying object types in the enterprise, the ways that these object types interrelate and what events must occur in order to change the state of objects. Models are built in greater detail as business areas are analyzed in greater detail. We want to build separate systems that relate to the same business model and that work together efficiently.

With object-oriented information engineering, enterprise models are created and extended into business area models to create systems that relate to the models. Use of entity models evolves to use of object models. With traditional information engineering, entity models are separated from processes that operate on data structures in the entity models. With object-oriented information engineering, object models combine processes (as operations or methods) with the data structures to form object classes.

In the past, traditional information engineering has focused on detailed models of entity types, subtypes and supertypes across an enterprise. A set of matrix diagrams connects processes to entity types in planning, and attributed data flow diagram objects and the associated mini-spec action diagrams connect process models to the underlying attributed entity relationship model using data views. Events may be modeled to describe how data/process groupings behave in response to external system stimuli. Object-oriented information engineering incorporates processes as operations and methods packaged with the data structures within an object model. Events describe the behavior of objects.

Information engineering aims to achieve extensive reuse of planning, analysis, design and construction deliverables across the enterprise. With object-oriented information engineering, this objective becomes much easier to achieve thanks to formal class structures developed during analysis and design and use of publicly available class libraries.

END NOTES

[1] Finkelstein, Clive. *Introduction to Information Engineering* (Reading, MA: Addison-Wesley) 1989, pp. 321–332.

[2] Martin, James. *Information Engineering*, 3 vols. (Englewood Cliffs, NJ: Prentice Hall) 1989–1990.

2

What Is Object Orientation?

2.1 WHY OBJECTS?

Object-oriented development is becoming quite popular these days. This kind of development promises solutions to the following problems, which are inherent in more traditional methods:

- long development times,
- difficult system maintenance and
- inability to adapt systems quickly to changes in requirements.

Object-oriented technology promises to produce a software revolution in terms of cost and quality that will rival that of microprocessors and their integrated circuit technologies during the 1980s. Object-oriented technology should provide us the ability to produce low-cost, highly reliable software repeatedly and efficiently.

The Need for Better Systems Development

Today, business organizations find themselves confronted with a serious dilemma. They are becoming increasingly dependent on information processing to handle almost every aspect of their operations, but their ability to handle information is failing to keep pace because the volume of information is increasing faster. The problem is not due to computing platforms (hardware and operating systems software). Rather, the failure to keep up with information processing demands lies in the inability of software developers to capitalize on the potential benefits of new technology. The main problem here is the need to maintain mountains of outdated software programs and databases.

This gap between computing power and the ability of software to adapt to the computing platforms gets wider all the time. Although everyone who uses computers is affected, large organizations with hundreds of thousands of lines of software code are most affected. It is a rare moment when a major information systems development project is completed on time and within budget. What is worse is that the systems that are built are usually full of flaws and so rigidly built that it can be impossible to enhance them without drastic changes, without major redesign and redevelopment.

The rate of change in global business and political environments exacerbates the problem to the point that many organizations are on the verge of a crisis in information management. Important organization-wide information systems can be obsolete before they are delivered. Even when they are delivered, they are not capable of evolving to address future organization needs. Some studies indicate that as little as 5 percent of all systems development projects create working systems. The rest are rejected and result in reconstruction, abandonment after completion or are never completed. In order to resolve this crisis in software development, a radically new way to approach the analysis, design and development of information systems is needed.

Modular programming, structured programming, CASE and fourth-generation languages each have attempted to address the development problem. They have had some degree of success. Despite all the efforts to date to discover better ways to build systems, the software development crisis is getting worse with the passage of time. We still build systems largely by hand. Better construction methods have been developed but tend not to work well on large projects. Current methods often produce systems of erratic quality and ones that are difficult to modify and maintain. Object technology can meet these challenges. The remainder of this book discusses how object technology can address many of the problems the software crisis presents us with.

Assembling Systems from Objects

Hardware is assembled from pretested components, which are used repetitively to design and build even larger assemblies, which are themselves reusable. The quality at each level of design is ensured by pretesting system components. Error-free assembly is ensured by interface standards that focus on the functionality and behavior of each system component at its interface. The same concepts can and are being applied in software development via object technology. Tools are available that support object-oriented design, analysis and system construction. Special libraries of reusable components are readily available, especially for graphical user interfaces. Object database management systems are becoming more widely used as well.

Today, much conventional software is written largely from scratch. Because such software is usually written to solve very specific problems, it can often be easier to write new systems than to convert existing ones. Objects, on the other hand, are general-purpose building blocks that closely reflect real-world entities, not special-purpose processing tasks. Objects can be made useful for subsequent application projects, even if the purposes of the new systems are different. As more and more object classes are constructed, they can be accumulated in an enterprise-wide systems building block library. Then development can shift from creating new object classes to assembling existing ones in new and innovative ways. It might be that experienced object system developers can spend as little as 20 percent of their time creating new classes and spend the rest of their time assembling proven system components into new, powerful and reliable systems.

Integration of Processing with Information

Development of information systems using object-oriented techniques involves more than just object-oriented programming languages. Rather, it embodies concepts of application architecture and development that can be implemented with existing languages.

Adapting a new approach to developing applications can mean starting from scratch. The object-oriented development approach is different from current programming procedures in basic ways. The barriers between data and the procedural instructions that manipulate these data are eliminated. This is accomplished by encapsulating data structures with program code that manages these structures.

Combinations of data and processing logic form objects. Objects are created to represent entities and functions of the business rather than the logical procedures of traditional data processing. Objects are created to represent real-world entities such as customers, products, invoices and employees. Object-oriented programs are built by stringing objects together in the order dictated by an application. The result is greatly simplified application development. In many cases, end users can actually build their own applications because the details are hidden inside the confines of object capsules.

Software systems are becoming increasingly complex. Numerous application systems of increasing size and complexity need to be connected and managed as a network of cohesive subsystems, not as the stand-alone systems of today. Tomorrow's systems must be understood at a high enough level to allow business planners and managers to grasp the systems as an integrated whole. These same systems must be modeled in enough detail to describe robust functionality at a conceptual rather than physical level.

As structured software engineering enthusiasts have long known, building models often takes longer during up-front analysis and design but saves much more time during system maintenance. Objects provide for not only greater simplicity but greater modeling power for system maintenance and growth. Object models tend to closely reflect natural systems in the real world. Rather than modeling static data structures separate from dynamic system behaviors, object-based systems incorporate processing logic along with static data structures.

Software reliability is becoming a real problem for older, often obsolete systems as well as the more complex new systems being developed today. Vendors of packaged software routinely send corrected upgrades to their users to repair problem software. System developers often make disclaimers about the software that they maintain or create. Object concepts can be used to model and implement much more complex but reliable systems via various levels of abstraction.

A significant opportunity exists for incorporating useful object concepts into older systems in order to evolve to object-based systems. An important goal of many organizations today is enhancing existing systems. Even small changes can have major impacts on systems because these changes may be propagated throughout a system. Object-based systems provide much protection from change propagation via encapsulation and information hiding. Subsequent changes to an object are localized to that object, unless changes are made to the public interface to the object.

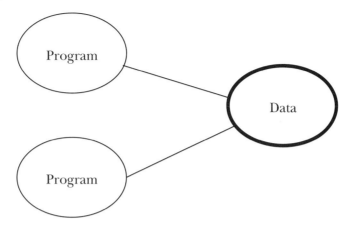

Figure 2.1   Traditional data processing

2.2 BENEFITS OF OBJECT TECHNOLOGY

The main benefits of object-oriented systems development are improved reliability and enhanced developer productivity. Reliability can be improved because each object is simply a "black box" to external objects that it must communicate with. Internal data structures and methods can be refined without impacting other parts of a system. Traditional systems, on the other hand, often exhibit unanticipated side effects when a section of code is modified. Object technology helps developers deal with complexity in systems development. Figures 2.1 and 2.2 contrast the ways that data are processed in traditional and in object-oriented systems.

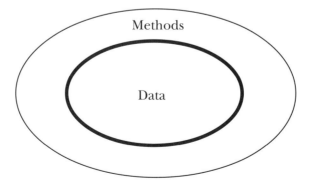

Figure 2.2   Object information processing

Developer productivity can be enhanced because classes of objects can be made reusable so that each subclass or instance of an object can use the same program code for the class. Developer productivity is also enhanced due to a more natural association between system objects and real-world objects. Application development becomes shortened once the object paradigm has been learned. Object models of the world are more natural because data and programs are stored together, hierarchical model structures are possible and successive layers can express increasing levels of detail. This all adds up to make object analysis models and systems designs easier to understand, enhancing system maintenance.

David A. Taylor[1] discusses these benefits of object modeling and development:

1. Faster development
2. Higher quality
3. Easier maintenance
4. Reduced cost
5. Increased scalability
6. Better information structures
7. Increased adaptability

Taylor[2] goes on to discuss some potential concerns we should have when evaluating object technology at the present time:

1. Maturity of the technology
2. Need for standards
3. Need for better tools
4. Speed of execution
5. Availability of qualified personnel
6. Cost of conversion
7. Support for large-scale modularity

Figure 2.3 lists the benefits of object technologies. Figure 2.4 compares traditional and object-oriented development.

- Reusability—Classes are built on other classes
- More reliable systems
- More rapid development
- More flexible development
- Models that more closely reflect reality
- Better handling of nontraditional data types
- Better technology independence and interoperability
- Focus on behavior, not low-level processing
- Better basis for client-server and distributed computing
- Commercial class libraries are available

Figure 2.3   Benefits of object technologies

2.3   WHAT ARE OBJECTS?

The idea of an object that combines both static data structure and dynamic processing behavior fits well with the way we view objects in the real world—at least objects that move or create or manipulate information (Figure 2.5). Although experts may disagree on how the term object should be used, for

	Traditional Approach	**Object-Oriented Approach**
Architecture	*Many sources of data *Many programs using one piece of data	*Networks of interconnected subsystems *One piece of data with one set of encapsulated procedures
Code Reuse	*Low-level code is not highly reusable if only a top-down approach is used	*Encourages building of complete definitions for key components
Abstraction	*Good at top model levels *Messy at bottom model levels	*Messaging approach encourages platform independent designs

Figure 2.4   A comparison of traditional and object-oriented development

our purposes an object is a single thing or concept as distinguished from other things or concepts. Strictly speaking, we should refer to a kind of an object (such as a person) as an object type and a specific occurrence of that kind of object (such as John Jones) as an object instance. In this book, an object type is an object class and an object occurrence is an object instance.

An object class describes a set of object instances that have similar

- data characteristics,
- behavior,
- relationships to other objects and
- real-world meaning.

A person may have a name, address, phone number, age and many other attributes. He or she may perform certain tasks as part of their job, report to managers and be reported to by other employees and be known to play the role of a certain type of worker. Thus a specific person is an instance of the person object class, as well as an instance of the employee object class (see Figure 2.6). Objects can be identified in a description of a system (in this case, a business) by nouns in sentences. The tasks performed by objects (the object behavior or operations) can be identified as verbs in these same sentences.

Objects that are members of an object class share some attribute types and behavior types. Individual object instances can be distinguished from other instances by differences in the actual values of the attributes and by associations with other object classes and object instances. Object instances that are members of the same class share a common real-world meaning in addition to their shared attributes and relationships.

2.4 ABSTRACTION

Abstraction allows for easier management of complex ideas. A description of a real-world object, situation or process can be simplified in an abstracted model to emphasize aspects that are important to a user of a model. Other details not needed for understanding are suppressed and displayed only in more detailed models. The idea of abstraction in object-oriented development models is to distill the essence of a problem to understand it better.

For our use in building models of systems of objects, an abstract model emphasizes the external view of an object, with the implementation details hidden inside the boundaries of the object (see the next section on encapsu-

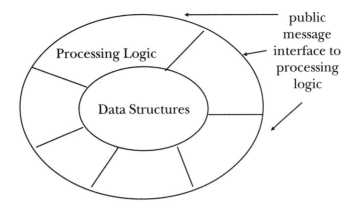

Figure 2.5   Representation of an object

lation). The external interface of an object describes only the essential behavior of an object. Classification (see Chapters 3 and 4) provides a way of building levels of abstraction into object models. Seidewitz and Stark[3] speak of kinds of abstractions useful in building models of objects:

Entity Abstraction	Represents a model of a problem-domain entity
Action Abstraction	Provides a generalized set of operations, all of which perform the same kind of function
Virtual Machine Abstraction	Groups together operations that are all used by some superior level of control or operations that all use some junior-level set of operations
Coincidental Abstraction	Packages a set of operations that have no relation to each other

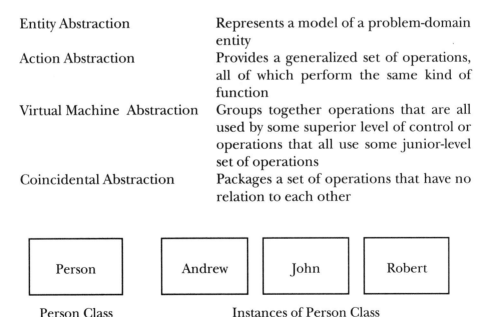

Figure 2.6   Class and objects

These kinds of abstraction provide the same logical groupings as the various types of module coupling found in structured systems design.[4] Object abstractions are used in analysis and design models to represent more naturally the concepts and vocabulary used in the particular problem domain that we are modeling. A problem domain might be the customer support area of a business or product research or product engineering design and development.

In a later chapter, this book covers clients that request the services of an object. Abstraction may be used to model systems of objects as networks of clients and servers. Using analysis and design models of the external characteristics of objects allows us to model only the interactions between clients and servers, not the details of how these interactions will be implemented. Implementation specifics will be covered in detailed object design and implementation models (Chapters 9 through 12).

2.5 ENCAPSULATION

In object modeling, as in traditional structured analysis and design, abstraction precedes the implementation details. Only the minimal details required in the enhanced understanding of an object should be used to represent that object in an abstract model. Abstraction leads us naturally to the concept of encapsulation, known as information hiding in structured design. See Figures 2.7a through 2.7c

Encapsulation provides a conceptual barrier around an object, preventing clients of an object from viewing its internal details. Thus encapsulation can

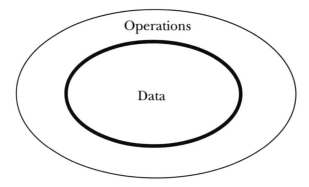

Figure 2.7a   Encapsulation

- Build a conceptual barrier around a collection of things.
- Group into a single capsule both data and operations that act on these data.
- Manage real-world complexity by allocating complexity to individual objects.
- Hide knowledge encapsulating within an object from other objects.
- Define *how* things are accomplished with object internals.
- Define *what* needs to be done with the external interface.
- Change private definitions without affecting the public definitions.

Figure 2.7b   Methods for encapsulation/information hiding

provide appropriate barriers for various levels of abstraction in a system model. In relational database design that uses Structured Query Language (SQL) to implement that design, application programs define what data they need to do their jobs, not how to navigate through relational tables. The logical view of a database is all that is required to access data within a relational database using SQL. Object databases can go to even higher levels of abstraction by accessing classes of objects using only the external protocol defined by encapsulation. Only the name of the object(s) being accessed and the operations to be performed on the object(s) are required to process object data. Higher levels of object abstraction are shielded from the encapsulated details of lower-level abstractions.

Each object class, then, must have an external interface defining the outside view of the class and an implementation that defines the mechanisms that provide the behaviors the object must exhibit.

External aspects of an object (public) can be separated from the internal implementation details (private).

A program change can be prevented from rippling through a system.

Private representation can be changed without effect on external applications.

Object-oriented systems tend to be much cleaner.

Figure 2.7c   Advantages of encapsulation/information hiding

2.6   HIERARCHIES AND INHERITANCE

Objects and their organization can provide the extra benefit of reusability of data and code. Programming procedures implemented in one object can be used in another object through a system of classes, hierarchies and inheritance. We need to combine data structures and processes to form a single unified set of structures and associated processing (see Figure 2.8). A business could have a consumer and a commercial customer. The consumer would inherit the behaviors of a customer object: the ability to maintain a name, address and account number. The consumer object would also have specific characteristics of a consumer customer as opposed to those of a commercial customer.

The consumer object does not need to have all characteristics rewritten for it. It simply inherits the data structures and code for all customers. This assists

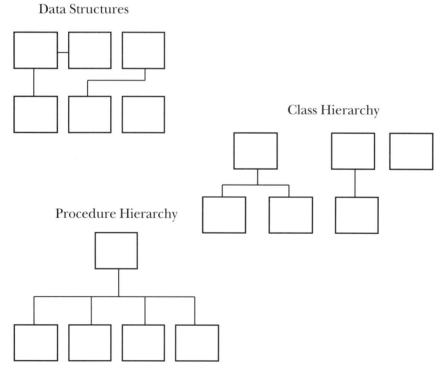

Figure 2.8   One unified hierarchy of objects

programmers in keeping applications current. If another class of customers is needed, a new subclass could be built to inherit all of the data and procedures of the common customer class. The data and procedures that are inherited are already designed, implemented and tested. This easy management of changes in a business environment makes object-oriented applications much more maintainable than they might be otherwise. A developer can be more productive when not having to rewrite all the details of a new business object and its associated functions. Productivity is improved by eliminating the need to design, implement and test key parts of a system.

Encapsulation

Encapsulation helps manage complex system models by hiding details at lower levels of abstraction. Still, more help is often needed in managing abstractions. Object models can be simplified by defining hierarchies of data structures. Two common kinds of data hierarchy are generalization ("kind of" or class structure) and aggregation ("part of" or object structure).

Generalization

This kind of hierarchy defines a relationship among classes (see Figure 2.9). One class shares the structures and behaviors defined in one class (single inheritance) or in more than one class (multiple inheritance). A subclass inherits characteristics from one or more superclasses and can refine the definition of the superclass(es). A general definition of a motor vehicle superclass can be refined by more specific definitions of the subclasses: automobile, truck and bus.

Aggregation

Aggregation relationships depict "part of" hierarchies (see Figure 2.10). An automobile is built of these subobjects: engine, body and chassis. The engine in turn is composed of fuel, cooling and ignition systems. Each of these systems is composed of subsystems and/or discrete parts. The higher-level abstractions are generalized while the lower levels are specialized. An automobile is modeled at a higher level of abstraction than any of its component classes.

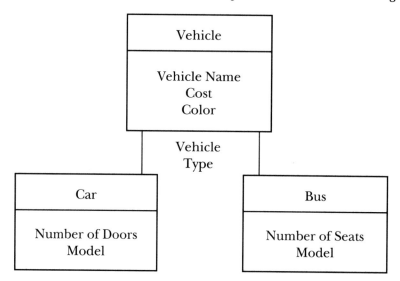

Figure 2.9   A generalization hierarchy

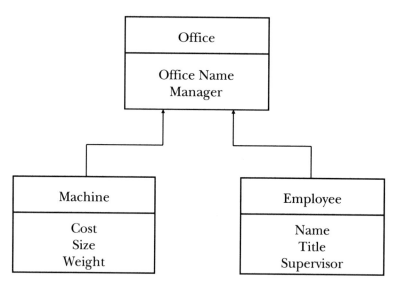

Figure 2.10   An aggregation hierarchy

2.7 ASSOCIATION

An association defines a conceptual connection between object classes with common structure and semantics (Figure 2.11). All of the connections between object instances that an association represents connect objects from the same classes. An association describes a set of object instance connections in much the same manner that a class defines a set of object instances.

Associations are bidirectional in that a connection may be traversed in either direction from one object to another. In structured analysis, entity types are connected via relationship types in much the same manner that object classes are connected via associations in object modeling. Associations may be binary, ternary or higher order, but in practice most are binary. Higher-order associations are difficult to model and build, so it may be better to try to work with associations that can be decomposed into sets of binary relationships. Object modeling in the future will likely consist of some form of extended entity-relationship modeling with much richer semantics than the various forms of data modeling in wide use today incorporate, but entity-relationship modeling is still a good place to get started.

The concept of association (or relationships) is not new, but it is not supported within many implementation languages or databases in use today. Still, associations can be very useful for modeling relationships between object classes. Associations provide a way to depict information that is not unique to a single class but that depends on two or more classes.

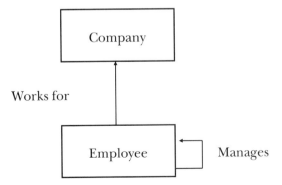

Figure 2.11   Association between objects

Figure 2.12a   Messages

2.8 MESSAGES

When objects have been encapsulated to insulate the outside world from the details of the object structures and behaviors, there needs to be a way to interact with these structures and behaviors. Messages provide this mechanism.

A message is composed of the name of an operation to perform on object data and any necessary parameters to qualify the operation (Figures 2.12a and 2.12b). When a client object sends a message to another object (a server), the client is asking the server to perform some operation and, perhaps, to return some information to the client. When a receiver of a message processes that message, it performs an operation in any way it can. The sender of the message does not (indeed, should not) know how the operation will be performed. Because of encapsulation, the details of how an object performs an operation are hidden from view of outsiders.

The total set of messages that an object can respond to comprises the behavior of that object. Some messages might be internal ones that are not part of the object's public interface. An object could send a message to itself to perform recursive operations, for instance. If a program needed to print the contents of a file, regardless of the type of the file, a PRINT message could be sent to the file object, causing the file to print. The details of how that print

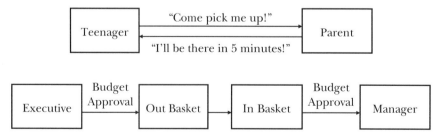

Figure 2.12b   Object messaging

operation is performed are hidden from the calling program's view. An EDIT operation, and subsequent COMPILE and LINK operations, could be performed on a program module with the actual implementations of each message hidden from view of the user or calling program. A PRINT message sent to another file of a different type would cause a similar action to take place by the other object (see the next section on polymorphism).

2.9 POLYMORPHISM

Polymorphism is the ability of two or more object classes to respond to the same message, but in different ways. The meaning of the commands that are passed between objects is packaged with the objects, so a client object does not need to be aware of which server object its message is being sent to. Polymorphism allows the similarities between different object classes to be exploited. Since it is possible to have different responses to the same message, the sender of a message can simply transmit it without regard to the class of the message's receiver. A PRINT, EDIT, COMPILE or LINK message could be sent to a program file without regard to the language the source program is written in or the type or version of editor (or other tool) the file invokes in order to respond to the message.

Implementing printer support in an object-oriented environment allows you to define a general printing interface that determines the way to communicate with that interface (Figure 2.13a). A print message could be responded to by a plain text file, a bit-mapped graphics file, a vector-mapped graphics file or a formatted report file. Each type of file is implemented as an object

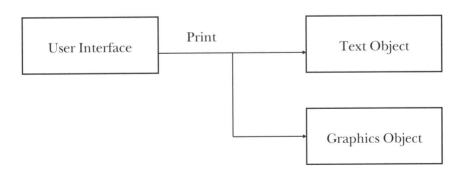

Figure 2.13a   Polymorphism

- Two or more object classes are able to respond differently to one message.
- An object does not need to know to whom it is sending a message.
- A method name can be implemented in different ways.

Figure 2.13b   Advantages of polymorphism

with a print method to respond to a print message, perhaps in conjunction with a set of optional parameters unique to each file type or the associated tools (print spooler, print queue, file formatter, printer, plotter, etc.) used for the print operation.

Polymorphism allows objects to communicate without knowing how other objects perform their functions (Figure 2.13b). A customer invoice object could obtain customer data from the customer object without having to include procedures for making the calculations upon customer data. Thus object-oriented software can be made to represent business objects and functions better and to help make applications more understandable for future modification and tuning.

- The gateway through the public interface for an object—the only way to properly access objects
- Consists of a name and any required arguments
- A request by another object does not specify HOW an operation is to be performed
- Consists of a reference to a method, whose implementation is known only to the object it belongs to

Figure 2.13c   Messages

END NOTES

[1] Taylor, David A. *Object-Oriented Technology* (Reading, MA: Addison-Wesley) 1992, pp. 103–107.

[2] Ibid., pp. 108–113.

[3] Seidewitz, E. and M. Stark. *General Object-Oriented Software Development,* Report SEL-86-002. (Greenbelt, MD: NASA Goddard Space Flight Center) 1986.

[4] Montgomery, Stephen L. *AD/CYCLE: IBM's Framework for Application Development and CASE* (New York: Van Nostrand Reinhold) 1991.

3

Business Information Requirements

Information systems built based on an information architecture rather than an application architecture have been proven to be more stable over time. Object databases will prove to be even more stable. Analyzing business information requirements and modeling them based on subject areas will provide a strong foundation for building object databases and migrating existing systems to an object-oriented environment.

One could view information processing as a succession of changes to data. At any point in time, a system or organization could be viewed as a data structure. Processes represent a series of changes to data structures: databases, working storage and data views. In a strictly object-oriented system, data are combined with logic, such as integrity checks and derivation rules. This provides a much cleaner framework for building information systems. Analysis of data subjects provides the beginning point for building architectures of stable systems.

3.1 TYPES OF INFORMATION MODELS

When we model information requirements for an entire business enterprise using an information engineering approach, we can visualize different views of the entire enterprise information model.

The Enterprise Planning Model

The enterprise planning model is a model of all of the information that an enterprise needs to store and process. This model focuses on several key dimensions of an organization: data, functions, strategies, missions, goals, etc. For our purposes in this book, the key component of the enterprise planning model for object modeling is the information (data) model. This provides a foundation for object structure modeling, discussed in this and the next chapter, and for subsequent modeling of object functional and control models.

The enterprise planning model depicts business information in a highly structured manner. This model is similar to an entity-relationship logical data model discussed in traditional information engineering, but contains richer semantic modeling constructs. The basic components of the enterprise planning model are the definitions of objects, associations between objects and attributes of objects. This is analogous to the modeling of entities, relationships and attributes discussed in entity-relationship modeling.

An enterprise planning model is a high-level view of the enterprise's use of information. The scope is broad and depth shallow. The scope includes all subject data areas (object classes) of the enterprise, depicting fundamental objects and key associations between these objects. The shallow depth results from hiding of associative, dependent and subtype objects and nonkey object associations that are too detailed to show on the summary level. Operational data needs are not necessary for high-level strategic planning, for instance. This lack of detail helps make the enterprise planning model easier to visualize and understand in the broader context of an entire organization.

The enterprise planning model is built as a top-down, strategic view of the information needs and activities of a business organization. This model forms the basis for analysis of the impact of planning cycles, new or changed business initiatives or strategic directions. When new organizational information needs arise, these needs are added to the enterprise planning model. Information strategy planning (ISP), business systems planning/strategic alliance (BSP/SA) or some other systems planning methodology is normally used to create and maintain the enterprise planning model. Business area analysis (BAA), business systems planning/architecture (BSP/A) or some other comprehensive business requirements analysis methodology is used to refine the business planning model (Figure 3.1). This refinement proceeds down into the increasing detail needed to form a comprehensive information architecture for designing and building integrated information systems.

	James Martin's Information Engineering	IBM's Structural Development Methodologies
Planning	ISP: Information Strategy Planning	BSP/SA: Business Systems Planning/ Strategic Alliance
Analysis	BAA: Business Area Analysis	BSP/A: Business Systems Planning/ Architecture

Figure 3.1   Planning and analysis methodologies

The Enterprise Logical Information Model

The enterprise logical information model is a fully detailed logical model of enterprise information requirements and forms an information architecture for integrating information systems across an enterprise. As with the enterprise planning model, the logical data model's scope is broad; unlike the enterprise planning model, this model includes all objects and associations. It is a refined, detailed representation of all of the information requirements for enterprise information systems.

All supporting objects (such as subtypes and aggregation components) along with all of their associations are built into the logical information model. The enterprise planning model, in contrast, does not necessarily have fully attributed, fully refined objects. The logical information model must depict existing information resources and thus is driven partly by projects that create new information systems or modify existing information systems. The enterprise logical data model is also an integration of individual application and project-level logical data models. Within any particular project logical information model, we usually see only subtype objects relevant to the project, but the enterprise logical information model must contain an exhaustive modeling of all subtypes and aggregation components.

The enterprise logical data model is so broad and deep that it usually depicts concepts of overwhelming complexity. Application projects and information systems require only a view of objects relevant to their own particular scope. Because project life cycles and change management schedules differ, their information models need to be refined and managed well before integration into the enterprise logical information model.

Systems Logical Information Models

Application system logical information models contain the same level of detail as does the enterprise logical information model, but their scope defines only those objects relevant within the context of the system being modeled. Several internal views of a project's information model may be created as a system progresses through analysis, design and development. The complete logical information model delivered as part of the project's final documentation package is the version that is merged into the overall enterprise logical information model.

The following sections of this chapter discuss how model building can progress from summary level to the most detailed logical information models. As the enterprise model is first being constructed, this process may be applied across much of an enterprise. After the enterprise planning model and the enterprise logical information models have been built, this complete process will occur only for those information requirements that are entirely new within a project, business area or the enterprise as a whole.

3.2 CHARACTERIZE SUBJECT AREAS

Subject area analysis is a way of defining major groupings of business data objects at a high level. This type of analysis helps to identify all information needed in an organization, in order that this information can be analyzed for its form and manner in which it is used. It also provides a basis for building an information architecture from which business data object analysis activities can be conducted and application projects defined. Example subject areas include:

- Products
- Parts
- Customers
- Vendors
- Employees

Purchasing

Parts

Vendors

Purchase Orders

Invoicing

Products

Customers

Customer Orders

Inventory Control

Products

Purchase Orders

Customer Orders

Vendors

Figure 3.2   Subject areas and their components

- Customer Orders
- Accounts

Application systems might use more than one subject (see Figure 3.2).

The planning phase of information engineering aims to divide the total set of data structures for an enterprise into manageable units—data subjects. One or more data subjects can be modeled in detail during the analysis phase.

Data subjects are sometimes referred to as object classes. Clustering techniques can be used to group existing data structures into data subjects, if desired. It is necessary to build a high-level model of an enterprise in order to plan what data subjects should exist. Enterprise planning must take into consideration not only data subjects but existing or new files and stand-alone databases for particular applications. Detailed modeling of what constitutes a subject database (derived from an enterprise model data subject) is performed during analysis of business areas. When databases can be quickly implemented based on enterprise model data subjects, application development becomes much more data-driven and, hopefully, fully object-driven.

Subject area analysis and modeling can be performed in facilitated group workshop sessions, or a series of interviews or by developing a straw model or an initial unverified model. The approach taken depends upon objects for subject area analysis and the resources and time available.

If at all possible, use a group-facilitated sessions approach for analyzing subject areas, as well as for analyzing functional and behavioral system requirements. This approach can be very difficult to use, especially if the technical and business team members are unfamiliar with it. A good session facilitator that continually challenges a group can quickly build strong ownership of a model and sponsorship. This is definitely the approach to take for analysis and design of a large system project.

Another approach to conducting subject area analysis involves serial interviews. This is particularly successful when one or more good subject area models exists. However, if the existing models are not fairly solid, using them can lead to much confusion. Interviews are often used to prepare for intensive group-facilitated sessions.

A straw model could be developed by a project team and later reviewed during a group-facilitated session. This technique can make effective use of a group's time, but the group may not take ownership of the model because members did not create the model in the first place.

An initial unverified model developed by a project team in isolation from business experts should be used only if contact with subject matter experts is not possible. Such a model will be inaccurate and may be rejected by subject matter experts. This author participated in such a model building exercise on a large project (out of necessity at first), and I and the other group members found that extensive rework of the model was needed. Still, the exercise did provide us with a set of questions to ask our subject matter experts once we could begin intensive group facilitated sessions (usually the preferred approach).

Once subject matter experts have given their input through one or more of the above information gathering approaches, you can begin to organize subject areas using a decomposition diagram. Each subject area needs to be agreed upon and defined by all people involved. The order and hierarchy of subjects need to be defined and agreed upon. A technique for identifying subject areas is to categorize them into persons, places, things or concepts. Identify all subject areas that fall into each category.

Produce a subject area decomposition diagram, from subject area headings, for visual completeness and consistency checking (Figure 3.3). The

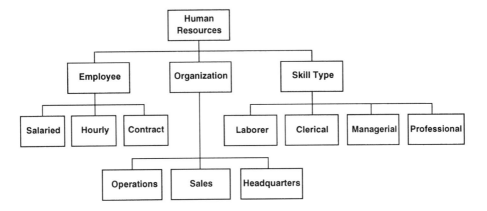

Figure 3.3   Subject area decomposition

initial categories can be discarded after a complete set of subject areas have been identified and defined, but the initial approach helps you get started in managing subject area decomposition.

Under a category of subject areas, the lowest level in the decomposition tends to result in data entities (or discrete objects). However, each level in the hierarchy is a valid subject and can become a class of objects. Subject areas and entities are closely related, as are classes and objects, but it is useful to start with higher-level subject areas than to jump right into detailed lists of entities.

3.3 REFINE SUBJECT AREA CLASSES

A subject area can be associated with many other subject areas and business functions. An important association is that between functions and subject areas. Information strategy planning within a comprehensive information engineering methodology often involves building of a matrix of functions that involve subject areas. This matrix can be refined to form a CRUD matrix of subject area data actions by process (operation): Create, Read, Update and Delete. See Figure 3.4 for an example subject area function CRUD matrix and Figure 3.5 for a subject area/process CRUD matrix. You build a CRUD matrix for subject areas in order to:

- analyze which functions act upon which subject areas
- determine the priority of subject area model and database implementation

Functions

		R	CRUD
C			
		U	
			R

Figure 3.4   Subject area/function CRUD matrix

- record the life cycle of a particular subject area
- ensure that each function creates or updates at least one subject area
- provide input into analysis project scoping efforts

Analysis of subject area life cycles can help you to verify a business function model by examining it against targeted subject areas. When all data states that a subject area can be in have been identified, a function model can be tested for its handling of life-cycle states. Later on in analysis and design we can use similar techniques for processes/operations and entities/objects and modules and database structures, respectively. When a function-subject area CRUD matrix is complete, you should find that:

- each function reads at least one subject area;
- each function creates, updates or deletes at least one subject area;
- each subject is read by at least one function; and

Processes

		C	R
			CRUD
R		U	

Figure 3.5   Subject area/process CRUD matrix

- each subject is created and deleted by only one function (usually), but updated by several functions

Your purpose in developing a subject area CRUD matrix is to be able to identify one function that is responsible for creation of data in each subject area. To achieve this goal, you may need to continue to decompose subject areas until you have achieved enough detail. At the leaf level of a subject area decomposition, you will likely find data entities. If you cannot identify one create function for each subject area, you need to decide whether you have analyzed the subject area in enough detail.

Two key concepts in an object-oriented model of a system are aggregation and generalization/specialization (both are discussed in the previous chapter as well as at other points in this book). Subject area decomposition analysis helps to identify these types of data hierarchies. During this initial analysis of groups of data objects, we are most concerned with identifying classes of data objects. Later on in analysis we can refine our subject areas into object hierarchies.

Subject areas (object classes) will ultimately be decomposed into one or more objects. Thus subject areas form the basis for partitioning and managing your entire enterprise data object model. You must be sure that the definitions are clear and agreed upon, that boundaries do not overlap and that subject areas are comprehensive. In future analysis efforts you will be glad that you have done your hard work up front during initial subject area analysis. Future efforts can leverage off previous analysis models in order to save significant time and effort. A properly architected business object model forms the ideal foundation for change, and the subject model is a good starting point. Such a model avoids having organizational or procedural changes impact systems in a major way (as would happen if you modeled functions and processes first and data classes and objects later).

3.4 CHARACTERIZE OBJECT CLASSES

Identifying Object Classes

At the highest level of data modeling, broad categories of objects (also referred to as data subjects) are identified:

- Customers
- Products

- Customer Orders
- Employees
- Sales Territories
- Equipment
- Vendors

and so on. Once broad object categories have been identified, we move on to identify specific object types for each object class. An object in the real world is a person, place, event or other real or conceptual thing about which the enterprise must store information. Object classes are used for all object structure modeling of business systems and computerized information systems.

In traditional information engineering, objects (known as entities) are strictly data structures. In object modeling, objects are data structures combined with procedures that manipulate object data structures. Operations for a customer order object might include create, update and cancel. These operations can only be accessed by sending a message to the customer order object, which activates its own methods to perform the operations. An object must be manipulated by objects that are defined for that specific object class. Some objects identified from object categories might include:

- Customers
  - Residential Customer
  - Commercial Customer
  - Industrial Customer
- Customer Orders
  - Customer Order
  - Customer Order Line Item
  - Customer Invoice
  - Customer Payment
  - Customer Balance Due

Guidelines for Selecting Object Classes

Once object class categories and object classes themselves have been identified it is necessary that you attempt to discard unnecessary and incorrect categories. Rumbaugh et al.[1] lists these types of situations to examine:

- *Redundant classes.* When two object categories depict the same information, the most descriptive name should be retained.

- *Irrelevant classes.* When an object class has little or nothing to do with the problem at hand, it should be discarded.

- *Vague classes.* An object class should be specific, not having ill-defined boundaries or being too broad in scope.

- *Attributes.* If an object type seems to describe another individual object, it probably should be defined as an attribute type, not an object type.

- *Operations.* If an object type describes an operation applied to objects and not manipulated in its own right, it is not an object class.

- *Roles.* The name of an object class should reflect its intrinsic nature and not a role it plays in an association.

- *Implementation constructs.* If a model construct is extraneous to the real world, it should be eliminated from an analysis model. It might be useful later on in design, but not during analysis.

3.5 DESCRIBE OBJECT ASSOCIATIONS

An association is a conceptual relationship between instances of an object. Each association can be defined as an ordered list of object instances. Associations describe groups of relationships with common structure and meaning; all instances of an association connect object instances from the same object type category. An association between objects is given a name in both directions so that the relationship name plus the associated object names builds a sentence (see Figure 3.6a).

Although associations are always defined as bidirectional, they do not have to be implemented in both directions. This concept of an optional association is used in some object-oriented languages that implement associations as pointers. Traversal of the associations defined in only one direction may be implemented for performance reasons.

Cardinality

The cardinality (also referred to as multiplicity) or number of instances of one object type that can be associated with instances of the other object type in an association is modeled like Figure 3.6b (using Martin notation).

Figure 3.6a   An association

This diagram says "a customer places many orders" and "an order is placed by one customer," where the vertical bar on the relationship represents 1 and the "crow's foot" represents many. Some modeling techniques (such as that used by Rumbaugh et al.) model cardinality (multiplicity) using an integer instead of a bar (1) or crow's feet (2, 3, 4, etc.).

Optionality

The optionality of a relationship ("may" or "must") is modeled as an "o" for optional or a vertical bar "l" (placed just inside the cardinality symbol) for mandatory (see Figure 3.6c).

This diagram says "a customer may place one or many orders" and "an order must be placed by one (and only one) customer." Other modeling techniques may use a solid circle to depict zero or more instances in an association and a hollow circle to indicate zero or one. The basic concept is the same—depicting constraints on an association.

The association modeled above is an example of a fairly simple binary association. More complex associations may include "composed of" (aggregation), inclusiveness and exclusivity, recursiveness and supertype/subtype (generalization/specialization) associations.

Guidelines for Selecting Associations

Rumbaugh et al.[2] lists some issues to be examined when determining which object associations to retain and which to discard:

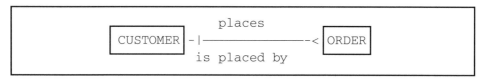

Figure 3.6b   Cardinality

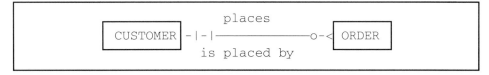

Figure 3.6c **Cardinality and optionality**

- *Associations between eliminated classes (object categories).* If one or more object categories in an association have been eliminated, the association must also be eliminated or restated in terms of other object categories.

- *Irrelevant or implementation associations.* Discard any associations outside the problem domain or deal with implementation constructs.

- *Actions.* Associations should describe structural properties of an application domain, not transient events.

- *Ternary associations.* Associations among three or more object types can be decomposed into binary associations or phrased as qualified associations.

- *Derived associations.* Eliminate associations that can be defined in terms of other associations because they are redundant. Also eliminate associations defined by conditions on object attributes.

- *Misnamed associations.* Avoid stating how or why a situation occurred; say what it is.

- *Role names.* Add role names to describe roles that an object type in an association plays from the point of view of the other object type.

- *Qualified associations.* A name is usually used to identify an object within some context, but most names are not globally unique. The context combines with the name to uniquely identify an object.

- *Multiplicity.* For multiplicity values of "many," consider whether a qualifier is needed. Also, ask if the objects need to be ordered in some way.

- *Missing associations.* Add any missing associations that are discovered.

3.6 DEFINE OBJECT ATTRIBUTES

Attributes are properties or characteristics of objects. An attribute describes a single object type although the same attribute name and concept might appear elsewhere in an object structure model to describe other object types. Example attributes for a customer might include:

Name

Street Address

City

State or Province

Zip or Postal Code

Country

Home Phone

Work Phone

Birth Date

These attributes describe a customer and are associated only with that object type. Attributes are usually named as nouns and might be modeled as object types in and of themselves, but their values may appear as adjectives, such as a color or size. During object structure modeling in analysis, we can usually ignore the formal modeling of derived attributes—such as age, which can be derived from birth date and the current date—in order to simplify the model. In design and implementation, we need to take these derived attributes into account, using methods to implement the derivation formulae, although we would probably not model these as operations in analysis.

The address might be a separate object type of "customer address" if more than one address is needed, especially if the number of addresses is variable from one to many. The phone numbers also might require a separate object type of "customer phone" if the number of phone numbers is variable (which is becoming more common with people working at multiple locations and using facsimile machines and cellular phones). Object modeling starts with identification of obvious object type categories and object types and progresses to identification of attributes. By examining attributes in detail you will often discover additional object types that must be created to handle situations such as the address and phone number examples.

Guidelines for Selecting Attributes

Before you consider attribute definition complete, consider these guidelines for keeping the right attributes (Rumbaugh et al.[3]):

- *Objects.* If an independent existence of an entity is important, rather than just its value, then it is an object.

- *Qualifiers.* If an attribute's value depends on a particular context, consider restating the attribute as a qualifier.

- *Names.* These are often better modeled as qualifiers rather than object attributes.

- *Identifiers.* Do not list object identifiers in object models—they are implicit in object models. List only attributes that exist in the application domain.

- *Link attributes.* If a property depends on the existence of a link, the property is an attribute of the link and not of a related object.

- *Internal values.* If an attribute describes the internal state of an object invisible outside the object, eliminate it from analysis.

- *Fine detail.* Omit minor attributes unlikely to affect most operations.

- *Discordant attributes.* If an attribute seems completely different from and unrelated to all other attributes, this attribute may be an object class that should be split into two distinct object categories.

END NOTES

[1] Rumbaugh, James, Michael Blake, William Premerlani, Frederick Eddy and William Lorensen. *Object-Oriented Modeling and Design* (Englewood Cliffs, NJ: Prentice Hall) 1991, pp. 153–156.

[2] Ibid., pp. 158–161.

[3] Ibid., pp. 162–163.

4

Detailed Object Modeling

4.1 AGGREGATION

An aggregation association depicts a complex object that is composed of other objects. A house may be characterized in terms of its roof, floors, foundation, walls, rooms, windows and so on. A room may in turn be composed of walls, ceiling, floor, windows and doors (Figure 4.1). The process of decomposing a complex object into its component objects can be extended until the desired level of detail is reached.

Object aggregation helps us describe models of the real world that are composed of other models, which are composed of still other models. Analysts describing a complex system of aggregates need to describe them in enough detail for the system at hand. A customer order is composed not only of header information but detail lines as well. The header and detail lines may each have public customer comments and private customer service comments attached. In an order entry system, detailed technical information about a product item appearing on a customer order line may be accessible as well (Figure 4.2). This complex object—called an order—can be very naturally modeled using a series of aggregations. An order processing system can then be constructed to model very closely the natural aggregations occurring in the real world.

Aggregation is a concept that is used to express "part of" types of associations between objects. An aggregate is conceptually an extended object, viewed as a unit by some operations, but it can actually be composed of

47

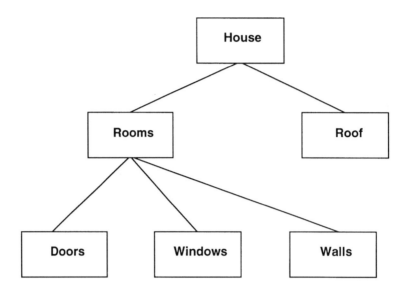

Figure 4.1   A complex object—a house and some of its components

multiple objects (Figure 4.3). One aggregate may contain multiple whole-part structures, each viewable as a distinct aggregate. Components may or may not exist in their own right and may or may not appear in multiple aggregates. Also, an aggregate's components may themselves have their own components.

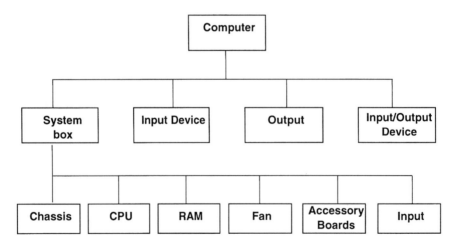

Figure 4.2   A complex object aggregation—a customer order

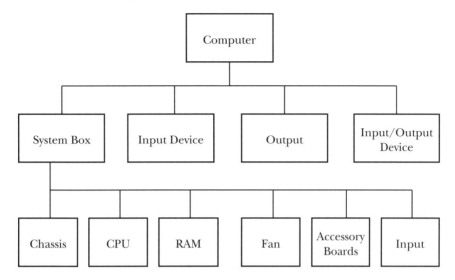

Figure 4.3   An aggregation hierarchy—computer hardware

Aggregation is a special kind of association, adding additional meaning in some situations. Two objects form an aggregate if they are tightly connected by a whole-part relationship. If the two objects are normally viewed as independent objects, their relationship is usually considered an association. Grady Booch[1] suggests these tests to determine whether a relationship is an aggregation:

- Would you use the phrase "part of" to describe it?
- Are some operations on the whole automatically applied to its parts?
- Are some attribute values propagated from the whole to all or some parts?
- Is there an intrinsic asymmetry to the association, where one object class is subordinate to the other?

If you answered yes to any of these questions, you have an aggregation.

An aggregation is not the same as a generalization. Generalization relates distinct classes as a way of structuring the definition of a single object. Superclass and subclass refer to properties of one object. A generalization defines an object as an instance of a superclass and an instance of a subclass. It is composed of classes that describe an object (often referred to as a "kind of" relationship). Aggregation relates object instances: one object that is part of another. Aggregation hierarchies are composed of object occurrences that

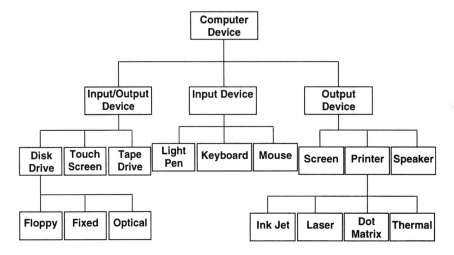

Figure 4.4   A complex hierarchy of aggregations and generalizations

are each part of an "assembly" object (often called a "part of" relationship). A complex object hierarchy can consist of both aggregations and generalizations (Figure 4.4).

4.2 ABSTRACT CLASSES

An abstract object class has no occurrences, but has child categories that contain the actual occurrences. A "concrete" class has actual occurrences. Only a concrete class can appear at the bottom of a class hierarchy. Figure 4.5 describes how abstract and concrete classes are related.

Abstract classes can appear in the real world and can be created by modelers in order to promote reuse of data and procedures in systems. They

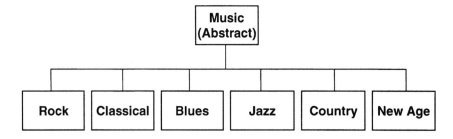

Figure 4.5   Abstract and concrete classes

are used to relate concepts common to multiple classes. An abstract class can be used to model an abstract superclass in order to group classes that are associated with each other or are aggregated together. An abstract class can define methods to be inherited by subclasses or can define the procedures for an operation without defining a corresponding method. The abstract operation defines the pattern of an operation, which each concrete subclass that uses the operation must define in its implementation.

4.3 GENERALIZATION

Generalization and specialization are the reverse of each other. An object type hierarchy that models generalization and specialization represents the most general concept at the top of an object type, hierarchy as the parent and the more specific object types as children.

We often organize information in the real world as generalization/specialization hierarchies (Figure 4.6). For instance, an employee may be either a salaried or hourly worker. A salaried worker can be a manager who, in turn, can be an executive, department manager or unit supervisor. The employee classification is most general, salaried worker is more specific and unit supervisor is most specific. Of course, you might not model the world exactly like this for all organizations, but you get the idea. Unit supervisor is a subtype

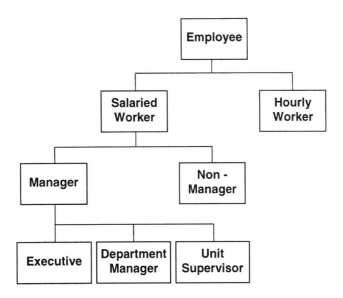

Figure 4.6   Employee generalization

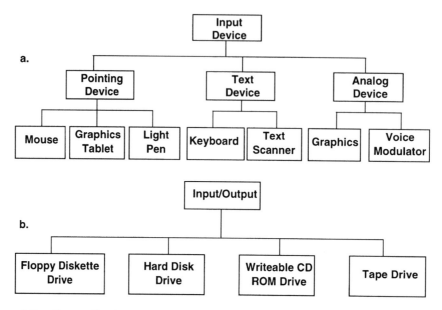

Figure 4.7   Generalization computer hardware

of salaried worker, which is a subtype of employee. Employee is the highest level supertype and salaried worker is the supertype of executive, department manager and unit supervisor. An object type could have several layers of subtypes and subtypes of subtypes. See Figure 4.7 for another example of generalization/specialization.

Generalization/specialization hierarchies help describe application systems and indicate where inheritance should be implemented in object-oriented programming language environments.

Any occurrence of a particular class is an occurrence of all ancestors of that class, so all features of a parent class automatically apply to subclass occurrences. A child class cannot exclude or suppress an attribute in a parent. Any operation on a parent must apply to all children. A child may modify an operation's implementation but not its public interface definition. A child class can extend parent features by adding new features. A child class may restrict the range of allowed values for inherited parent attributes.

In design and construction, operations on object data types can be overridden, which could substantially differ from the original methods (rather than just refining them). Method overriding is performed to override for extension, for restriction, for optimization or for convenience. Rumbaugh et al.[2] proposes the following semantic rules for inheritance:

- All query operations (ones that read, but do not change, attribute values) are inherited by all subclasses.

- All update operations (ones that change attribute values) are inherited across all extensions.

- Update operations that change constrained attributes or associations are blocked across a restriction. A scale-x operation is permitted for class Ellipse, but must be blocked for subclass Circle.

- Operations may not be overridden to make them behave differently in their externally visible manifestations from inherited operations. All methods that implement an operation must have the same protocol.

- Inherited operations can be refined by adding additional behavior.

The authors indicate that the implementation and use of many existing object-oriented languages violates these principles.

4.4 MULTIPLE INHERITANCE

Inheritance allows a class to inherit features from a parent class. Multiple inheritance extends this concept to allow a class to have more than one parent class and to inherit features from all parents. Thus, information may be mixed from multiple sources. A more complex kind of generalization—multiple inheritance—does not restrict a class hierarchy to a tree structure (as does single inheritance). Multiple inheritance provides greater modeling power for defining classes and enhances opportunities for reuse. Object models can more closely reflect the structure and function of the real world, but models can become more complicated to understand and implement. See Figure 4.8 for an example of multiple inheritance.[3]

Working with multiple inheritance can be difficult in implementation if only single inheritance is supported, but analysis and design models can be restructured to provide a usable model. Rumbaugh et al.[4] discusses the use of delegation as an implementation mechanism by which an object can forward an operation to another object for execution. The recommended techniques for restructuring include:

- *Delegation using aggregation of roles*: a superclass with multiple independent generalizations can be recast as an aggregate in which each component replaces a generalization.

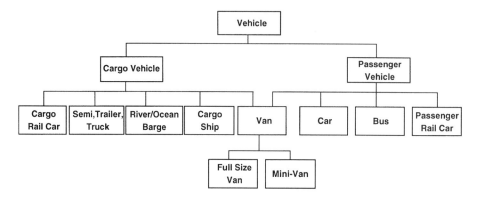

Figure 4.8   Multiple inheritance from overlapping classes

- *Inherit the most important class and delegate the rest*: a join class is made a subclass of its most important superclass.
- *Nested generalization*: factor on one generalization first, then the other, multiplying out all possible combinations.

Rumbaugh suggests issues to consider when selecting the best work around:

- If a subclass has several superclasses, all of equal importance, it may be best to use delegation and preserve symmetry in the model.
- If one superclass clearly dominates and the others are less important, implementing multiple inheritance via single inheritance and delegation may be best.
- If the number of combinations is small, consider nested generalization. Otherwise, avoid it.
- If one superclass has significantly more features than the other super-classes or one superclass is clearly the performance bottleneck, preserve inheritance through this path.
- If nested generalization is chosen, factor on the most important criterion first, then the next most important, etc.
- Try to avoid nested generalization if large quantities of code must be duplicated.
- Consider the importance of maintaining strict identity (only nested generalization preserves this).

4.5 KEYS

Object instances may be identified by an attribute (or combination of attributes) called a *key*. A *primary key* is an attribute (or combination of attributes) that uniquely identifies an object instance and corresponds to the identifier of an actual object. Customer number would usually be used as the primary key for customer object instances. Two or more attributes in combination sometimes must be used to uniquely identify an object instance. For example, the combination of last name, first name and middle initial might be used to identify a customer or employee object instance. Last name alone would not suffice because many people might have the same last name. First name would help, but there is still a problem with uniqueness. All three parts of the name are better still, although a system-generated customer or employee number is best used as an identifier if absolute uniqueness is desired. Possible primary keys that are not actually selected and used as the primary keys are called *candidate keys*.

A *secondary key* is an attribute (or combination of attributes) that may not uniquely identify an object instance but can describe a set of object instances that share some common characteristic. An attribute (customer type) might be used as a secondary key to group customers as internal to the business organization (subsidiaries or divisions) or external. Many customers could be typed as internal or external at the same time, but the secondary key is useful to identify customers for pricing and customer service reasons.

4.6 CONSTRAINTS

Referential Integrity

Optionality constraints on associations should be examined for referential integrity implications in the database models. Ask when referential integrity rules should be enforced—immediately or at a later time? When modeling object instances over time, you may need to introduce extra object classes to capture situations where attribute values can change over time. For instance, if you need to keep an audit trail of all changes to an order or invoice, you could add a date and time attribute to the order or invoice objects to allow for storage of a historical record of their instances. Each change to an instance would result in another instance of the object, stamped for data and time of instance creation.

Insert Rules

These rules determine the conditions under which a dependent class may be inserted and deal with restrictions the parent classes impose upon such insertions. The rules can be classified into six types:[5]

Dependent	Permit insertion of child class instance only when the matching parent class instance already exists.
Automatic	Always permit insertion of a child class instance. If the parent class instance does not exist, create one.
Nullify	Always permit insertion of the child class instance.
Default	Always permit insertion of a child class instance.
Customized	Allow child class instance insertion only if certain validity constraints are met.
No Effect	Always permit insertion of the child class instance. No matching parent class instances need exist, and no validity checking needs to be done.

Delete Rules

These rules determine conditions under which a parent class instance can be deleted, including possible restrictions imposed by child class instances. Six delete constraint types determine valid deletion of a parent class instance.

Restrict	Deletion of a parent instance is allowed only when no matching child class instances exist.
Cascade	Always allow deletion of parent class instances and delete all matching child class instances.
Nullify	Always allow deletion of parent class instances.
Default	Always allow deletion of parent class instances.
Customized	Allow deletion of parent class instances only if certain validity constraints are satisfied.
No Effect	Always allow deletion of parent class instances. Matching child class instances may or may not exist. No validity checking is performed.

Domain Integrity

These integrity rules define constraints on valid values that attributes can assume. A *domain* is a set of valid values for a given attribute—a set of logical or conceptual values from which one or more attributes can draw their values. For example, U.S. state codes might constitute the domain of attributes for employee state codes, customer state codes and supplier state codes. Domain characteristics include such things as:

- data type
- data length
- allowable value ranges
- value uniqueness
- whether a value can be null or not

Domains describe the valid set of values for an attribute, so domain definitions can help you determine whether certain data manipulation operations make sense. Two examples would be comparing two values for equality and forming an association between two classes based on two attributes.

One way to define domains and assign them to attributes is to define the domains first and then associate each attribute in your logical data model with a predefined domain. Another way is to assign domain characteristics to each attribute and then determine the domains by identifying certain similar groupings of domain characteristics. The first way seems better because it involves thorough study of domain characteristics before assigning them to attributes. Domain definitions can be refined as you assign them to attributes. In practice, you may have to use the second method of defining domains due to characteristics of available repositories or CASE tools, which may not allow you to define a domain as a separate modeling construct.

Domain definitions are important because they:

- Verify that attribute values make business sense.
- Determine whether two attribute occurrences of the same value really represent the same real-world value.
- Determine whether various data manipulation operations make business sense.

A domain range characteristic for *mortgagee* in a mortgage financing system could prevent a data entry clerk from entering an age of five years. Even though *mortgagee age* and *loan officer number* can have the same data type, length and value, they definitely have different meanings and should not be related to each other in any data manipulation operations. The values 38 for age and

Data Characteristic	Example
data type	character
	integer
	decimal
data length	8 characters
	8 digits with 2 decimals
allowable data values	x >= 21
	0 < x < 100
data value constraints	x in a set of allowable customer numbers
uniqueness	x must be unique
null values	x cannot be null
default value	x can default to the current date
	x can default to a dummy inventory tag number (for ordered items)

Figure 4.9   Typical domain values

38 for officer number represent two entirely unrelated values in the real world, even though numerically they are exactly the same.

It makes little sense to match records based on values of *mortgagee age* and *loan officer number*, even though it is possible. Matching *customer number* in a customer class and *customer payment* in a customer transaction class makes a great deal of sense. Typical domain characteristics that can be associated with a class attribute are shown in Figure 4.9.

Triggering Operation Integrity Rules

Triggering operation integrity rules govern insert, delete, update and retrieval validity. These rules involve the effects of operations on other classes or on other attributes within a class and include domains and insert/delete and other attribute business rules. Triggering operation constraints involve:

• Attributes across multiple classes or instances.

• Two or more attributes within a class.

• One attribute or class and an external parameter.

Example triggering constraints include:

- An employee may only save up to three weeks time off.
- A customer may not exceed a predetermined credit limit.
- All customer invoices must include at least one line item.
- Order dates must be current or future dates.

Triggering operations have two components:

- The event or condition that causes an operation to execute.
- The action set in motion by the event or condition.

When you define triggering rules, you are concerned only with the logic of the operations, not execution efficiency or the particular implementation of the rules. You will implement and tune the rule processing later when you translate the logical database model to a physical database implementation. It is important to avoid defining processing solutions (like defining special attributes to serve as processing flags such as a posted indicator for invoices) until all information requirements have been defined in the logical object model and fully understood.

Triggering operations can be similar to referential integrity constraints, which focus on valid deletions of parent class instances and insertions of child class instances. Ask specific questions about each association, attribute and class in order to elucidate necessary rules regarding data entry and processing constraints.

Triggering operation rules:

1. Define rules for all attributes that are sources for other derived attributes.
2. Define rules for subtypes so that when a subtype instance is deleted, the matching supertype is also deleted.
3. Define rules for time-initiated integrity constraints.

END NOTES

[1] Booch, Grady. *Object-Oriented Design with Applications* (Redwood City, CA: Benjamin/Cummings) 1991, p. 59.

[2] Rumbaugh, James, Michael Blaha, William Premerlani, Frederick Eddy and William Lorensen. *Object-Oriented Modeling and Design* (Englewood Cliffs, NJ: Prentice Hall) 1991, p. 64.

[3] Ibid., p. 65.

[4] Ibid., pp. 67–68.

[5] Fleming, Candace C., and Barbara von Halle. *Handbook of Relational Database Design* (Reading, MA: Addison-Wesley) 1989.

5

Business Functions and Subject Areas

Information engineering's planning phase describes the executive view of an organization, including the mission, goals, strategies, organization structure, functions, processes, subject areas, entities, problems, critical success factors, critical assumptions and other information important in supporting the strategic direction of the organization. This book does not cover these topics in any detail except for functions, processes, subject areas and entities.

The astute reader may wonder why I cover planning issues in the middle of analysis modeling. The idea is to cover the data structure component of object modeling before attempting to examine business functions, the typical starting point for process modeling in conventional information engineering. Analysts who are very familiar with process modeling may be tempted to jump into a process-driven approach if the object data structures are not defined first. As with conventional information engineering, object-oriented information engineering places great emphasis on the data model, but more so on objects. Functions and subject areas will be retained as enterprise model components, but processes will not be modeled in the same manner. Subject areas and entities will become object classes.

When enterprise planning is conducted, an overview model of the organization is built that describes organization units, locations, functions and entity types, among other items. Functions are performed at certain locations. Organization units reside at certain locations, entity types must be related to

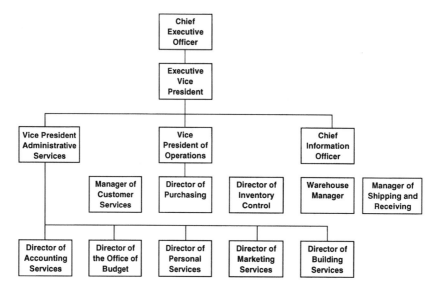

Figure 5.1   An organization chart

processes and so on. A variety of detailed matrices are built that associate entity types and subject areas together, entity types and functions and entity types and processes. Data (subject areas and entity types) must be related to functions and processes. With object modeling, this linking of process and data together will be a natural byproduct of model creation.

An organization chart is a convenient place to begin building planning models. Note that as an organization is an object, so are the organization units. An organization chart depicts an object aggregation hierarchy (Figure 5.1). The difference in object modeling is that both data and process are grouped together. This level of detail isn't modeled in planning yet, but rather later on in analysis. However, organization units can be useful in defining the scope of an analysis project. Many organizations are simply too large to model in a single analysis project. The organization chart can be used to identify a portion of the enterprise on which to focus modeling efforts. Information strategy plans encompass an entire organization if possible, but analysis projects must have a much smaller span of information in order to be workable.

An organization typically has operations at multiple locations, perhaps only rooms in a single building but often locations at cities around the globe. Locations are important to business modeling because they form the basis for models of distributed information systems. A planner would build a matrix of organization units to locations, and analysts would also be interested in entities (object classes) and processes (high-level objects or lower-level object operations) versus locations.

5.1 CHARACTERIZE BUSINESS FUNCTIONS

Once an organization chart has been constructed, a planner typically proceeds to model the decomposition of business functions. A business function represents a group of activities that are conducted together to support one key aspect of supporting the enterprise mission. Functions are named with nouns or gerunds. In larger organizations, functions may be grouped together into higher-level functional area objects:

Finance

Marketing

Production

Accounting

Human Resources

Functions can be decomposed into processes. A function is an ongoing, continuous set of activities, but a process relates to a specific task that has a definite beginning point and ending point. Processes have identifiable inputs and outputs and are usually named with a verb:

Record Customer Order

Select Product

Update Employee Records

Maintain Tax Tables

Functions are useful for defining scope of object models. Processes could serve this purpose, as in conventional business area analysis, but I discourage use of traditional processes in object-oriented information engineering. The reason is that processes are really object operations (components of objects)

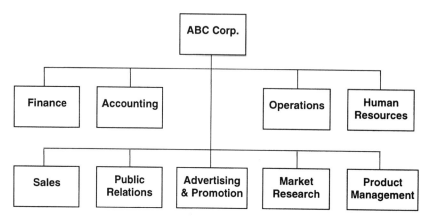

Figure 5.2   A business function decomposition chart

or messages sent to objects. Therefore, within the scope of a function or subfunction, an external agent object will likely send a message to a system object to begin a possibly complex set of activities in response to the external event's message.

Decomposition of functions and subfunctions (Figure 5.2) should be conducted independently of organization structure because the organization may change its form frequently, but the functions and process structures tend to remain more stable. (Data structures are even more stable.) You should strive to make your enterprise models stable over time, and organization structure is definitely not stable in many enterprises these days. Functions should define what activities must be performed in order to manage an organization, not how these activities are to be conducted. Procedures that define how activities are to be performed will be described during systems design, not during analysis.

5.2 CHARACTERIZE OBJECT CLASSES WITHIN EACH FUNCTION

In object structure modeling (Chapters 3 and 4), we discussed hierarchies of object classes. Subject areas are used to define groupings of related entity types in conventional information engineering, but really represent high-level object classes in object modeling. From the planning model point of view, they are the same. Example subject areas might be:

Customers

Products

Supplies

Equipment

Employees

Suppliers

Within each subject area (high-level object class), we identify more detailed object classes. These object classes represent a person, place, thing, concept or event about which the enterprise needs to store information. Examples include those shown below and in Figure 5.3:

Purchasing
Order
Material Type
Service Type
Property Type

Human Resources
Employee
Organization
Skill Type

Payables
Supplier Invoice
Disbursement
Dividend

Finance
Category
Classification
Property
Allocation Cost
Depreciation/Amortization
Revenue Type
Expenditure Type
Hournal Event

Work
Material
Schedule
Storage Location
Service
Task
Receipt

Figure 5.3   **High-level clases**

Customer

    Customer

    Locations

    Contacts

    Account

Orders

    Customer Order

    Order Item

    Invoice

    Invoice Item

    Payment

Sales Organization

    Region

    Territory

    District

    Branch

    Salesperson

See Chapter 3 for more examples of subject areas. Each of these object classes might be decomposed into other object classes. Once a fairly complete list of subject areas has been developed, each can be decomposed into its constituent object classes. Object classes that have already been identified might be grouped into a logical subject area. The subject area itself may be so generic that it contains no actual attributes—it is a conceptual tool used only for modeling at this point.

An example of a very generic subject area might be that of *person*, composed of employee, manager, supplier and so on. The person class might contain an identifier and name of the person later on when detailed analysis is conducted, but at this point it is useful simply to group concrete object classes (ones with obvious attribute content) into one or more subject areas. Note that if a member belongs to more than one subject area, an object may exhibit

Object	Operation			
	1	2	3	4
A	C	R		RU
B	CRUD	R		R
C	R	CU	R	
D	R	R	R	CRUD

Figure 5.4   A CRUD matrix for objects

multiple inheritance due to its multiple parent classes. The details of inheritance implementation are not of concern at this point but one can readily prepare for rich models with multiple inheritance. Chapter 3 covered identification of subject areas and object classes in some detail, so we will not repeat the discussion here. What we do need to cover is the analysis of object classes within a business function (or business area).

Object life-cycle analysis is described in detail during object behavior analysis. For now, it is sufficient to identify basic object access actions from the standpoint of a function. The CRUD matrix can be used to document operations that act upon objects and analyze how the use of information within an object changes over the life cycle of the object (see Figure 5.4). The matrix is especially useful after operations have been identified with a business function. At this point, operations can be mapped against class data structures, as processes are mapped against entities in conventional information engineering. The next section discusses the identification of these operations.

5.3   IDENTIFY OPERATIONS FOR OBJECTS WITHIN A FUNCTION

When object class structures have been defined well enough and key business functions identified, you can begin writing descriptions of each function that include information requirements (ties to the object structure model). Be sure to focus on what functions do, not how to implement them. Don't worry just yet how operations (business processes) are to be defined—just identify them and get an idea of which functions use them and which object classes contain them. The traditional process decomposition hierarchy chart will not be used. Rather, a set of object structure hierarchy charts, which may include object operations, will be used.

When defining functions and their associated operations, you may use a declarative description to describe relationships between input values and output values and the relationships between the various output values. The next chapter discusses object interaction models, where these various relationships can be described graphically using message flow diagrams and data flow diagrams.

The approach used in this book does not dictate that operations be completely defined early in the analysis process, but that operations be identified and placed in the proper context before complete specification. It is easy to keep adding useful operations to analysis models, without knowing for sure when to stop. This is perfectly natural when the problem space is large and little structure is available yet for modeling operations in regard to owning objects and operations in other objects.

A prototyping or iterative development approach defines only parts of a complex system design in order to zero in on some of the key features of a system. When detailed analysis and design models are available, they greatly assist designers in building prototypes. Otherwise, a prototype is built first and the models built either in parallel with prototypes or before prototypes and designs are considered to be anywhere near complete. Likewise, a fairly complete, structured set of object models for placing operations in context should be used when available. For now, the focus is on identifying operations without concern for the details.

Operations can correspond to queries of object attributes or associations in an object model, events in the behavioral models and functions and processes in the interaction model. Operations that can be derived from object structures include reading and writing attributes and navigating association connections. Events are a source of information about operations because each event message sent to an object corresponds to an operation on that object. Event messages may be shown as labels on transitions in object state diagrams. Each object on a message flow diagram contains some operation that responds to the messages being sent into the object.

Bertrand Meyer[1] speaks of a "shopping list" of operations observed from the real-world behavior of object classes. Operations need not be dependent on a particular application. Shopping list operations permit consideration of any future needs while the object class structures are still not completely defined. They allow widening analysis efforts beyond an immediate problem, to the overall functioning of an entire enterprise business information system.

Once you have a fairly long list of possible object operations, look at your object structure models for operations that seem to be similar. Look for variations on a single operation. Often redundancy in operations can be eliminated by examining class inheritance structure and by placing common operations as high in the class inheritance hierarchy as possible. Consider promoting a new subclass to handle such operations. Using fewer operations simplifies analysis models greatly and enhances reuse.

5.4 CHARACTERIZE INFORMATION REQUIREMENTS ACROSS FUNCTIONS

Object classes can be associated with business functions using a matrix (see Figure 5.5). First, build a simple matrix that associates high-level object classes (subject areas) with functions. Then refine the associations to include the basic operations of create, read, update and delete. Chapter 3 discussed using such a matrix with these operations indicated in each function/object cell. Start with functions versus high-level classes in the fashion of a function/subject area matrix and work down to fundamental classes to depict individual operations within a function mapped against fundamental objects.

Create, read, update and delete values are often determined during the data modeling discussed earlier. Definitions of lower-level functions should allow some identification of data access actions taken on classes and hierar-

Business Function

Class	1	2	3	4
A		X		\
B	\	X	\	
C			\	
D	\		X	\

Figure 5.5 **Object class involved in business functions**

chies of classes. Sometimes, several functions will create or delete an object. When this occurs, each function's action must be determined against each attribute in the object, not just the overall object. Each function should update a subset of the attributes of an object. Problems may exist when multiple functions create or delete the same attribute. During analysis, business people and analysis modelers should identify only possible duplication problems. Building and reviewing a CRUD matrix help detect problems that can be addressed during detailed analysis. The process is useful in building and validating subject areas and low-level functions and their associations.

5.5 BUILD AN INVENTORY OF BUSINESS EVENTS

Objects interact with each other, sending messages that stimulate responses. An event is something that occurs at a point in time, such as customer inquires about order, sales manager requests sales report or end-of-day processing deadline arrives. In concept, an event is instantaneous. One event may be unrelated to other events or two or more events could follow in sequence. An event in the modeling sense is a unidirectional transmission of information from one object to another. Responses are modeled to events within the behavioral and interaction models, but here interest is in building lists of events for organizing subsequent detailed analysis.

A system event may represent a signal that something within the system has occurred, but this book does not cover these types of events. What is covered are those events that business people care about, hence the name *business events*. Business information is identified that comes into the function from outside the function, information system or the enterprise itself, as well as information the function needs to produce as output to be sent to the external environment—other functions or objects outside the information system or enterprise as a whole.

The function under study produces outputs in response to events, stimuli from the function's environment. All events are to be identified that occur in the function's external environment and to which the function must respond. An event list is a narrative list of stimuli that occur in the function's outside world to which the function must respond. These events can be categorized as flow-oriented (triggered by message flows), temporal (triggered by arrival of points in time) or control events (triggered by stimuli that occur at some unpredictable point in time). See Figure 5.6 for examples of each of these types of events.

Flow-oriented
- customer places order
- customer sends payment
- vendor shipment arrives

Temporal
- time arrives for daily transaction closing
- time arrives for month-end processing

Control
- customer credit limit guidelines need to be changed
- estimated lead time for vendor shipments changes
- product item inventory level falls at or below reorder level

Figure 5.6   Types of business events

5.6 BUILD FUNCTION CONTEXT MODELS

Before describing interactions between multiple objects within the scope of a business function, a very high level interaction model should be built to define the external interfaces of the function itself. An actual physical system may or may not be built to implement a particular business function, but it is useful to view the function as an object for modeling purposes. The context diagram used in conventional information engineering process modeling can serve this purpose well.

A context diagram, accompanied by a list of events and description of the function being modeled, completes what Edward Yourdon[2] calls the *environmental model* for the function. Yourdon's *behavioral model* corresponds to the combination of the interaction model and behavior model here. The environmental model describes the function interfaces and key inflows and outflows of information, along with those objects that send and receive that information. Figure 5.7 lists some characteristics of context diagrams.

Within the function (or system) defined on a context diagram, the object structures, object behaviors and object interactions are covered in detail. The context diagram helps to keep discussions and analysis and modeling efforts confined to a portion of an enterprise's information systems requirements.

- Central idea is depicted as one business process
- Central process is surrounded by related external agents
- Data flows to/from external agents describe main activities
- Scope and boundaries of a project are defined
- Related external agents (external objects) are identified
- Main inputs and outputs are shown
- "Big picture" of a single business function or the entire system is communicated
- All input and output messages, external agents and a single function or system are shown in a single message flow diagram
- If it represents a system, the central object is named for the system
- If it represents a business function, the central object is the function name

Figure 5.7   Characteristics of context diagrams

Business functions can have dozens of incoming and outgoing message flows and a large system can have hundreds of flows. Message flows will be documented in detail later, but first key flows in and out of the function are identified in order to ensure proper interfaces between functions.

If every function in a system is modeled in this way, a larger, higher-level message flow diagram can be constructed to depict concisely function interfaces present in a very complex enterprise model. Many development methodologies do not connect application models together to build an enterprise model, but information engineering has promoted this idea for some time now. The entire enterprise may be depicted on the highest level message flow diagram, the context diagram for the entire enterprise. Building such a diagram is mechanically the same as what is described here, but the message flows will be very high level abstractions of numerous lower-level flows.

Be sure to spend a lot of time building the context diagrams and event lists for business functions before embarking on detailed analysis projects. If this is not done, opportunities to define key system interfaces and messages flowing between parts of the system can be missed. Many refinements and revisions will likely be made to high-level business function models because no one person can usually understand the function as analysis first begins. Business people should be encouraged to build a vision of what a function should do in the future, not what it does today. Extensive analysis of the functioning of a business enterprise and the associated modeling of business functions affords an ideal opportunity to reorganize for greater effectiveness in achieving business goals and strategies, furthering the organization's enterprise mission. Don't just throw a context diagram and event list together and consider the job done. Make sure that the environmental model for the function is complete before proceeding on to more detailed analysis and modeling.

END NOTES

[1] Meyer, Bertrand. *Object-Oriented Software Construction* (Hertfordshire, England: Prentice Hall International) 1988.

[2] Yourdon, Edward. *Modern Structured Analysis* (Englewood Cliffs, NJ: Yourdon Press, Prentice Hall) 1989, p. 337.

6

Individual Object Behaviors

As the object structures are identified and modeled, basic processing requirements for each object can be identified. How each object responds to messages from other objects needs to be defined. Object structure models describe data statically whereas object behavior models describe how object data structures change values over time. Because change over time can be difficult to comprehend in a complex system, the structure of objects and their relationships to each other are modeled first. This is consistent with information engineering's focus on data before process, in order to ensure that systems are nonredundant. With object behavior modeling, however, processes are modeled in the context of classes and objects, so there are a natural normalization of behaviors as well as data structures. This chapter views object behavior from the point of view of one object, in isolation of other objects. Chapter 7 deals with modeling networks of intercommunicating objects—object interaction modeling. When object interaction modeling is performed, individual object behaviors need to be revisited.

Object behavior modeling involves describing object states and the conditions and events that cause an object to change from one state to another, actions that an object performs and actions that are performed on an object. Some systems also need any exceptions to normal behavior to be recorded as well as any real-time constraints imposed on the behavior of objects.

Aspects of an information system concerned with time and changes are often referred to as the dynamic model.[1] Control of a system describes sequences of operations that occur in response to external stimuli, with no consideration of what these operations do, what they operate on or how they are implemented. This chapter describes how systems of objects must deal with flow of control, interactions and sequencing of operations. A later chapter deals with these topics again in more detail. The purpose here is to capture any behavioral requirements early—before any attempt is made to build models that follow more traditional functional decomposition (see the next chapter).

6.1 IDENTIFY OBJECT STATES

A good starting point for modeling object behavior is to describe the various states that an object exhibits. States represent object status, phase, situation or activity. Each object may go through many different states, from object creation until object termination. An object's state is represented by the values that the object's attributes can take on. A change in any attribute's value constitutes a change in the object's state.

There are a few different ways to discover object states. One way is to observe objects within a system and then to record the observed states. A customer order may be recorded but not filled, filled but not shipped, shipped but still active or inactive, for instance. The state of customer orders is recorded by some attribute of the order (and possibly of the individual items on the order as well). The status attribute changes value as the customer order changes state throughout its life.

Another way to discover object states is to examine the attributes directly. Each change in an attribute's value reflects a change in the state of the object that owns that attribute. First examine the potential values for attributes and then determine whether the system requirements include different behaviors for those possible attribute values. This is the approach used by Coad and Yourdon.[2]

Processing requirements for an entire system can be described in terms of the behavior of its objects and the corresponding changes in object states. The behavior of an object can be described over time as a series of state changes. An object state diagram can be used to depict the states that an object can be in over time. This kind of diagram identifies states and transitions from one state to another. Object state diagrams can be drawn using the "fence"

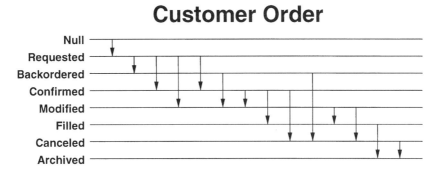

Figure 6.1   An object state diagram—fence notation

notation of Martin and Odell[3] (Figure 6.1) or a network diagram, with bubbles or boxes for states and lines or arcs for transitions between states (Figure 6.2). A third notation used to describe object states and transitions between states is an object state matrix (Figure 6.3).

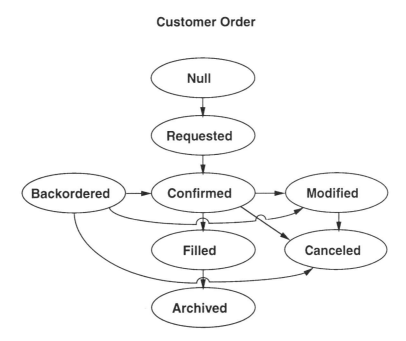

Figure 6.2   An object state diagram—network notation

Customer Order

	A (Null)	B Requested	C Back ordered	D Confirmed	E Modified	F Filled	G Canceled	H Archived
Record Order	B							
Record Backorder		C						
Confirm Order		D	D					
Modify Order		E	E	E				
Fill Order				F	F			
Cancel Order			G	G	G			
Archive Order						H	H	

Figure 6.3   An object state matrix

Detailed behaviors and changes in behavior are defined within the specification of each behavior operation (just as the processing logic and data accesses of fundamental processes are specified using mini-spec action diagrams during business area analysis).

The object state diagram using a network notation represents states by oval bubbles. Each of these bubbles corresponds to a single state of an object. The name of each state is placed inside the state bubble. The arcs connecting the states represent the state transitions and may or may not be labeled, depending upon the needs of a project or the methodology used to model object behavior. It is important to remember that a state is either on or off at any point in time. A state is on when the object is currently in that state; it is off when the object is in some other state.

As Martin and Odell[4] point out, a useful technique for object behavior specifications is the *finite-state machine*, a hypothetical machine that can exist in only one of a finite number of states at any given point in time. Each finite-state machine changes its state and produces output in response to a stimulus from the external environment. This technique is used to depict object state transitions by having each machine describing a single set of objects. External stimuli are responsible for triggering state changes and responses are in turn returned to the invoking external environment. Figures 6.4a and 6.4b show the basic notation for a finite-state machine.

Martin and Odell[5] list these primary components of a finite-state machine and its interface with the external environment:

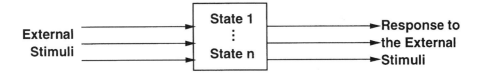

Figure 6.4a   Finite-state machine—external view

1. An event in the external environment stimulates or triggers an operation within a machine.

2. Each operation is invoked to change the state of exactly one object.

3. Each operation is specified in terms of object types that must apply to an object before the operation and those that apply after. These prestates and poststates are guaranteed by each operation.

4. Within each finite-state machine, a specific operation is selected on the basis of trigger and state preconditions.

5. Before an operation is invoked, some adaptations of finite-state machines require that a control condition be evaluated. Only if the condition is true will the operation actually be invoked.

6. When the invoked operation is successfully completed (there is a state change), an event occurs.

7. The occurrence of an event indicates that a response should be sent to the external environment.

In the process of modeling states and their transitions, the relationship of one state to another within the operation of a system needs to be considered.

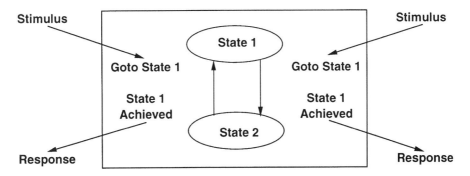

Figure 6.4b   Finite-state machine—internal view

Expected business events and system conditions that activate a change of object state need to be described. The process of moving an object from one state to another is a transition. Events and conditions that activate these transitions are triggers. In the customer order example, the event "receive customer order" becomes the trigger for recording the order. The condition "item out of stock" triggers the recording of a backorder.

An object state diagram should relate triggers and states. When a trigger stimulates an object, the next state depends on the current state as well as the trigger. A change of state caused by a trigger is the transition, performed by an object operation (implemented as a method in design). On a state diagram, the transition is drawn as an arc or line with an arrowhead showing the direction of the state change. An object state matrix (Figure 6.3) depicts explicitly the dependencies between states and the operations that cause transitions to occur. All transitions from a state represent different triggers and thus different operations.

An event or condition causing a state transition operation to occur can be specified on an object state diagram, but an event scenario diagram can also be used for this (see Chapter 7). If an object is in a state and a trigger identified with one of its possible transitions occurs, the object enters the state on the target end of the transition. This is depicted on an object state matrix as the identifier or name of the target state and is placed in the cell at the intersection of the starting state and the operation that performs the transition. If more than one transition leaves a state, the first trigger to occur causes the corresponding operation to execute the transition. If a trigger occurs that has no leaving transition defined for the starting state, the trigger is ignored. A sequence of triggers (events or conditions) can be depicted on an object state diagram as pathways through the network of states.

An object state diagram can be used to describe the behavior of an entire class of objects. By definition, all instances of a class have the same structure and behavior, so they can all share the same state diagram. Each object has its own distinct attribute values (and, therefore, distinct states) so it goes though state transitions uniquely as the different triggers occur.

6.2 CHARACTERIZE OBJECT OPERATIONS

An operation represents what an object does in response to a specific triggering event or condition. Operations are performed in response to a combination of starting object states and the specific trigger that occurs. Each trigger and any conditions associated with it that may cause a transition operation to execute need to be identified. Then the action that takes place during the transition between states needs to be defined. This action may be composed of several simpler actions, each of which may or may not execute each time the overall transition operation is triggered. This means that a transition may have multiple threads of execution, each of which must complete before the overall transition is through. An example of this might be the multiple data accesses required to record information when a customer places an order (read customer record, read product item record, write order header, write order line, etc.).

Many notations may be used to define object operations, but a convenient one might be to use a mini-spec action diagram. The name of the diagram is the name of the transition operation and the diagram itself describes the overall operation. Conditional logic is easily depicted using condition blocks; repetition blocks depict looping actions. Using an action diagram has the advantage that it is fairly consistent with traditional information engineering techniques, thus providing a workable migration path to full object orientation.

As with more traditional process modeling, a complex object operation may be decomposed into separate operations. A conventional process decomposition diagram could be used to depict levels of operations. The difference between this use of a process decomposition diagram and the traditional way is that object behavior modeling would use a process decomposition within the context of a class, not an entire system (although one could argue that a system is a class, modeling processes at such a gross level has serious problems).

Once object structures have been modeled and operations identified for class structures within the object model, a process decomposition diagram and the associated mini-spec action diagrams provide a nice way to both specify object behavior and to migrate from traditional structured analysis models. Within an object model, the decomposition diagram depicts processes within an operation and the mini-spec action diagrams depict methods to support parts of the overall operation. An operation may affect multiple object state changes via its own methods. These methods (fundamental operation processes) will likely cause one or only a few state changes and will have specific processing logic defined for making these state changes.

When specifying logic for methods, it is important to avoid building in knowledge of what triggers may cause method execution. Just as an external object must not be aware of how another object implements its methods, those methods must be totally unaware of what external triggers cause their own execution. Also, each method needs to be unaware of what happens after it executes. Methods are, however, aware of their triggers through the parameters passed in from outside. This information hiding from the inside of a method allows for greater method and operation reuse.

When it is necessary to analyze and model very large, complex systems, consider some additional features of object behavior modeling, suggested by Martin and Odell:[6]

- Operation Scripting: Express how an object's state changes over time with step-by-step script aids experts who are accustomed to starting problems in a sequential manner. The script entails an orderly sequence of finite-state machines as a way to carry out an operation.

- Specification Leveling: Compose or decompose each script using levels of process specification. Analysis can proceed from high levels of generality to more detailed ones and vice versa.

- Operation Reusability: Define operations as processing units. Define kinds of required inputs and outputs. The same operation can be included within any number of operation scripts—each operation is an object type whose instances are its various invocations.

- Process Concurrency: In the real world, processes occur simultaneously. Events can trigger multiple, parallel operations. Parallel operations can simultaneously result in different state changes. Concurrently produced results may require synchronization before invoking further operations.

6.3 DEFINE TRIGGER CONDITIONS AND EVENTS

A trigger causes a state transition operation to execute for a particular object when certain events occur or when certain conditions are met. These events and conditions can be external or internal to the object. In any case, a trigger represents a boolean logic expression for expected events and conditions that result in a true or false result.

A condition is a logical requirement for the current state of an object, the current state of the system, the existence or absence of an object or the existence or absence of relationships among objects. Condition-based triggers cause an operation to execute when a logical statement is true. For instance, an operation to reorder product inventory would execute for a specific product inventory object only if that object's attributes defined that the inventory level is at or below a certain reorder level. As another example, consider a bad customer credit action. If a customer's credit valuation is good, the bad credit action is not taken.

An event is a change to a system. Examples might be the receipt of a customer order, vendor shipment or product inquiry. When an object responds to an event, it does so as a result of some change to the system. Events can be detected in object state networks using triggers by employing what Embley et al.[7] refers to as an event monitor. These monitors are conceptual devices that observe a certain type of event in a system. The name of an event monitor associates the trigger with the type of event it monitors. An example might be "product reorder condition met" as the name for the monitor that evaluates whether product inventory levels are adequate.

For this discussion, an event triggers an operation only at the instant that the event occurs. A condition triggers an operation during the entire time that a particular condition is present. A trigger based on an event monitor can only cause an operation to execute if the operation is enabled at the time the event occurs. If the operation is not enabled, the event is ignored by the object.

6.4 MODEL OBJECT LIFE CYCLES

In order to build a comprehensive system of interoperating objects, how an object moves to and from various states needs to be fully described. The previous discussion of object state diagrams and object state matrices gives some idea of how object life cycles might be modeled.

You could use a formal notation for describing object life cycles (the event schema of Martin and Odell or the state network configuration of Embley et al.) or just document the details within the descriptions that support the diagrams and the method specifications. The actual life cycle of some objects is quite complex. However object life cycles are documented, it is important that they are examined in detail.

Subsequent states follow a state transition. Each state could have several follow-on states defined for it (but only one subsequent state is chosen for the next transition), as shown in the previous object state diagrams and the object state matrix. Prior states precede a state transition. Multiple states may lead to a single state (but not at the same time). Initial transactions activate initial states, those states that exist when an object comes into existence. Initial states have no prior states and have no conditions necessary for placing an object in those states. Common operation names assigned to initial state transitions are: create, record, initiate and establish. State diagrams in this book use a NULL state as a conceptual state for an initial operation to start from when establishing an object.

Final states require no subsequent states. As an operation executes to place an object in a final state, prior states are turned off. When a final state is reached, the object ceases to exist (at least, it is not active in the system but may be archived). Common names for operations that place objects in final states include: cancel, terminate, destroy, finish, close or end.

Build an Object State Matrix

Begin object life-cycle modeling by identifying all known states that an object can be in. Then place these states on an object state diagram. Starting with the NULL state, draw a transition arc or line to the next state. Label the next state and continue mapping transitions from state to state. Be sure to include the final state(s) on the diagram. Label the transitions using operation names if desired at this time, but be sure that all states are identified and named.

Once the object state diagram is complete, build an object state matrix for those objects whose state networks are fairly complex. Label the columns of the matrix with the states depicted on the object state diagram (I use a letter as an identifier of each row) and the rows with the names of the operations that perform the state transitions (for simplicity, number these rows for subsequent mapping back on the arcs or lines of the object state diagram).

Starting with the NULL state, locate the row that represents the initial state transition operation. In the cell that represents the intersection of the NULL state and the initial operation, place the identifier for the next state that the operation will place the object in, based on the current state (the NULL state initially). The transition from NULL to the initial state requires no more states, so begin defining transitions to subsequent states from that initial state (identify states to place in the cells under the initial state column).

Progress along each column, identifying subsequent states, the operation to make the transition to each of these subsequent states and the code for the subsequent state in which each operation places the object. Place the subsequent state code (a letter in this example) into the cell that represents that starting state and that transition operation. For each state (column), identify all subsequent states (column codes) and the associated operations (rows) that make the transitions to those states. Indicate the subsequent state codes in the cell for that row and column.

After all states of the matrix have been examined, be sure that each column has at least one cell below it that contains a state code and that each row has at least one cell that contains a state code. Each state may have multiple transitions from it to subsequent states and each operation may have more than one starting state (but only one ending state). Figure 6.3 shows what the finished matrix should look like.

Hierarchies of Object States

Ordinary, flat state diagrams lack the modeling power needed for large, complex systems. When the system being modeled is very complex, it may become necessary to use layered object state diagrams in the same way that objects are layered in a hierarchy.

Each object state diagram in a hierarchy of such diagrams would have one associated object state matrix (if needed). Rumbaugh et al.[8] discusses ways to model object state networks as generalization and aggregation hierarchies.

Generalization of object states allows states and events to be arranged into generalization hierarchies with inheritance of common structure and behavior (similar to the inheritance of attributes and operations in classes). Aggregation of object states consists of breaking them into their components as processes are decomposed in a process decomposition hierarchy. Aggregation is equivalent to concurrency among states. Concurrent states can correspond to object aggregations—even entire systems—that have interacting parts.

Operations in a complex state can be expanded as a lower-level object state diagram, with each state representing one step of the operation. Nested diagrams of this type show input and output transitions, and the set of nested diagrams forms a lattice structure. A nested object state diagram represents a kind of generalization on states, with the generalization being the "or" relationship. An object in a state in a higher-level diagram must be in exactly one of the substates depicted on the child diagram for that state. States on nested child diagrams refine the states in their parent diagrams.

When a customer asks a telephone company to install a new telephone line, a service order is created. From the customer's point of view, the service order is either open or completed, but from the phone company's viewpoint, the service order can be in a multitude of states, one of which is waiting to be installed. The actual installation of the telephone line by the phone company (actions taken during the waiting-to-be-installed state of the service order) places the telephone line in an operational state. This operational state in turn consists of substates and operations representing the running of a computerized telephone switch as it manages the telephone line. The computerized telephone switch system is itself a complex system, probably having its own nested object states.

States could have substates that inherit operations from their superstates, as subclasses inherit attributes and operations from their superclasses. Any operation that applies to a state automatically applies to all its substates unless overridden by an equivalent operation on the substate. State transitions of a superstate are inherited by each substate.

Embley et al.[9] discuss ways to interrelates state networks and class generalization/specialization hierarchies.

END NOTES

[1] Rumbaugh, James, Michael Blaha, William Premerlani, Frederick Eddy and William Lorensen. *Object-Oriented Modeling and Design* (Englewood Cliffs, NJ: Prentice Hall) 1991, p. 238.

[2] Coad, Peter, and Edward Yourdon. *Object-Oriented Analysis*, 2nd ed. (Englewood Cliffs, NJ: Yourdon Press, Prentice Hall) 1991.

[3] Martin, James, and James J. Odell. *Object-Oriented Analysis and Design* (Englewood Cliffs, NJ: Prentice Hall) 1992.

[4] Ibid., pp. 320–325.

[5] Ibid., p. 323.

[6] Ibid., p. 326.

[7] Embley, David W., Barry D. Kurtz and Scott N. Woodfield, *Object-Oriented Systems Analysis: A Model-Driven Approach.* (Englewood Cliffs, NJ: Yourdon Press, Prentice Hall) 1992, p. 67.

[8] Rumbaugh, et al., *Object-Oriented Modeling and Design*, p. 238.

[9] Embley et al., *Object-Oriented Systems Analysis: A Model-Driven Approach*, pp. 88–93.

7

Object Interactions

Object structure models describe object data structures and the relationships between them. The behavior model describes the behavior of individual objects in isolation from other objects in a system. Now how to describe the interactions between objects is covered. As business events occur in an organization, the people and information systems objects must respond to these events in order to support the mission, goals and strategies of the enterprise. An object interaction model consisting of event scenarios and message traffic between objects helps to describe fully the coupling between objects in a system. As new objects and attributes or new object states and operations are discovered, it may be necessary to revisit the object structure and behavior models to update them and validate the interaction model.

7.1 BUILD FUNCTION CONTEXT MODELS

During the information engineering planning phase (using Martin's IE approach[1]), a business analyst works with executives to describe the missions, goals, strategies, business functions and subject areas (classes) among other executive-level business system characteristics. These business system characteristics are very important to analysts and modelers because they form a high-level framework from which to define and build strategic information systems.

Enterprise functions and subject areas form the basis for high-level analysis, the beginning of business area analysis. Decomposition of functions into subfunctions does not change with object orientation, but decomposition of processes does. A function is a very high level business enterprise object, with many data structures (class structures) and processes (class operations). A subject area may become an abstract class that further defines concrete object structures that appear in our object models later on in analysis. The business functions and subject areas serve to help scope the analysis efforts.

One good technique often used in structured analysis and information engineering for defining project scope and boundaries is the building of context models for functions and processes. These context models use a simple data flow diagram, called a context diagram, to define all inputs and outputs to a single high-level process (actually, a process, function or entire system). External agents are placed around the process, and one data flow into the process from each external agent and one out of the process to each external agent are drawn and labeled. These single inflows or outflows are usually fairly complex, composed of all the information flowing to or from an external agent, which may be a person, organization or another information system that interacts with the process depicted on the context diagram. Figure 7.1 shows an example context diagram for an order entry function.

Some modelers choose to depict each individual flow to or from an external agent. This can result in very busy context diagrams for complex functions, high-level processes or information systems, but can be very useful when depicting the interfaces to an individual class as in object behavior modeling.

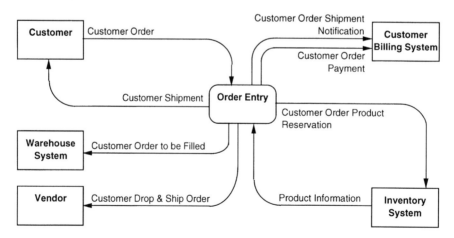

Figure 7.1   Order entry function context diagram

Indeed, context modeling via context diagrams is extremely useful in facilitated workshop sessions to describe project scope and external interfaces for a variety of analysis project topic areas.

7.2 BUILD EVENT LISTS

An event represents an external system stimulus, something that happens at a certain point in time and that requires a response by a system. Lists of events are helpful when characterizing the overall behavioral requirements for a system. At about the same time that the context diagram is built for a function, it is useful to create a complete list of business events (system events will be addressed in design) to accompany the context diagram .

Using the list of events created when function context models are created, data flows can be described in much more detail. Either just before, during or just after creating function context diagrams, lists of business events need to be built that stimulate the system, requiring some system response (Figures 7.2 and 7.3). Figure 7.4 shows an event context diagram.

7.3 DESCRIBE EVENT RESPONSE SCENARIOS

A scenario is a sequence of events that occurs when a part of a system operates. This sequence of events might include the major events in a system or just a few events. Think of an event scenario as the step-by-step actions that take place when an event stimulates the system.

A Simple Event List

External Agent	Stimulus	Response	External Agent
Customer	Retail Sales	Receipts	Customer
Supplier	Shipment Info	Purchase Order	Supplier
	End of Day	Deposits	Bank
	End of Week	Sales Reports	Sales Manager
	End of Year		CPA Firm

Figure 7.2   A simple event list

External Agent Stimulus	Stimulus	Response
Customer	Places Order	Verify Order
		Generate Price List
Shipper ◄———————————————		Generate Shipping Instructions
		Assemble Product
Customer ◄———————————————		Ship Product
Inventory Management System ◄————		Generate Inventory Reduction
Finance ◄———————————————		Generate Order/Shipped Value
Sales Manager ◄—————————		Generate Sales Report

Figure 7.3   A structured event list

For each event identified in an event list, list each detailed response that the system needs to make. As an example, the scenario for using a telephone line (adapted from Rumbaugh[2]) might appear as shown in Figure 7.5.

A business event example might be one for a telephone order entry system (Figure 7.6). Because the process of entering an order can be quite complex, this is only one example of many scenarios that might occur in practice.

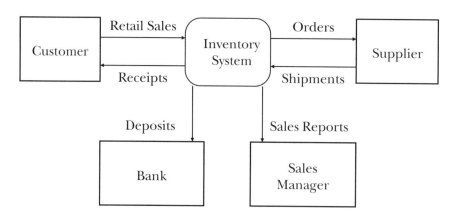

Figure 7.4   An event context diagram

1. The caller lifts receiver.
2. A dial tone begins.
3. The caller dials a digit (5).
4. The dial tone ends.
5. The caller dials a digit (5).
6. The caller dials a digit (5).
7. The caller dials a digit (5).
8. The caller dials a digit (1).
9. The caller dials a digit (8).
10. The caller dials a digit (4).
11. The called phone begins to ring.
12. A ringing tone appears in the calling phone.
13. The called party lifts the receiver.
14. The called phone stops ringing.
15. The ringing tone disappears in the calling phone.
16. The two phones are connected.
17. The called party hangs up the receiver.
18. The two phones are disconnected.
19. The caller hangs up.

Figure 7.5   An event response scenario for a telephone call

Actually, each of these examples contains elements of both business requirements and system requirements (analysis and design requirements), but the overall responses are to external events. In both examples, there are additional system events involved behind the scenes, but these details will be addressed in design. The key idea here is to capture a system's overall requirements from the users of the system. A facilitated group workshop serves this purpose well, but it does require that the problem scope is agreed upon by system users and analysts so that a detailed meeting can be conducted within the scope of the context model and not outside the immediate problem domain.

1. Customer call is received at the switchboard.

2. The computerized telephone switch sends the phone number to the order entry system.

3. The order entry system routes the session to a sales agent's terminal.

4. The order entry system searches the phone file to identify the caller as a customer.

5. The caller is identified, and the customer record is retrieved.

6. The customer's recent order history is retrieved.

7. The customer's recent account information is retrieved.

8. The sales agent's phone rings.

9. The sales agent's terminal displays the customer information.

10. The sales agent picks up the phone.

11. The sales agent receives and verifies the customer name and account number.

12. The sales agent retrieves information on a potential product sale.

13. The product sales information is verified and placed on a working order line.

14. The customer shipping information is verified.

15. The customer billing information is verified.

16. The order is confirmed and recorded for subsequent fulfillment by the warehouse.

17. The customer hangs up.

18. The sales agent hangs up.

19. The order entry system sets up a blank screen for the next phone call.

20. The computerized phone switch disconnects from the network and waits for another call.

Figure 7.6   A possible event response scenario for an order entry system

7.4   BUILD AN EVENT RESPONSE MODEL
FOR EACH EVENT

Once an event scenario has been constructed for a particular business event, the objects involved in the response to the event (performance of the steps described in the event scenario) are described. Rumbaugh[3] calls this next task building an event trace, and Embley et al.[4] refers to it as building a sequence of interactions. The process of building what we'll call an event response model consists of describing the sender and the receiver of each message indicated in the event response scenario steps and then drawing an event response diagram.

   Starting with the very first step in an event response scenario, we identify the object that sends the message that causes the first response to occur. In our telephone example, the caller is the first object. The message is that the receiver is being lifted and is sent from the caller to the telephone line (actually, the local telephone company's computerized switch is the receiver of the message, but this is at a much more detailed level than we need to examine here). We model this by identifying all objects needed for the event response and then drawing a vertical line (or bar) for each object being modeled. Then we draw a horizontal line from the sender of the message to the receiver of the message, placing an arrowhead on the receiver end of the message line. Figure 7.7 shows how this is done for the entire telephone call event response scenario listed earlier.

   The same process can be performed for an order entry system. Our possible order entry event response scenario would look something like that shown in Figure 7.8 when completed.

7.5   BUILD AN OBJECT INTERACTION MODEL

Before we can model interaction between objects in a system, we need to know what objects are involved in a particular interaction (a component of an event response model), how objects act or react for the interaction and the detailed nature of the interaction. The list of business events, event response scenarios and event response models created earlier for each business function gives us a good starting point for identifying specific interactions to examine. The event response models for each event should have identified the objects involved in each interaction, as well as the message(s) being sent.

Calller	Phone Line	Callled Party
lifts receiver		
dialtone begins		
dials a digit (5)		
dial tone ends		
dials a digit (5)		
dials a digit (5)		
dials a digit (5)		
dials a digit (1)		
dials a digit (8)		
dials a digit (4)		
ringing tone appears	phone begins ringing	
	lifts receiver	
ringing tone stops	phone ringing	
phone connected	phone connected	
	hangs up	
disconnected	disconnected	
hangs up		

Figure 7.7   An event response diagram for a telephone call

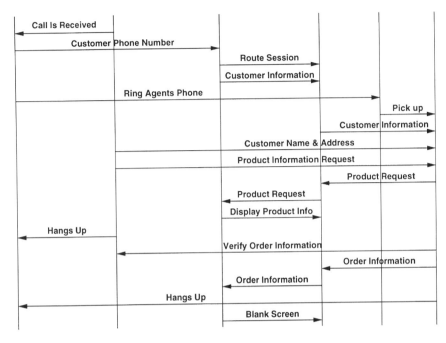

Figure 7.8   An event response diagram for an order entry system

We can define the behavior of each object using object state diagrams and object state matrices (discussed in the previous chapter). These same diagrams can be used to help characterize object actions and reactions in an object interaction. We need to describe an activity that comprises the interaction and describe the information or objects transmitted or exchanged in an object interaction.

Message Flow Diagrams

A conventional data flow diagram, used in structured analysis, can be a useful tool for depicting information flowing between objects via object interactions. Indeed, Rumbaugh et al.[5], Martin and Odell[6] (object flow diagrams), Embley et al.[7] (object interaction diagrams), Coad and Yourdon[8] (message connection), Booch[9] (object diagrams), Wirfs-Brock et al.[10] (collaboration graphs) and others use some form of data flow diagram, although only Rumbaugh and Schlaer-Mellor[11] (and perhaps a few others) use data stores. Such a diagram depicts, at a minimum, messages flowing among objects in a system.

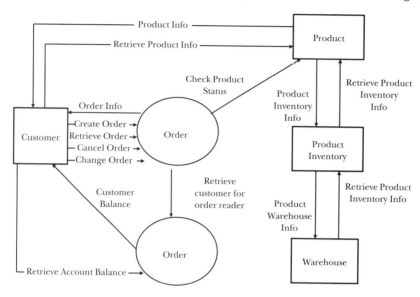

Figure 7.9   A message flow diagram for order entry

It may depict external agents and data stores, but these are less important than the message flows between objects if the individual object characteristics are documented well enough using a technique other than data flow diagrams. These diagrams are useful for describing flows within an object, where data stores may be introduced.

A data flow diagram used to describe interactions between object classes is different than the data flow diagram used in structured analysis. When object class interactions are being modeled, we don't model processes but rather object classes and their associated behaviors when we describe high-level business function objects (the topic of a high-level object message flow diagram). It is useful to depict individual operations as processes on lower-level data flow diagrams, but this is done only within the context of an individual object class. For now, we will focus on analyzing and modeling high-level classes within the context of a business function and refer to the flow diagrams as message flow diagrams (Figure 7.9).

Control Flow Diagrams

Another useful tool for describing object interactions is a process dependency diagram, which depicts control flow between objects in a system. Some object-oriented analysis and methodologies use variations of these diagrams, with certain strengths and weaknesses existing for each approach and application (Martin and Odell call these event schema diagrams and Rumbaugh extends state models to include control flow). For our purpose, describing a set of techniques for migrating from structured analysis-based information engineering to a pure object-oriented information engineering environment, the message flow diagram and control flow diagram together seem to form a very useful starting point. Other more sophisticated techniques can be used to model complex real-time systems, for example.

As a particular application or system component needs more sophisticated modeling rigor, such as that required for real-time systems, the models described here should form a strong foundation for more elaborate modeling efforts. The key here is to use objects as the basis for data flow and process dependency modeling, not pure process modeling, as is the case in traditional structured analysis. Traditional process modeling is truly obsolete, but the diagramming techniques are useful when properly applied in an object context.

Use of Message Flow Diagrams

An object interaction model consists of multiple message flow diagrams, each of which specifies a message and its sender and receiver. Like a data flow diagram, a message flow diagram is a graph that shows flows of data values from sources to destinations. The object model's message flow diagram, however, does not depict data stores except at the very lowest level inside the capsule that surrounds the actual data structure of an object. A message being sent between system objects or to or from an external object (external agent) is normally shown as unidirectional, with one arrowhead defining the direction of the flow.

A message flow diagram, like a data flow diagram, does not depict control information, such as when messages are sent, the order that multiple messages are sent or control decisions made along the path of a message. The behavioral model shows this kind of information in the object state diagram. A message flow diagram also does not show the organization of object data—the object structure model does this.

Objects

In a data flow diagram, a process transforms data inputs into data outputs. In an object model, the message flow diagram depicts active objects and their associated operations sending and acting upon messages. At the very lowest level of detail in an object interaction model (within the confines of an object capsule), operations are implemented as methods which may store and retrieve object attributes from a static data store. This is not really necessary to show in a pure object-oriented language and/or database implementation in design (because object data are always encapsulated with methods in these systems), but in analysis we may need to depict systems that will be implemented using traditional languages and database management systems that use traditional static data structures.

The technique of modeling object data structures as static data stores (only within the boundary of a fundamental object) serves a useful purpose in providing an implementation-independent model for subsequent design specification. You could choose to omit the data stores or even the message flow diagrams at the fundamental object level entirely, but this is not recommended unless an adequate modeling technique is used as a substitute.

For a message flow diagram, the entire message flow graph represents an object. The messaging model does not uniquely specify the result of an operation, but only dictates the possible functional paths of messages. It does not show which path will actually be taken in any given situation. The result of an object operation execution depends on the behavior defined for the object. An object receiving one message may receive messages from many objects, and an object may send multiple messages. The processing logic that defines how messages get sent is defined within the sending object. The logic for the processing of the message once received is defined in the specification of the operations for the receiver(s) of the message. Remember, messages define *what* operations should be performed, not *how* they are to be performed.

A message flow diagram depicts only the pattern of message inputs and outputs. Transformation of inputs into outputs must be specified in the various object operations (the internal object details). A high-level object can be expanded into an entire message flow diagram in the same way that a high-level process can be expanded into an entire data flow diagram. At the lowest level in an object interaction model of leveled message flow diagrams, a fundamental or atomic object may explode to a message flow diagram (really, almost a traditional data flow diagram) for the object itself. The difference here, though, is that the operations within an object have no idea who is sending inbound messages, but parameters can help characterize the message in detail. The operations will know who the outbound messages are addressed to.

External Agents

An external agent is an active object that interacts with the object described by a message flow diagram. Such an object sends input messages into the message flow diagram and/or receives output messages from the diagram. Usually, external agents appear on the edge of the message flow diagram, serving as sources or sinks for the data conveyed in the messages. On a data flow diagram, an external agent is sometimes called a terminator, actor or external entity. Examples of external agents include people interacting with the system via a user interface, a device sending or receiving information to or from the system or perhaps another information system interacting with the one being modeled. The details of how an external agent operates are outside the scope of a message flow diagram model but may be included in part of the behavioral model. In our message flow diagrams, an external agent is drawn as a shaded rectangle.

Data Stores

A data store is a passive object defined to be within the scope of a data flow diagram model. It stores information in an object data structure for permanent storage. A data store does not generate or modify data in any way, but reacts only to object operations that access the data. Files and databases store information in this way, and data stores are used to model them in data flow diagrams. In our object interaction models, message flow diagrams will not contain data stores. A data flow diagram may be used to depict messages being stored to or accessed from object data structures modeled as data stores.

Control Flows, Stores and Transforms

Some analysis modeling methodologies use control flows, control stores and control transforms to extend data flow diagrams for handling complex control situations like those that appear in real-time systems. Normally, a data flow diagram shows all possible computations and control decision paths for data values, but does not show which paths are navigated and in which order. A control decision affects which activity is performed (or even if any are performed), without producing data as output.

A control flow represents a boolean value that determines whether a process gets evaluated. This flow is not a data value for input to the process and is shown as a dotted control flow line rather than a solid data flow line.

Control flows, stores and transforms can indeed be useful, but we can usually model their meanings in an object behavior model. Therefore, we will not use them in this book. Refer to Ward and Mellor's methodology for a good coverage of the use of control constructs in real-time systems modeling.[12]

Describing Object Interactions

A message sent between objects, representing one of many possible interactions between the objects, needs to be described in detail before we can consider our interaction modeling complete. All or part of an object may be sent in the message, or part or all of several objects may be sent. This is equivalent to linking a data flow to the data model via entities and attributes in the flow's data view.

A data flow expression contains a definition of the contents of a data flow in terms of entities, attributes and how many occurrences of the entity may be present in the flow at any one time. Likewise, in an object interaction model, a message definition needs to define objects, their attributes and the number of instances that may be transmitted in a message. For a customer order, the flow to the order object when the order is created will contain the order header and its attributes, perhaps one-to-ten instances of order detail records and zero-to-many instances of order comments.

The details of a message flow between objects need to be documented in a model repository or dictionary, not necessarily on a message flow diagram. Each flow on a diagram should be named, however. The repository or dictionary entry for a message flow needs to indicate the frequency of message flow occurrence, the peak flow volume and peak time and whether the interaction is immediate or delayed (synchronous or asynchronous). An immediate interaction might involve retrieval of product information for an online order entry clerk's request (Figure 7.10). A nonimmediate interaction might be appropriate for an electronic mail or facsimile transmission system using a store and forward type of messaging (Figure 7.11).

If a message interaction is immediate, then the message sender and receiver must be ready before the interaction can be completed. If an interaction need not be immediate, then a temporary holding place for the message can be used. With traditional data flow diagrams, a transient (buffer or temporary file) data store might be placed between interaction objects to handle a delayed flow, but this is probably best deferred until design begins. Likewise, it is not necessary to show an intermediate, transient object between a sender and receiver of an object message until design. The nature of the

Figure 7.10   An immediate (synchronous) object interaction

interaction should be documented in the flow's repository or dictionary entry.

Describing Object Interaction Activities

It is possible to simplify analysis efforts and the resulting models if the focus is on those common interaction activities used across any information system (Embley et al.[13]). First, identify activities that make the transition to initial and final object states: "create," "establish" and so on for the initial state; and "cancel," "withdraw," "terminate," etc., for the final state. Activities that make transitions to intermediate object states need to be included, too.

Operations that read, write or update attributes or associations of objects should be given special attention, at least before object design models are complete. In design access operations that are private to objects must be described, but in analysis the focus should be on ones that are public. Message flow diagrams will depict public object accesses, while data flow diagrams (if used in the analysis models) depict private object data structure accesses. Access operations may be derived from attributes and associations of a class in an object structure model.

All interactions that read information within objects can be grouped under a category called "read." This can become the generic name of messages being sent to objects, with the specific requested information identified in the arguments of the message. This can form the name of data flows, which are now named as messages. For instance, when the customer object is read to obtain the current credit rating, this request can be named as *read customer credit rating*. Figure 7.12 shows how this interaction might be drawn.

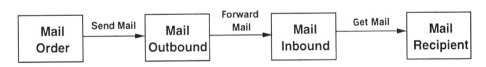

Figure 7.11   A nonimmediate (asynchronous) object interaction

Figure 7.12   A READ access interaction between objects

All interactions that modify information within objects could be categorized as *update* activities. For instance, a request to the customer object for customer credit rating for the purpose of modifying the value could be named *update customer credit rating*. The data flow for this object interaction could be depicted as an outflow from the customer object to the requesting object (in analysis, a customer service agent; in design, the customer update screen) and a corresponding flow from the requesting object to the customer object, but it is often simpler to show only the flow into the customer object (or use an arrowhead on each end of the flow to depict bidirectional flow). See Figure 7.13 for a graphic example of this.

Deletion of an object from its class needs to be performed for all classes, at least as a utility operation. A deletion operation would delete an object from the class but not necessarily from the entire system. For instance, if an employee were defined as having both salaried and hourly employment at an organization, the hourly payroll information could be *deleted* using a *delete hourly employee* message, but the employee record and salary payroll information would be retained (Figure 7.14). The employee and salaried employee classes still contain information about the employee, even though the hourly payroll record is deleted.

If an entire employee record, including all specialization records, needs to be deleted, a *destroy* message can be sent to the employee class to *destroy employee record*. This would cause the deletion to propagate to all specialization records and all related associations linking the object classes (Figure 7.15).

A *create* message could be used to bring an object into existence within a system. If a product manager needs to create a new definition of a product to be carried in the new company catalog, he or she can send a *create new product* message to the product object (Figure 7.16). Before the *create new product* message is sent to the product object, a product number needs to be

Figure 7.13   An UPDATE access interaction between objects

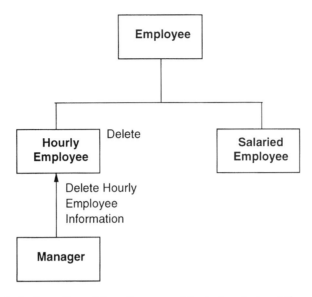

Figure 7.14   Deletion of an object from an object class but not the system

defined to identify the new product (unless the system is allowed to generate a new product number). Some basic product information might also be supplied along with the identifier. If the product object actually contains other objects with information such as product technical information, product record changes and product catalog releases, these other object records may have to be created when the base product record is created. These details

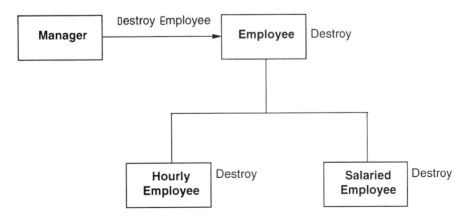

Figure 7.15   Destruction of an entire employee record across the system

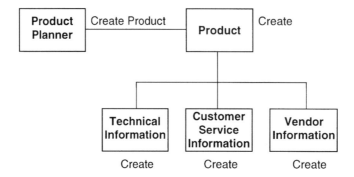

Figure 7.16   Creation of a product record

do not need to be covered in design, but this can be modeled by sending a *create product* message to the higher-level product object, which takes care of these details.

Operations that are nontrivial may be categorized as queries, actions or activities.[14] A query is an operation that has no side effects on the externally visible state of any object; so it is a pure function. Such an operation that has no parameters—only the target object name—represents a derived attribute. Age is an attribute derived from a birth date and the current date. An action is a data transformation that has side effects on its target object or objects the target object is in contact with. An action is instantaneous (in theory, anyway). All actions must be definable in updates to base attributes and associations because an object's state is defined by attributes and associations. Actions can be defined in terms of the state of an object or group of objects just before and after the action is executed; they can be derived from processes in a process model or operations in an object model.

When describing actions, the specification should be clear and unambiguous. An algorithm could be used, but the action diagram format can be used in conventional information engineering modeling. The operation name needs to be specified, along with its inputs and outputs, the transformation of data and any constraints.

An activity operation has duration in time, unlike queries and actions, which are instantaneous, so it has side effects. Model activities only for external agents and active objects. System monitor processes might be activities, such as print demons or system clock-driven task schedulers. These types of operations are described by an object behavior model as well as the interaction model and can be depicted using object state diagrams.

A procedural description of an operation specifies an operation by stating an algorithm used to compute output values from input values. The algorithm should specify only what an operation does, not how it is implemented. Implementation details are covered during design. If there is a choice, try to use a declarative description rather than a procedural one to avoid getting too detailed and perhaps getting into design issues too soon. However operation requirements are specified, try to specify what will happen with all combinations of input values. The very detailed operation specification process will likely be completed after object interaction modeling is completed, but capture all information possible at this point while working with the users of the system.

When specifying operations, try to identify all constraints between objects—functional dependencies not related by an input/output dependency. These constraints can be on multiple objects at one time, between instances of the same object at different times or between instances of different objects at different times (usually input/output functions). Preconditions on functions constrain input values, and postconditions specify output values that are guaranteed. Specify times or conditions under which constraints hold.

One constraint may specify that no product inventory levels may be negative (no backorders are allowed). This constraint would not specify what should be done if the product inventory level falls to zero; the same constraint needs to be built into the behavioral and interaction models in order to complete the constraint specification.

Values to be maximized, minimized or otherwise optimized need to be specified, and if optimization criteria are in conflict trade-off decisions need to be made. The messages sent between physical locations or locking time for database objects may be minimized, if desired.

END NOTES

[1] Martin, James. *Information Engineering*, 3 vols. (Englewood Cliffs, NJ: Prentice Hall) 1989–1990.

[2] Rumbaugh, James, Michael Blaha, William Premerlani, Frederick Eddy and William Lorensen. *Object-Oriented Modeling and Design* (Englewood Cliffs, NJ: Prentice Hall) 1991, p. 86.

[3] Ibid., p. 87.

[4] Embley, David W., Barry D. Kurtz and Scott N. Woodfield. *Object-Oriented Systems Analysis: A Model-Driven Approach* (Englewood Cliffs, New Jersey) pp. 192–195.

[5] Rumbaugh et al., *Object-Oriented Modeling and Design.*

[6] Martin, James, and James J. Odell. *Object-Oriented Analysis and Design* (Englewood Cliffs, NJ: Prentice Hall) 1992.

[7] Embley, et al., *Object-Oriented Systems Analysis: A Model-Driven Approach.*

[8] Coad, Peter, and Edward Yourdon. *Object-Oriented Analysis,* 2nd ed. (Englewood Cliffs, NJ: Prentice Hall) 1991.

[9] Booch, Grady. *Object-Oriented Design with Applications* (Redwood City, CA: Benjamin/Cummings) 1991.

[10] Wirfs-Brock, Rebecca, Brian Wilkerson and Lauren Wiener. *Designing Object-Oriented Software* (Englewood Cliffs, NJ: Prentice Hall) 1990.

[11] Schlaer, Sally, and Stephen J. Mellor. *Object-Oriented Systems Analysis: Modeling the World in Data* (Englewood Cliffs, NJ: Yourdon Press, Prentice Hall) 1988.

[12] Ward, Paul T., and Stephen J. Mellor. *Structured Development for Real-Time Systems,* 3 vols. (Englewood Cliffs, NJ: Yourdon Press, Prentice Hall) 1985.

[13] Embley, et al., *Object-Oriented Systems Analysis: A Model-Driven Approach,* pp. 178–185.

[14] Rumbaugh et al., *Object-Oriented Modeling and Design,* p. 131.

8

Integrate and Validate Analysis Models

8.1 WHY MODEL INTEGRATION AND VALIDATION ARE SO IMPORTANT

Before moving into design, it is important to take the time to ascertain that various analysis models and their components fit together. This is most important when large teams or multiple teams are involved in extensive analysis. The separate views of the entire system must be integrated into a cohesive, comprehensive whole. Object structural, behavioral and interaction models need to be constructed to represent different views of the same subject, not totally separate entities. The order in which each of these models is examined does not matter, and it is not necessary to completely validate the models before design begins, but it is very important that an audit is done before design proceeds too far.

Architectural or strategic design assumes complete requirements are available from analysis models. The repository or model dictionary can help to balance horizontal and vertical system components in various sets of diagrams. Graphical models, although valuable for communication between analysts, designers and end users, do not ensure that the requirements for a system are complete.

Message flows between objects must be fully described at the attribute level. The repository or dictionary must assist in validating completeness of requirements. Physical requirements for the system to be implemented must also be collected and organized (see more about this topic in the chapter on general system design). Analysis models must depict system requirements, and the end products of various object state transformations must document each decision used to make these transformations. End users and quality assurance team members should be able to trace all mappings from analysis to design models.

Analysis model integration and validation ensure that models of object structures, behaviors and interactions with other objects fit together. Examination of the life cycle of each object (or just the important objects) and the use of object structures by object operations is important. This helps clarify the use of object structures by various operations and improves the definitions of object structures and object state transitions and message flows.

It can be helpful to begin the model integration and validation at the top levels of abstraction, at the business function level (if working with enterprise models) or at the system context level (if working with a single system). The top-down approach works well because it is possible to decompose the large task into smaller chunks. Once the various models have been examined at the context level, how to move down progressively to lower levels can be decided, just as a problem domain is first analyzed. At each lower level, the models depict increasing detail and decreasing scope. The top-down approach also enhances integration of the entire model. In the next three sections, Embley's integration techniques for the OSA methodology are presented.[1]

8.2 COMPARE DIAGRAMS

Various model diagrams must be compared in order to ensure that corresponding objects are modeled consistently. Two basic kinds of inconsistencies may exist: naming conflicts or structural conflicts. Name conflicts result from use of synonyms or homonyms. Synonyms exist if a component in two diagrams has multiple names; homonyms exist if different components have the same name. An example of a synonym is the name *client* and the name *customer*, used for the person to whom your company sells products or services. Another example might be *part* and *component* for a product item. An example of a homonym is the use of *end date* to describe several types of completion dates: *service end date, engineering end date, installation end date*, etc.

A structural conflict could exist when different types of structures represent the same concept or due to conflicting restraints. In some modeling techniques, it might happen that some analysts model a data element as an attribute and another analyst models the same concept as an object. This is more common when analysts survey users for attributes before identifying objects or entities. By listing and examining potential classes and objects before describing their attributes, this structural mismatch problem tends not to exist in object structure modeling.

Another way that structural conflicts can result is when a modeling concept is depicted at a high level on one set of diagrams and at a lower level on another set of diagrams. This problem can exist when traditional process decomposition is used to describe processes at various levels of abstraction. Different people may model the same set of requirements in two very different ways but have the same total set of requirements accounted for. A given process might appear at a middle level on one analyst's models and at a lower level on another analyst's models.

Data structures can exhibit the same problem if both high-level and lower-level data stores and data flows are used to describe data structures. This problem might occur in object structure modeling, which is hierarchical in nature. Classes of objects tend to quickly get validated, however, when the associations and attributes are described in detail. Modelers using leveled data stores or data flows tend to leave the details of data store or flow contents for the lower levels in a process model. Data structures are accounted for at the lowest level, but the data store or data flow partitioning may not come close to matching those appearing in another analyst's models.

In object structure models, use of associations might differ, depending on the particular view of the object data that an analyst has from the particular subset of the problem domain. If the transactions or user views of object structures studied by one analyst and set of users are different from those studied by another analyst and set of users, the modeled associations are likely to differ. Besides using different names for associations between classes, examine the types of association and their constraints (optionalities and cardinalities); these may differ significantly across problem domains.

Analysts who incorporate time-dependent requirements (storing object instances over time) will model different optionalities for associations than those who view only the current set of instances for objects. For instance, one analyst may model the situation where order detail records may be retained in archives when the order header records have been destroyed (an optional association). Another analyst may model the situation such that order detail records may not exist in a system unless the order header records also exist (a mandatory association). Constraints on an association may contradict each other; others may refine concepts that are incomplete.

8.3   RESOLVE DIAGRAM CONFLICTS

Inconsistencies in model concepts across diagrams must be resolved once identified. The models that result must reflect the real world or the way that users need the system modeled for the future real world. The original requirements must be reviewed for completeness and consistency. Model conflicts may not be the fault of the modelers but rather that of the users, who have differing views of the system (if not the world). Problems among the users may be resolved via workshops or meetings between members of different groups. Sometimes a difficult political issue will arise from examining inconsistent requirement statements. Such an issue must be resolved or a proposed system will not fulfill its mission.

Modeling problems of synonym and homonym conflicts are easier to resolve than political issues (except when they become political among the various modelers). Model component names may be changed or aliases allowed. Attribute names within object structures do not need to be unique; they are unique by virtue of being placed in different object structures. Classes and objects must, however, have unique names. Associations that model the same concept should be merged and one name used. Constraints on these associations must be correctly modeled. Object structures that have the same attributes and associations (or largely the same ones) may need to be merged. Objects that have the same identifiers are candidates for merging, as are ones that have a one-to-one cardinality for the main association between them.

8.4   EXAMINE THE RELATIONSHIPS BETWEEN MODELS

The object structure model describes static data structures and their relationships to each other. The behavioral model specifies permissible sequences of actions on objects modeled in the object structure model. The object state diagram describes behavior for individual objects in a class. Events can be modeled as operations on object data structures. The functional model shows requirements for what tasks a system needs to do. The object model depicts the actors that perform system tasks. The behavioral model shows the sequences in which these tasks are performed. All three models merge as method implementations are specified, just as the process, data and control models of structured analysis come together when processes are specified in detail.

The behavioral model is constrained by the structures in the object structure model. States and substates in an object state diagram describe attribute and association link values that an object can take on. Temporary differences between objects in a class are modeled in the behavioral model. Permanent differences appear in the object structure model.

Like object structures, the behavior of a superclass is inherited by its subclasses. Subclasses have their own state models. Each subclass must refine the states of the superclass, with any state in the superclass represented in subclass state diagrams. Thus, parent and child state diagrams must be vertically balanced, just as leveled data flow diagrams must be leveled in process modeling. No new states or transitions must be introduced at the parent diagram levels without being represented on a lower-level diagram as well.

Event hierarchies depicted in the behavioral model are normally independent of class hierarchies. Events may be defined across classes, unlike states and transitions that more closely match class structures. States and transitions are caused by interactions between objects via event. Transitions in the state diagrams may be modeled as operations on objects, with operation names matching event names. Events depend upon not only the class structure of an object, but also the object state.

The interaction model describes what functions a system must perform and how objects pass information among themselves. The object structure model describes the actors that perform tasks. Responses to messages sent between objects are modeled as operations on objects. Messages sent to a high-level object identify a primary target for the message, with parameters to be used by the receiving operation in the target object. The target object thus acts as a client for the requesting object and may request operations to be performed by other objects not visible to the client, or at least not known to be involved in servicing the initial target object.

Objects depicted on message flow diagrams are actual objects described in the object structure model. Message flows to or from these objects represent requests for operations and the results of these requests. Values contained in message flows are operation arguments from the requesting objects or responses to requests from the server objects. The message flow diagrams do not describe *how* operations are performed, only *what* operations are requested by which objects and *what* the responses are to the requests. The behavioral model describes how operations are performed, and the object structure model describes what data structures are involved.

Message flows represent data values in the object structure model or perhaps data derived from object structure data. Input flows sometimes represent objects that are the target of other operations. A *customer order* sent to a *customer order maintenance* object would be the target for order maintenance operations. A message flow might also contain an object that is not changed by the receiver of the message. A completed *invoice* object is contained in a message flow sent to a print queue for subsequent printing or to a communication queue for subsequent transmittal to another network node.

The object model shows the structure of objects that act on messages that flow in the behavioral model, the flows themselves and the structures that store information about these objects. The behavioral model describes object states and operations performed on objects as they receive events and change their states.

8.5 PERFORM OBJECT LIFE-CYCLE ANALYSIS

This set of techniques helps discover fundamental operations on objects, identifies states that objects can be in and validates components of behavioral and interaction models. Object life-cycle analysis generates these deliverables:

- object state diagrams
- object state matrices
- more complete object definitions
- more complete operation definitions
- newly identified operations
- elimination of duplicate operations

Object states follow a few basic rules:

- Each object must have a state.
- An object cannot be in two states simultaneously.
- State changes must come as the result of an operation.
- An object may have multiple states throughout its life.
- An object may pass through several states in a variety of sequences.

At a minimum, an object must have a *create state, intermediate states* and a *termination state.* To model the create state, a null state (the state before the object exists) is introduced. Object state diagrams and object state matrices (discussed in Chapter 6) are used to document the findings of object life-cycle analysis. They are reprinted here for convenience in Figures 8.1 and 8.2. Note that we may only walk through our existing state models during model

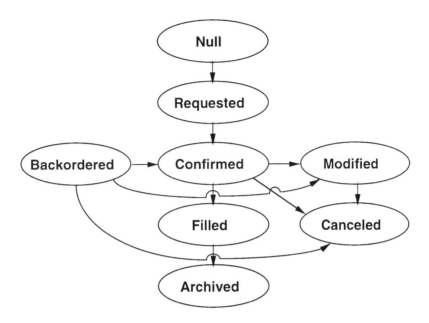

Figure 8.1   An object state diagram

integration and validation here rather than create new ones. Usually, detailed work was done to create such models during object behavior analysis.

8.6   PERFORM DATA USE ANALYSIS

The technique uses a data navigation diagram (discussed by Martin and McClure[2]) to depict the accesses to object structures and the associated processing logic. This technique asks these questions about how operations act on object data structures:

- What data are used as input?
- What stored data are needed?
- What new data are created?
- What data are updated?
- What data are deleted?

Customer Order

	A (Null)	B Requested	C Back ordered	D Confirmed	E Modified	F Filled	G Canceled	H Archived
Record Order	B							
Record Backorder		C						
Confirm Order		D	D					
Modify Order		E	E	E				
Fill Order				F	F			
Cancel Order			G	G	G			
Archive Order						H	H	

Figure 8.2   An object state matrix

Data navigation defines what procedures are required to handle the access and update of stored data within an object structure model. The data navigation diagram (Figure 8.3) shows object actions and association actions and involves process specification (using action diagrams) to describe the operations that perform detailed processing logic. It uses an object structure diagram to show data accesses. Figure 8.4 shows the steps involved in data use analysis. The data actions depicted in that figure describe the following portion of the process specification for the operation to record a customer order:

1. Read customer
2. Create customer order
3. Read product
4. Create customer order detail OR create customer back order
5. Read product order statistics
6. Update product order statistics
7. Update customer order

Of course, these are only the data accesses (messages sent to the various objects for data actions). Conditional logic and algorithms must be added to make the process specification for the operation complete.

Note that data navigation can be used to build process specifications for operations from the basic data access logic or used to validate existing process

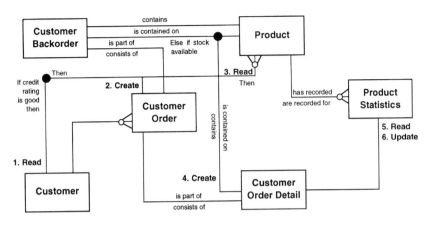

Figure 8.3   A data navigation diagram

specifications. In the former case, additional processing logic would be added to the basic logic of data accesses. In the latter case, data accesses could be built without knowledge of the existing process specifications. These data accesses would then be matched against those existing in the process specification for the operation being examined. This shows if the object structure model and object interaction models are integrated properly via the process specification. Data use analysis prepares analysis models for database design.

1. Determine the main object classes for the operation.
2. Examine the neighborhood of each main object class.
3. Omit unneeded classes.
4. Form a data navigation diagram.
5. Consider modifications to the use of object data: conditions, options, alternate paths and error situation.
6. Verify that all required attributes are present in the class structures.
7. Identify object and attribute actions.
8. Analyze sequences for exceptions.
9. Perform object life-cycle analysis.
10. Add to operation process specifications any needed algorithms and procedure calls.

Figure 8.4   Steps in data use analysis

The operations modeled here represent methods that act on database objects.

Before data access requirement modeling can be considered complete, describe within the analysis model some other characteristics of data accesses by operations—the transactions in a design model:

- the source of the transactions
- the mode of information capture
- the types of transactions
- the size of individual transactions (average and peak values)
- frequency of transaction arrival (low, average and peak values)
- priorities among transactions
- any important processing considerations

8.7 VALIDATE OBJECT STRUCTURES

Various business rules described in the object structure model must be validated. Redundant associations must be evaluated to make sure that they provide no additional information. If they do not, remove one or more of the redundant associations.

Modeling Time

Time should also be considered. Try to get accurate estimates of the cardinalities of associations between objects. Take a look at snapshot (the current state of an object model) versus the long-term view. Decide upon which associations and constraints are relevant. Should previous or future instances of an object be accounted for or just the current instances? Be careful to ensure a consistent view of time everywhere in the object structure model.

One-to-One Associations

Associations with one-to-one cardinalities need to be examined. Are both association memberships mandatory? Are the object identifiers identical? Do the objects involved have many identical attributes and associations? If the answer to these questions is yes, consider merging the objects into one object on the model. Do not merge them if both association memberships are optional, most attributes and associations are different or corresponding attributes can take on different values.

Parallel Associations

Multiple associations between objects should be examined to see if they are valid. Valid parallel associations might be *person pays for policy (policy is paid for by person)* and *person is insured under policy (policy insures person)*. An invalid pair of parallel relationships might be *person codes module (module is coded by person)* and *person writes module (module is written by module)*. *Codes* and *writes* are redundant, so the parallel associations should be merged.

Recursive Associations

Recursive associations, pairings between instances of the same object class should be examined. Parallel associations for a single object can exist, too. Consider the association of *employee manages employee* and *employee works with employee*. These are really separate association concepts, so should be retained.

Summary of Object Structure Validation

Validation of the object structure model should result in a complete model. It can help identify business operations that need to be performed on object data and forms the basis for database design. All object classes must have states and transitions defined for them in the object state diagrams of the behavior models. The process of developing analysis models is iterative, but the validation and integration process often represents the last chance to get the models right before design begins (or before design gets too far along).

END NOTES

[1] Embley, David W., Barry D. Kurtz and Scott N. Woodfield. *Object-Oreinted Systems Analysis: A Model-Driven Approach* (Englewood Cliffs, NJ: Yourdon Press, Prentice Hall) 1992.

[2] Martin, James, and Carma McClure. *Structured Techniques: The Basis for CASE* (Englewood Cliffs, NJ: Prentice Hall) 1988.

9

Object Structure Designs

9.1 DESIGN CLASSES

Classes in analysis may map directly into classes in design, but they may need some adjustments.

When classes instantiate themselves (create instances of their type), they set up storage spaces and the initial values that the class attributes will take on. Object instances are created so that all integrity constraints are adhered to. Referential integrity constraints for creation of object instances must be enforced at instantiation. If there is a customer order to create for a new customer, but association constraint rules define that the order must belong to a customer in order to exist (see Figure 9.1), an instance of customer must also be created. The customer instance is created first, then the customer order instance.

Most, if not all, object-oriented programming languages provide for each class an operation to allocate storage for new instances, but in some the operation makes it difficult to add constraint checking. In addition, if programming languages and database management systems are not object-oriented, constraint checks need to be handled manually. Consider implementing class instantiation as a *create* and *initialize* operation, as suggested by Martin and Odell.[1] The first allocates storage for new objects, and the second constructs the object to adhere to specifications and constraints. The create operation may be already provided in object-oriented languages, but the initialize operation needs to be provided in most cases.

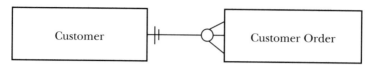

Figure 9.1   A referential integrity constraint

When it comes time to delete an object, referential integrity constraints must also be checked. For example, when a customer is to be deleted, first delete customer orders, accounts and any other information dependent upon the customer object via a mandatory association. Either specify that all dependent object instances be deleted before the customer instance is deleted or cascade all deletes down to all dependent object instances. The second option can involve a complex set of referential integrity checks because some of the dependent objects may themselves have dependent objects.

As with object instantiation, design for object termination can benefit from implementation of two operations for each class—a *finalize* and a *terminate* operation. A finalize operation breaks associations with other objects, ensuring data structure integrity. Terminate frees up storage no longer used by classes that have been deleted. Object-oriented languages support the terminate operation, but usually the finalize operation needs to be provided to ensure referential integrity.

9.2   DESIGN FOR OBJECTS

Objects in analysis models are designed and implemented as objects, much in the same way that entities in a data model may be implemented as a record in a database or program data structure. Some of the object models described in analysis may require that an object in design be changed from being a member of one class to being a member of another class. An employee may change from one job classification to another or may change from being employed to being retired or otherwise terminated. Some object-oriented database management systems support this type of dynamic classification, but support for this from object-oriented programming languages is limited. Consider implementing initialize and finalize operations to handle this. Use the finalize operation to handle associations before transfer to a new class and then the initialize to handle the reassignment.

There may be situations where objects need to be members of more than one class. A subtype object is a member of all superior classes in an inheritance hierarchy. For instance, a car is an instance of the car class, an instance of the automotive vehicle class and an instance of the vehicle class (Figure 9.2). Multiple inheritance defines that a subtype with multiple supertypes be handled differently than if it had only one supertype (single inheritance). It is possible that an object might be an instance of multiple classes other than via an inheritance hierarchy. A car is an instance of both automotive vehicle and licensed vehicle, for example. Some object-oriented programming languages and database management systems support modeling of multiple inheritance hierarchies, but do not support class/subclass hierarchy situations.

Additional classes may need to be created to handle multiple class membership. It is possible to implement a licensed automotive vehicle class to handle membership of a car in both the licensed vehicle and automotive vehicle classes. Car becomes a subclass of the licensed vehicle and automotive vehicle classes using this technique, but it requires that a class be implemented for each combination of multiple class membership.

When designing for dynamic and multiple classification situations, surrogate objects could be used to represent "sliced" versions of an object, in addition to the original "unsliced" version of the object. The surrogate objects implement recorded views of the intact object. Martin and Odell[2] suggest building two new classes: an implementation object and a conceptual object. Instances of the implementation object represent object views or "slices," while instances of the conceptual object are the base, "unsliced" objects.

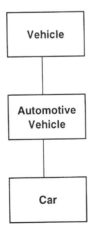

Figure 9.2   A subtype object is a member of multiple classes

Multiple object views can thus be maintained for each base object that needs to have these multiple views available to applications.

Changes in class membership can be addressed by adding or removing surrogate objects and changing the respective pointers in the conceptual object class. The create, initialize, finalize and terminate operations discussed earlier are still used, but the object view approach requires addition of new class-level operations to ensure integrity among multiple object states. An object could be a member of one class while simultaneously being a member of another class. Changes in membership of one class should not affect membership in any other classes, and simultaneous membership in mutually exclusive classes (say, licensed vehicle and unlicensed vehicle) must not be allowed.

9.3 DESIGN ATTRIBUTES

When beginning to design applications, two types of attributes need to be addressed: base and derived. A base attribute is a fundamental part of an object structure model and thus will appear in design as well. A derived attribute will likely be missing from an object structure model in analysis yet still need to be handled in design. Fields in design must reference either other objects (they might be foreign key pointers to other objects) or data values stored within a data structure (information-bearing database fields). Different programming languages handle these types of attributes differently. Several types of attribute operations need to be considered when implementing attributes as fields in design. At a minimum, some basic operations are needed.

Some kind of operation needs to be designed for establishing a field value or reference. Another needs to be defined for retrieving attribute values or references. Multivalued fields need more operations, such as inserting and removing elements from a collection of fields. Sometimes it is useful to have an operation that allows selection of previous or next values in a collection of fields. Fundamental operations would include adding, removing, detecting, selectively retrieving and updating multivalued fields.

When a field needs to be modified, all necessary constraints must be checked. Add operations must check cardinality upper bounds and remove operations must check optionality rules, such as whether the fields can be null. An optionality constraint of zero means that an attribute value is optional. If the constraint is defined as one, the attribute value is required.

9.4 DESIGN CLASS HIERARCHIES

Handling class/subclass (generalization/specialization) hierarchies can be accomplished in more than one way: public subclasses, private subclasses, object views or status flags. The most natural way is to implement a subtype as a subclass that is available to any other class, but for performance reasons the other approaches may need to be examined.

Private subclasses (ones accessible only by a superclass) can be used. The subclass retains all of its attributes but its operations are placed—protected—in the superclass. The object view approach allows reclassification of an object dynamically, with each subtype implemented as a subclass. The flag approach avoids implementation of a subclass by adding a flag field to the superclass in place of an actual subclass. The flag by itself indicates whether an object is conceptually a member of another class. The flag approach also requires that all fields and operations of the subclass be located in the superclass. Control conditions need to be placed on the usage of these attributes and operations.

9.5 DESIGN FOR DERIVED DATA

Derived (computed) attributes may be implemented as operations that define algorithms to calculate the resulting values. These operations may call other operations when performing their tasks. Thus operations that compute attribute values can be made reusable. A computed attribute may be derived whenever a change occurs in one of its component mappings or whenever a specific change request is made. The decision of when a derivation is performed might be based on performance requirements. Waiting to derive an attribute until a query is run is an example of a delayed strategy. When constraints are placed on attributes, derivation should be immediate so that integrity violations may be prevented.

The result for an attribute can be derived and stored in a database, just as with any other information system design, but such an attribute needs to be managed carefully. Data redundancy is to be avoided in most cases, but for query operations this technique makes perfect sense when the attribute being stored does not change often but is retrieved continuously.

At the time that an attribute value changes, the new value must be calculated and the stored value updated. This cost will not be prohibitive if the value is fairly stable over time (relative to query operations against the derived attribute value). Actually, there are three ways to detect that a computed attribute value may be updated: explicitly, periodically or by using active values.[3]

With an explicit update, each derived attribute is defined in terms of one or more base objects. Then a designer decides which of these attributes is affected by each change to a base attribute. The designer then inserts logic in the update operation on the base object to perform an explicit update on the derived attributes that depend on the base attribute.

Periodic recomputation allows for update of derived attributes in batches. It is possible to recalculate all derived attributes periodically without needing to recompute them when each base value changes. This can improve performance because some derived attributes can depend on several base attributes, requiring one update for each update of a base attribute. Periodic recomputation could be performed as a batch operation, when online transactions are at a minimum. It may not work if an object changes a few instances at a time because too many recalculations are performed for the few actual ones required.

Active values have dependent values, each of which registers itself with the active value. The active value maintains a set of dependent values and update operations. When an update of the base value is requested, updates of all dependent values are triggered. The initial update request does not need to perform the update of dependent values; the separation of the calling operation logic from that for the dependent objects aids in modularizing operation logic across a system.

9.6 DESIGN FOR EFFICIENT ACCESS

A nicely constructed analysis model may not perform well when implemented. Like any other design, object-oriented design must consider performance tuning issues before a system gets placed into production. The analysis conceptual model should always be the first point of reference for design. It captures conceptual information about the system, to which design must add details. Performance tuning helps make a system run faster but can make maintenance difficult, if not a nightmare. Both clarity of design and efficiency in implementation must be considered.

In analysis, always eliminate redundancy wherever possible to keep the model concise. In design consider creating or deleting associations between objects. Often redundant associations between classes can be added to minimize access costs and maximize overall system convenience. An additional index can also be added to improve query performance. Analyze the set of associations in an object structure model and examine each operation.

- Examine associations a query must traverse; consider implementing one-way traversals as one-way pointers.
- Determine how often an operation is executed and how costly it is to do so.
- Estimate the average number of "many" associations encountered; multiply cardinalities to determine the number of accesses on the last class in a path.
- Determine objects that meet selection criteria and are operated on; for rejected objects, avoid simple nested loops in operation algorithms.

Once the design is adjusted to handle frequent traversal of associations, seek to optimize operation access algorithms. Often it is possible to optimize by eliminating attempted retrievals of unwanted data. For instance, to determine all of the products supplied by two of the vendors, consider narrowing the search by retrieving vendor products first and then examining which are carried by the retailer. If a large array of products is carried but each vendor sells only a few, the performance improvement by answering the query in this manner can be dramatic compared to searching all products first and then inquiring about vendor products.

9.7 DESIGN FOR DATA MANAGEMENT SYSTEMS

When preparing to implement database designs, whether flat file, relational, object-oriented or some other type, consider both data structures and the operations that act on those structures. Each type of data management system requires a different kind of design. For flat file systems, define a first-normal form table for each class and its attributes, and, for relational systems, define third-normal form tables. Consider and test performance issues and adjust designs accordingly. Measure storage and performance needs and consider denormalizing as necessary. Object-oriented database systems may not need normalization assistance. For a discussion of data normalization, see Montgomery, 1990.[4]

Once tables have been defined, add attributes and their operations to each object in the database design. In an object-oriented design, objects need to know how to store and retrieve themselves. With multiple inheritance situations, an attribute and a corresponding storage operation could be defined. These would then be inherited by subclasses that need to store objects, as suggested by Coad and Yourdon.[5]

A flat file system needs to know:

which files or files to open,

how to position the file at the correct record,

how to retrieve existing values, if any, and

how to update fields with new values.

A relational system needs to know:

which tables to access,

how to access the correct rows,

how to retrieve existing values, if any, and

how to update columns with new values.

An object-oriented system does not need to have extra storage attributes and operations added because it allows objects to know how to store themselves over time. The database management system automatically handles any object marked as needing to be held over time. See Coad and Yourdon[6] for examples of this within a design for a sensor monitoring system. For relational systems, see Rumbaugh et al.[7] for a discussion of ways to implement object structures in relational database management systems.

9.8   GENERAL DATABASE DESIGN CONSIDERATIONS

Object-Oriented Database Characteristics

While each database application is a bit different from others, there are some fundamental characteristics that an object-oriented database should exhibit, including:

- support for complex data structures
- complex relationships
- retaining unique object identifiers
- maintaining versions of data structures

A database that supports object-oriented applications should be based on a data model that supports representation of sometimes complex real-world objects as one database object. In this chapter we deal mostly with the modeling aspects of object databases. The chapter dedicated to object databases discusses some of the physical features of several commercial object database management systems available today. The physical features that must be addressed in implementation of a database design include the usual services provided by a database management system:

- recovery
- security
- transaction management
- concurrency control

Modeling of Objects

Most applications require that a database object support associations with other objects. Database objects might also contain component objects involved in associations. Objects that contain other objects are complex, not like the typical databases or file structures in use today. Complex database objects might include those shown in Figure 9.3.

The last two types of complex objects shown in Figure 9.3 might appear in a systems development environment that coordinates and integrates CASE tools, but is representative of all kinds of aggregation objects that need to be stored in a database. Complex objects like these can have their internal structures made invisible to external objects that must access them. A program specification, engineered product component specification, or an

- Documents consisting of sections, subsections, text, graphics and bit maps
- Hypertext documents that have complex links to other hypertext documents or graphics
- Engineered product specifications including drawings with sub-drawings and component descriptions
- Programs consisting of modules, data structures, statements
- Libraries of programs, modules and database structures

Figure 9.3   Types of complex objects

entire multiple component document may be defined to have a text type attribute. This attribute is seen as simple text to an outside object, even though it is itself composed of many other text objects (or even graphics). This approach is simplistic but useful in many applications that do not need to address individual database object components.

When an application needs access to the component objects of a certain database object, we need to allow the structure of an object, its component objects and associations, to be visible through the object's public interface. For a design and programming tool environment, we would need to define programs composed of modules. Common, reusable modules would be stored in a library for public access. Each of these types of objects is complex: programs are composed of modules, which are composed of other modules, and libraries are composed of some of these same complex modules.

External relationships between different object classes and their associations must be distinguished from the same classes and associations that are internal to an object. Otherwise, if we use only one model for both internal and external object details, our database models are complex from the public view but not complex enough from the internal view. Also, the internal structure of objects is difficult to change when external objects need to know the structural details of each database object.

Some database management systems (the object-oriented ones, but some others as well) are structurally object-oriented (see Dittrich[8] and King[9]). When the complex structure of database objects is explicitly defined, it is much easier for users and applications to determine which details to focus on while ignoring other aspects of object structure. The database management system can manage the structure and control all integrity issues and application and user views.

Identifying Object Instances

Programming languages, especially the object-oriented ones, provide ways to represent and access database records via properties of the records (by the value of some record field). This can be a problem when object attribute values change over time. Also, associations between objects must be maintained when the value of an attribute used as a foreign key changes (as with relational databases).

Using a unique object identifier for each objects that is independent of object attribute values can simplify database designs and applications that use those designs. Attribute values are bound to change but a system generated and system maintained object identifier can serve an object throughout its life. Using unique identifiers for database objets is not a new idea; semantic database models have used the term "surrogates" for this.

User-Definable Database Operations

With traditional database management systems, any operation on complex objects requires that the component parts of those objects be know and stated explicitly. To delete a complex object, delete commands must be issued for the components of the object before the parent object can be deleted (true, some systems today do support cascading deletes). This requires much effort for program developers and users, but also reduces system modularity and information hiding. When the structure of such a complex database object changes, many programs must change. Use of a library module for handling complex deletes is helpful, but does not address the main problem. A better solution would be to design in operations that allow creation and deletion of entire complex objects at one time. Object structures can then change but the applications using the more powerful operations are stable.

Operations on database objects should be defined across class structures. Components of higher-level classes need not redefine these operations, and application programs are much simpler. Operations defined across an entire class might include:

- add to class
- query class
- return last update time stamp
- delete from class

When implementing complex objects in a non-object database environment, it makes sense to build and maintain specialized applications for those objects so that functionality and flexibility are high while not sacrificing performance. At any rate, it is reasonable that a database administrator be in charge of maintaining not only database structures but the key operations on those database components. This person must be aware of all key transactions and queries that access each part of a database.

Design for Encapsulation

In earlier chapters we discussed the definition of basic operations on objects, using a CRUD matrix to map create, read, update and delete operations against operations in application objects that require a database object. We will always implement these operations for any database object. Complex objects require much more powerful data manipulation operations, however.

We can combine fundamental operations to perform more complex operations. To remove a complex document and all of its components from a database, we need to check that the document is not in use before attempting the deletion. Then we need to lock the object and all of its components, each of which has a fundamental delete operation defined for it. The high-level delete operation needs only to send a delete message to each component, which in turn communicates with each of its components.

Some database management systems allow object designers to define a set of operations for each complex object type along with specifications for object structures. If we do not have this luxury, we need to ensure that object data structures are accessible only via special operations defined for those structures. At all times, the implementation of each object should be kept private to the designers and maintainers of that object.

Design for Class Hierarchies

Inheritance can be viewed as a form of *coupling* between superclasses and specialization classes. A high degree of inheritance coupling is desirable. To accomplish this, each subclass should really be a specialization of its more general superclass. If a subclass explicitly rejects a lot of the attributes of the superclass, the subclass is only loosely coupled to its superclass. Try to design for inheritance in which subclasses inherit and use attributes and operations of the superclass.

Attributes and operations should be highly *cohesive* within a class, with no unused components. For each subclass within an inheritance hierarchy, try to ensure that the specialization is a valid one, not arbitrary. If it does not make sense to view the subclass as a type of the superclass, the specialization is not valid. Perhaps the subclass should be place higher in the hierarchy or within some other place in this or another class structure.

Some object-oriented database systems are based upon class hierarchies, with structural and behavioral inheritance between related classes. You may need to implement support for inheritance manually.

9.9 ISSUES IN OBJECT DATABASE DESIGN

Transactions

Typical transactions in business information management systems involve only a few database records and occur logically as one activity (either the entire transaction succeeds, or it fails and records are "rolled back" to their previous state). During transaction execution a database passes through inconsistent states while moving the system from the pre-transaction state to the post-transaction state. Transaction integrity must maintain database integrity to prevent external users or applications from accessing intermediate states within a transaction unit-of-work.

Although the traditional transaction processing systems used in commercial business systems tend to treat transactions as complete units-of-work, object databases may exhibit other transaction characteristics:[10]

- Transactions may be "conversational," requiring frequent interaction between end user and the database system before transaction completion
- Transactions may last for hours.
- Transactions may use many records when objects are complex and highly interrelated
- Transactions may be non-atomic (part of the transaction may be committed or rolled back)

A conversational transaction might be one to produce a design specification for an engineered product using a CAD tool, or an information management system being built using a CASE tool. Before a final design is produced, the user may produce a diagram via frequent interaction with a set of diagram tools.

Transactions that last for hours might occur when producing design diagrams built over several hours or days (the "complete" design is actually never complete). Transactions that consist of many records may involve browsing through complex documents, referring to other documents, and examining previous versions of documents produced for related projects.

Some applications require support for data sharing during these transactions. Many object-oriented database management systems support this. The traditional models of transactions might need to be replaced or higher-level mechanisms built on top of existing transaction models. See Brown[11] for a discussion of database issues when dealing with these types of transactions.

Concurrency Control

When a very large number of objects needs to be locked for a long transaction, it is not feasible for applications or users to wait for lock release in order to proceed. One approach to this problem is an optimistic approach to concurrency control. This approach relaxes the usual locking approach to perhaps allow two applications access to the same object. Information would be sent to each application to make it aware that a possible conflict exists. Users of the object must ensure that inconsistencies do not arise.

Greater concurrency control is possible when multiple object versions are created and maintained. With this approach, access to an object is to a particular version of that object. With this approach, many applications and users can simultaneously access multiple versions of that object, without creation of a new version of the object. One application or user can then change a version of an object while all others are reading that version.

When two copies of that version are updated simultaneously, a conflict can still occur. Library management systems that need this type of functionality usually implement a "check-in/check-out" type of concurrency control system. When a user or program needs to change an object, a version is checked-out into a private workspace and a write-lock is placed on the object version in the database. Once changes have been made, the application or user holding the write lock checks-in the object, creating a new version.

Another approach to concurrency control is to make it type-specific. When two transactions attempt to access the same object concurrently, there may not be a conflict if one attempts to remove an item from a queue while another is adding an item to the end of the queue. By use of queue types, a system can allow transactions to execute in parallel. To abort such a transaction by rewriting the original one may remove concurrent changes. Some complex transaction rollback mechanism is required for this to work well in practice.

Database Implementation

Any database system can be implemented as a logical database component, thus separating lower-level physical issues from higher-level database semantics. In a true object-oriented database management system, an object storage server allocates disk space to objects and places the objects appropriately. Likewise, we can implement complex database objects in layers that insulate higher-level models from the implementation details.

As a higher-level system interprets application and user database operation requests within the context of an object structure model and converts these requests to ones for specific objects, higher-level classes within complex objects can use a layered model approach as well. This requires that each model level define specific operations to be performed by lower-level models. Each model level maintains minimal semantics about the objects it describes, treating them as black boxes. Lower levels hide the details.

While an object storage server may identify objects using physical addresses, a higher-level server needs to use some logic object identifiers. If two separate references are maintained for each object, mappings between the two must be maintained for the appropriate translations between models. This translation may cause some extra processing overhead, but it does provide powerful database semantics. When an internal physical address is used in higher level and storage models, physical data independence is lost. Changing an object's physical allocation will have effects on the higher-level models.

Clustering

When a single database operation involves many different types of data, clustering may be used to group data by type. Rows of a relational table might reside in consecutive blocks so that record prefetch capabilities of the database manager may be used. When different data types are involved, this can be difficult to make work efficiently. On the other hand, using a different object server for each data type might not be very efficient, either.

When a simple, high-level representation of a complex object is used as the basis for design, it can lead to inefficient transactions and queries. This is similar to the way that relational set operations are conceptually simple but require sophisticated optimization routines in the database management system in order to execute well. Conventional clustering techniques thus may not work well when applied to certain kinds of transaction processing.

Some research has been conducted on both static and dynamic clusterings. The static approach decides about data clustering only when an object is created. Dynamic clustering allows objects to be clustered again later.

Large Databases

Another implementation problem can occur when you try to store and manage very large amounts of data. Techniques must often be devised for decomposing large objects into individual pieces. Data distribution often involves this kind of decomposition when multiple physical locations capture different transactions that map to the same logical database. Queries may reconstruct the logical database for reporting purposes, or a centralized database might be implemented on a large mainframe system.

Distributed design should be dealt with early when it is known that instances of objects will be distributed, but designs and implementations could be changed after the initial implementation if absolutely necessary. Similar techniques can be used to break up a large centralized database.

END NOTES

[1] Martin, James, and James Odell. *Object-Oriented Analysis and Design* (Englewood Cliffs, NJ: Prentice Hall) 1992.

[2] Ibid.

[3] Rumbaugh, James, Michael Blake, William Premerlani, Frederick Eddy and William Lorensen. *Object-Oriented Modeling and Design* (Englewood Cliffs, NJ: Prentice Hall) 1991, p. 238.

[4] Montgomery, Stephen L. *Relational Design and Implementation Using DB2* (New York: Van Nostrand Reinhold) 1990.

[5] Coad, Peter, and Edward Yourdon. *Object-Oriented Design* (Englewood Cliffs, NJ: Yourdon Press, Prentice Hall) 1991.

[6] Ibid.

[7] Rumbaugh, et al., *Object-Oriented Modeling and Design*, Chapter 17.

[8] Dittrich, Klaus R. "Object-Oriented Database Systems: The Notion and the Issues (Extended Extract)." In *International Workshop on Object-Oriented Database Systems*, September 1986, edited by Klaus R. Dittrich and Umeshwar Dayal. (New York: IEEE Computer Society Press) 1986.

[9] King, R. "My Cat Is Object-Oriented." In *Object-Oriented Concepts, Databases and Applications*, edited by W. Kim and F. H. Lochovsky. (New York: ACM Press) 1989.

[10] Brown, Alan W. *Object-Oriented Databases: Applications in Software Engineering* (London: McGraw-Hill) 1991.

[11] Ibid.

10

Application System Object Behavior

10.1 PROCEDURE-DRIVEN CONTROL

Most conventional information systems use this type of control, whereby a program's state is determined by the location of control within the program. A finite-state machine (see Chapter 6) can be built as a program, with each state transition mapping to an input statement. When input data are read, the program's control branches according to the input event. This requires that each input statement be able to handle any values that could be input at that point. With a deep application structure, lower-level modules must accept unknown inputs and pass them up the hierarchy, so modularity is lacking in this approach.

It is possible to convert an object state diagram to procedural code using these steps:[1]

1. Identify the main control path. Begin with the initial state and identify a path through the diagram that corresponds to the normally expected sequence of events. Write the names of states along this path as a linear sequence, the sequence of statements in the program.

2. Identify alternate paths that branch off the main path and rejoin it later. These become conditional program statements.

3. Identify backward paths that branch off the main path and rejoin it earlier. These become loops in the program. If multiple backward paths exist that do not cross, they become nested loops in the program. Backward paths that cross do not nest and can be implemented with GOTOs if all else fails, but these are rare.

4. The states and transitions that remain correspond to exception conditions. They can be handled by several techniques, including error subroutines, exception handling supported by the language or setting and testing of status flags. Exception handling is a legitimate use for GOTOs in a programming language. Their use frequently simplifies breaking out of a nested structure, but do not use them unless necessary.

10.2 EVENT-DRIVEN CONTROL

This approach is very straightforward, using states and transitions defined for an application. Rumbaugh[2] suggests that a general state machine engine class could allow execution of a state machine, represented by a table and actions provided by an application. Each object instance contains its own state variables but calls on the state machine engine to determine the next state and response.

With this approach, it is possible to move quickly from the behavior models in analysis to a rough prototype of an application. This can be done by defining classes from the structure model, state machines from the behavioral model and then creating stubs of the operations. A stub only defines a point where a more detailed part of an application (a subroutine, for instance) would be called. In structured design, stubs can be used to flesh out the high-level architecture of an application without implementing all of the details. Note that some generic methods and attributes in a subclass may actualy be implemented in the superclass (see Figure 10.1).

Operations appearing in analysis models can be implemented as operations in design. One type of design operation accesses objects with only a read access—object states do not change. Attribute operations that derive values are examples of this type of operation. Operations that modify objects do change object states, implementing the transitions on an object state diagram.

Martin and Odell's analysis and design methodology[3] includes trigger rules. A trigger detects an event and then completes arguments for its operation, evaluates control conditions and calls the operation. Each component of a trigger rule can be implemented from the initial event detection as:

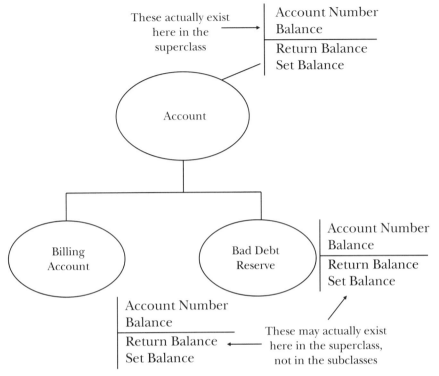

Figure 10.1 Implementation of attributes and methods

1. *Detect the event.* Actively poll the system environment for a predefined event or use a demon to activate the triggering mechanism.

2. *Fill operation arguments.* Triggers must provide those arguments required by an operation for invocation. Unless the argument is the same as for the event, one or more functions must be invoked. These functions should be implemented as operations in their own right.

3. *Evaluate the control condition.* This is a separate operation that returns either a true or false value. When the condition is true, the operation-invocation portion is executed.

4. *Invoke the operation.* Send a request (or message) for a specific operation. This part of the trigger can be implemented simply as an object-oriented program request.

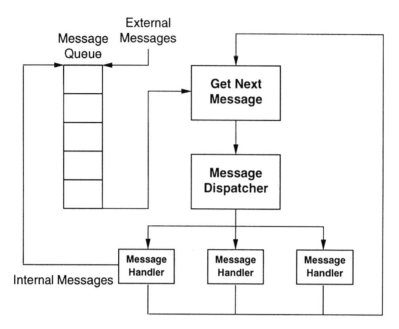

Figure 10.2   An event scheduler

This type of triggering mechanism is not often used but rather is built into the code of a preceding operation. This means that if trigger logic is embedded in an operation, the logic is stable only as long as its trigger logic is stable.

Operations need to be viewed only in light of their inputs and outputs. An operation should not need to be aware of what triggers it and what operations it triggers upon its completion.

An event marks a point in time when a state change will take place. Event types can be used to express the kinds of events that an application is required to respond to. Graphical user interfaces (GUIs) support event processing explicitly but most programming languages do not. An event schedule mechanism (like that used by powerful GUIs) can be implemented to handle event types (Figure 10.2).

Operations have procedural logic specified in analysis. This logic will be implemented as a method in design. One way to build a method is to have each specified action performed in a specific order, much as an ordinary program would be written. Another way is to implement an event scheduler. With the second approach, an application is controlled by an event scheduler program that pulls (pops) an event from a queue of events and performs processing for that event before starting to work on another event. GUIs prompt the user for input. In an application, operations can generate vents so that as an operation completes, an event is generated. This generated event can have triggers that evaluate control conditions and execute other operations.

An event scheduler's processing steps proceed something like this:[4]

1. Each time an operation defined on an event schema completes, an event occurs. This event is created by the event scheduler when an operation ends successfully.

2. Each instance of a particular event type is also an instance of its supertypes. All event supertypes are identified and an event created for each.

3. For each event created above, associated trigger rules are identified.

4. For each trigger rule, invoke functions that supply those argument objects required by the triggered operation.

5. The control condition of each operation to be triggered is evaluated. If the condition is true, allow triggering.

6. The event and all its components are placed onto the event queue.

7. A queued event is pulled from the event queue.

8. Operations for each trigger are requested. In multitasking or parallel processing environments, invoke several processes to run concurrently; in single-threaded environments, schedule operations one at a time.

10.3 CONCURRENT TASK CONTROL

This is a general approach in which objects may be implemented as tasks in programming languages or operating systems. Events are constructed as interprocess communications. A task identifies its state using its location within a program. Some languages support concurrency, but very few are available for production use.

Multiple, concurrent tasks are often required for:

• complex GUIs with multiple windows,

• data acquisition and control responsibility for local devices,

• multiuser systems,

- systems that must communicate with other systems and
- multiprocessor hardware architectures.

Tasks represent activities that a system must perform. They can simplify the design and development of systems, especially when they implement separate system behaviors that must be executed simultaneously. Multiple, concurrent tasks can be implemented on separate object processors or by using a single processor and a multitasking operating system environment.

When tasks are not used to implement multiple behaviors, design and development can become difficult. Implementing systems as large, monolithic programs has resulted in complex, unmanageable systems. Breaking systems into tasks can simplify the design of concurrent behaviors. Identifying and designing tasks can follow a procedure similar to this (discussed by Coad and Yourdon[5]):

Identify tasks (event-driven, clock-driven)

Prioritize tasks

Identify a coordinator

Justify each task

Define each task (description, how it coordinates, how it communicates)

Some tasks are driven by events and may be responsible for communication with:

- devices,
- multiple screen windows,
- other tasks,
- subsystems,
- other processors and
- other systems.

END NOTES

[1] Rumbaugh, James, Michael Blaha, William Premerlani, Frederick Eddy and William Lorensen. *Object-Oriented Modeling and Design* (Englewood Cliffs, NJ: Prentice Hall) 1991, p. 239.

[2] Ibid.

[3] Martin, James, and James Odell. *Object-Oriented Analysis and Design* (Englewood Cliffs, NJ: Prentice Hall) 1992, p. 424.

[4] Ibid, pp. 428–429.

[5] Coad, Peter, and Edward Yourdon. *Object-Oriented Design* (Englewood Cliffs, NJ: Yourdon Press, Prentice Hall) 1991.

11

User Interface Requirements

Any information system that must interact with users needs to have careful attention paid to the user interface. The look and feel of this interface must be appropriate for each of the users that must interact with the system. Systems analysts need to identify attributes and operations that will be specified in the system design. Design then adds user interface design specifications and details of how their users will interact with the interface. The user interface design describes the format and functioning of windows, screens and reports. Prototyping the interface can help refine user requirements and get some important users heavily involved in the development process for the first time. Prototyping can be a very powerful tool for gathering requirements, especially for those people who have difficulty describing what a computer system should do for them.

User interface issues are discussed in the design portion of this book; some developers address the topic in analysis. Modeling the user interface, which is covered in this chapter, can be successfully handled at several points during development, as long as the conceptual, functional requirements of analysis are modeled separately from the implementation-dependent specifications modeled in design.

11.1 ANALYZE USERS

To best design a user interface, first it is necessary to understand how users need to gather information from the system and enter information into it. Good user interface design can help sell the system to key users or groups of users who have certain opinions about what an information system is supposed to look like. Analysts must study the way people perform their work today and examine how that work may change with a new information system. Designers must then continue studying these users of the system, at least during user interface design. Whereas the analysts define what information users need, designers need to describe user interface interaction capabilities that will be used.

Designers wishing to fully analyze how users perform their work can benefit from working side by side with these people. Better yet, perform some of their work for a while. There is no better way to begin to understand what a computer user interface should do than to experience what the users experience in their everyday jobs. Of course, a designer would be considered an advanced user from the standpoint of computer interaction sophistication (not the business knowledge but the technical knowledge required). The designer can get the essential information captured very quickly this way.

The user interface designer needs to examine tasks that users need to perform and envision what system functions or features can be used to support the performance of these tasks. It is not usually important to describe individual people's characteristics, but it will be important to categorize groups of users by their levels of skill (novice, intermediate, advanced) and perhaps also by organization level (executive, manager, clerk). Try to identify for each category of user what the most important criteria for the user interface are and some sample scenarios that they are likely to act out when using the computer system to perform their jobs.

11.2 DESIGN MENU/COMMAND STRUCTURES

Consider using a standard design guideline and format such as IBM's Common User Access (CUA) component of their Systems Application Architecture (SAA) for those situations where a hierarchy or other command structure is needed. (See Montgomery[1] for coverage of the basic characteristics of IBM's SAA as well as IBM's AD/Cycle framework for building applications that adhere to SAA guidelines.) These standards and guidelines change over time but incorporate some solid design principles that have been implemented across tens of thousands of systems users. Always look for, evaluate and incorporate user interface standards and guidelines. Doing so can save a lot of headaches after system implementation.

To establish a command structure, use combinations of menu screens, menu bars (action bars), pull-down (or pop-up) menus or combinations of graphic icons that invoke system functions when selected and activated. View the options on the command interface as operations that are sent to application system objects from the user.

Basic action to include on a GUI screen begins with basic functions such as file, edit, view and help. The main action bar menu for Microsoft Word for Windows (word processing software running under Microsoft Windows, which was used to write this book) appears like this:

File Edit View Insert Format Tools Table Window Help

With each of these command categories, other commands need to be identified and, at the lowest level of a command hierarchy, the final action to be taken once the user has selected from the menus. From the word processing example, under file, these options can be found on the pull-down menu:

New...

Open...

Close

Save

Save As...

Save All

Find File...

Summary Info...

Template...

Print Preview

Print...

Print Merge...

Print Setup...

Exit

Under the exit option are the names of the last four documents that were edited. Click the left mouse button while pointing to any one of these file names to cause the file to be loaded immediately for editing. Point to any one of the menu options that has no ellipsis (. . .) to take immediate action, which might include prompting the user for more information. Choose save to store the current document to disk immediately with no further prompting for information. The open option requires information about the drive, directory and file name to search for. Options that have an ellipsis (. . .) after the name of the option will prompt the user with an additional pull-down menu upon their selection and activation. This, then, is an example of a menu hierarchy used for the Microsoft Windows user interface.

Microsoft Word for Windows also provides a toolbar—a list of icons displayed horizontally just under the main action bar menu. This is an example of an icon-based command structure. Each icon, when pointed to by the mouse and activated with the left mouse button, causes an application function to execute immediately, just as if the user had selected options from the menu and the subsequent prompting dialogs. Word for Windows and other Windows applications provide users the capability of building their own tool icons. These icons can be placed on the user interface for the convenience of their various users. Thus, it is possible to give the user the opportunity to customize the predesigned user interface to some degree. This would be very convenient for building standard queries in a decision support system, for instance.

Once a general idea of what the command structure should look and behave like has been developed, begin to refine it. Coad and Yourdon[2] list four techniques for refining command hierarchies:

- Ordering
- Whole-part (aggregation) chunking
- Breadth and depth chunking
- Minimal steps

Ordering involves careful selection of distinct operation names. These names are ordered within each section of the command hierarchy, with the most frequently used operations listed first and in the customary work-step order.

Whole-part chunking involves examining aggregation patterns across operations themselves to assist in organizing and grouping operations within the command hierarchy.

Breadth and depth chunking aim to avoid overloading human short-term memory capabilities with too many system operations at one time. The depth versus breadth dimensions of the command hierarchy are examined and an attempt made to moderate depth to about three and breadth to about three groups of three operations.

Minimal steps focus on minimizing the number of mouse clicks and drags and keyboard keystroke combinations used to select operations. Provide shortcuts for advanced users.

11.3 DESIGN THE USER INTERFACE INTERACTION

Once user interface options have been identified for a portion of the system (and perhaps grouped and placed into an initial command hierarchy or other structure), it is time to move on to design the detailed user interaction. Many good references are available to assist in this effort, such as the example below, adapted from the steps and guidelines suggested in the STRADIS methodology from Structured Solutions, Inc. of Marietta, Georgia (Figure 11.1).

Figure 11.2 shows suggestions for user interface design, also adapted from the STRADIS methodology:

Coad and Yourdon[3] list some human interaction criteria to aid interface design:

- Consistency
- Few steps required
- No "dead air"—lack of feedback to the user
- Closure—using small steps leading to a well-defined action
- Undo
- No memory storage in "human RAM"
- Time and effort to learn
- Pleasure and appeal (look and feel)

Figure 11.3 shows a graphic example of menu/screen navigation dialogs.

1. List all operations to be performed by the user.

2. Place operations on the list into functional groups so that each operation contributes to the performance of a single overall function.

3. Place listed and grouped operations into a function tree that shows their relationships to one another.

4. Create a detailed description of the steps to perform each operation on the function tree (usually only a single step for each operation).

5. Design the physical screen layout.

6. Consider providing a terminal dialog option if there are to be both novice and expert users. Novice users need an option to provide full prompting of dialog, feedback on each input, extensive help features and descriptive messages. Expert users need to be able to select a dialog option that has minimal prompting and feedback, but includes a summarized help feature.

7. Write the dialog.

Figure 11.1   Designing for user interaction

11.4 BUILD A PROTOTYPE OF THE USER INTERFACE

Although user interface prototyping is covered in this chapter, building the prototype may occur before analysis is complete. The technique of prototyping is actually a form of analysis, but since it also involves design and construction issues, it is presented here. Prototype the user interface to explore human requirements for interaction with a computer system. The interface needs to enhance a person's ability to work with the system, minimizing the effort required and possible confusion that may result. The interface should do more, though. It needs to be able to enhance the work experience, not just support it.

The last section discussed the use of menus and command shortcuts to tailor the system to user needs. Normally, assumptions about this structuring of system command structures would be implemented quickly, using a screen painter and the various screens and menus linked together in a tool that simulates the actual production environment proposed for the system.

- Always remain conscious of legibility.
- Be conscious of dialog flow.
- Watch the tone of the dialog.
- Be careful with terminology.
- Use blinking and other forms of highlighting sparingly (preferably for urgent action messages).
- Always provide a help function.
- Give the user the option of escaping from the dialog at any time.
- Provide feedback on each input.
- For alphanumeric information, group characters for maximum legibility.
- Make sure that recurring information always appears in the same place in every screen on which it appears.
- If possible, use normal upper- and lowercase letters.
- Always list items in their natural order (or list them numerically or alphabetically).
- Provide defaults whenever possible.
- Make sure that error messages are clear and that any faulty items entered are flagged.

Figure 11.2   Suggestions for user interface dialog design

The goal of prototyping is to gather requirements more effectively by presenting the user with a portion of the system to use and react to in order to avoid problems from users who only know what they want when they see it. Prototyping does not solve all analysis design problems, even in the interface area, but it is one more approach to system development that should be considered.

A prototyping approach can improve system design by getting users involved early in the development process (a key goal of information engineering) and getting them to experience what the system can do for them. Users get immediate feedback, and their interest can be stimulated and enthusiasm kept high. It will be easier to find out early what the user's business needs, work habits, work patterns and system behavior expectations are. Communi-

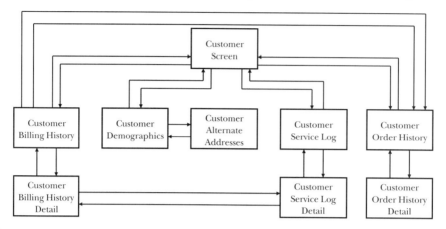

Figure 11.3   A state diagram for a user dialog

cation between users and developers of the system is greatly enhanced through prototyping.

Two basic types of prototypes may be built and evaluated: discovery and production. The discovery prototype is used only for analysis and must be rebuilt for production use. It may include any or all of the following:

- Screen and report layouts
- Menu layouts, navigation, declaration and execution
- Help screens
- Application screens with editing capabilities and limited or full function
- Working reports

A production prototype can be moved directly into production and may include all of the above plus screens with full functionality, working reports and storage capabilities for database data.

Not all systems can achieve great benefits from a prototyping approach. Good candidates for prototyping include systems that:

- incorporate user work patterns,
- are highly interactive,
- have high degrees of data manipulation,
- have large numbers of potential users,
- have vague user needs,

- exhibit high risk and cost,
- give important hands-on experience for users,
- have developers who are not familiar with the business area and
- have requirements that are constantly changing.

System candidates that are poor ones for prototyping include ones that:

- require little or no user interaction,
- have well-specified requirements,
- have few users,
- are static and well-understood,
- involve many algorithms but few data structures and
- can easily be substituted with a package.

11.5 DESIGN USER INTERFACE CLASSES

During this phase of user interface design, it becomes helpful to consider constraints placed on the production system environment, such as accuracy, control, privacy and security. Also, close attention should be paid to the physical devices that will be used for various user interfaces. All kinds of devices may play a role in user interface design and implementation:

- Intelligent workstations
- Video terminals
- Voice response units
- Point-of-sale (POS) terminals
- Portable terminals
- Light pen terminals or workstations
- Touch-screen terminals or workstations

Selecting the right terminal device for the application at hand improves the effectiveness of the user interface. It may not be possible to influence the device selection decision due to technical or management constraints, but try to incorporate the powerful features provided by GUIs running on personal computers or more powerful workstations.

The specific user interface classes that are selected and built in detailed design will necessarily differ based on the actual GUI selected (such as Microsoft Windows, OS/2 Presentation Manager, Motif, Macintosh MacApp, etc.). With a GUI, begin by structuring the interaction using windows and their components. Each main window class will contain definitions for menu bars, pull-down menus and pop-up windows. The classes each define the operations required for menu creation, item selection and invoking application functions and are responsible for presenting information within the window itself. These window classes need to encapsulate all of the details of the user dialog.

Design of user interface classes often consists of using inheritance to specialize the existing window classes. Lower-level classes may not need to include a lot of new operations but instead refine those operations present in their superclasses. Knowing what operations to override may involve a trial-and-error process but often is fairly straightforward. New interface classes may need to be invented when it is expected that requirements are likely to change, but refinement of superior classes makes this easier.

Figure 11.4 shows example window classes and inheritance among them for the Smalltalk environment, which can be implemented on many of the previously mentioned GUIs. In Smalltalk, you deal with types of windows,

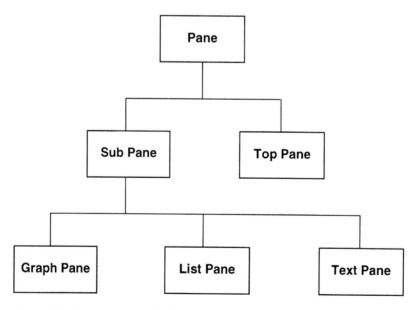

Figure 11.4   Window classes and inheritance in Smalltalk

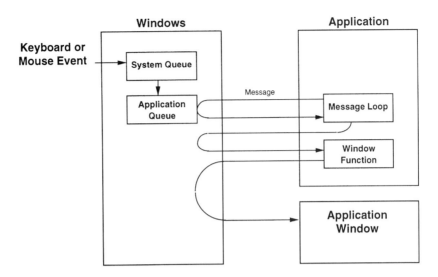

Figure 11.5   Processing of keyboard or mouse events in Microsoft Windows

which the GUI implements physically. Smalltalk windows are called Panes, all of which handle menus, pop-ups and fonts. Panes handle variables and methods appropriate for a window subarea. SubPanes refine these capabilities, adding knowledge of variables and methods for scroll bars hidden inside. GraphPanes further refine variables and methods, adding hidden bitmap and graphics tools. ListPanes add the handling of indexed collections of strings to SubPanes, and TextPanes handle individual strings—displaying, scrolling and editing. The TopPane handles color, border, frame and label functions.

Following user interface class development is development of application domain-specific classes. These classes act on the messages sent by the user via the user interface to the application system. These domain-specific classes are invoked via the user interface system's event loop processing mechanism. A method reacts to a user interface event message by invoking an event dispatch method. This dispatch method then invokes the application method to process any command that the event handler might have created.

Figure 11.5 shows how this works in the Microsoft Windows environment. First, the user presses a key or clicks the mouse button on a window object. This event is received by the system queue and routed to the application queue. There, a message is sent to the message loop within an application in the WinMain function, which processes the message and sends it back to Windows, which dispatches the message to the application window. The application window function sends a TextOut message to Windows, which sends a message to the application window. All of this processing is invisible to the end user. Even though it is complex, it provides great flexibility to the system user. Unlike traditional user interfaces, GUIs like Windows allow the users to decide how to navigate through the command structure. Processing is based on what should be done; the application programmer does not need handle the events in detail.

END NOTES

[1] Montgomery, Stephen L. *AD/CYCLE: IBM's Framework for Application Development and CASE* (New York: Van Nostrand Reinhold) 1991.

[2] Coad, Peter, and Edward Yourdon. *Object-Oriented Design* (Englewood Cliffs, NJ: Yourdon Press, Prentice Hall) 1991, Chapter 4.

[3] Ibid.

12

General System Designs

12.1 DESIGN PROBLEMS ADDRESSABLE DURING ANALYSIS

At about the time that analysis models are complete, design issues need to be addressed in order to avoid designing and building systems that don't quite work out the way planned. Object orientation gives developers a big advantage when it comes time to take conceptual analysis models and make the transition to a logical and then physical design. Figures 12.1 and 12.2[1] show how an object design might begin to view how a model of an object should be implemented. Often, design problems can be characterized as:

- acceptance of incomplete requirements,
- problems in partitioning and decomposing models,
- problems in mapping models to design,
- service-level (performance) problems and
- human interface problems.

Programming normally deals with small, well-bounded, stable tasks. It makes few strategic decisions about systems design—very good analysis and design models need to be completed before programming can begin. Analysis deals with the entire system, making no particular decisions as to how requirements are to be implemented. Design expands upon analysis, which

155

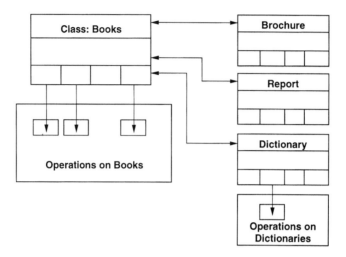

Figure 12.1   Objects, classes and inheritance

is the essence of what a system should do. The design process deals with constraints placed on the system's physical environment and any managerial or technical choices that have been made.

Poor decision making during design can wreak havoc for detailed design and development. Many poor decisions are difficult, if not impossible, to discover and correct during later stages of design and development.

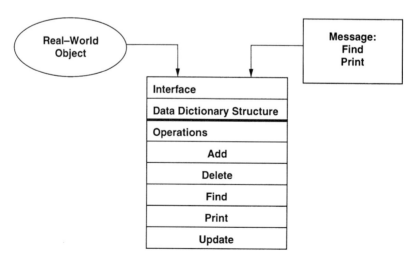

Figure 12.2   Software representation of an object

Acceptance of Incomplete Requirements

Acceptance of incomplete requirements should be avoided by careful and complete analysis and modeling of system requirements. The various analysis models and miscellaneous documentation are of little benefit if the process of gathering requirements was not complete and rigorous. Various repository or encyclopedia reports can be used to cross-check models for consistency and completeness, but designers often inherit the task of validating that analysis models are feasible to implement. Ideally, designers are involved in the detailed analysis stages of modeling and can correct some potential design problems early. In addition to gathering a system's logical requirements (the job of an analyst), a designer needs to get an early start gathering a system's physical requirements such as:

- data and transaction or user view volumes,
- locations for data storage and user processing,
- response time requirements and
- data volatility.

At a minimum, analysis deliverables should provide to design those items listed below:

- System functions
- Inputs and outputs
- Interfaces with other systems
- Performance requirements (throughput, response time)
- Constraints on the system
- Security issues
- Usage patterns

Problems Partitioning and Decomposing Analysis Models

Analysis model partitioning and decomposition problems must be addressed before analysis is considered complete. Partitioning (horizontal splitting) and decomposition (vertical splitting) of system models during analysis and design should allow for any expected changes. The most detailed portions of an analysis model should probably be partitioned, or at least described in terms of, the probable implementation environment. Object models are quite structured, and partitioning is thus much easier than with conventional structured analysis and structured design models. It can be helpful, though, to capture any design and implementation constraints during detailed analysis in order to allow designers enough time to work out any problems with the analysis models before constructing decent design models.

It can be very useful to isolate software and hardware interfaces early in design, using information hiding to insulate possible changes from applications and users. One obvious way is to design user interfaces, databases, communications and business logic as distinct from each other. Many application environments for development and systems implementation that are supported today by hardware vendors and industry standards organizations support this idea. If object standards are not available or are not comprehensive enough, begin to think of design and implementation object types. The result will be a much higher resilience to changes in underlying technologies.

Distributing objects to physical locations (discussed in Chapter 13) should be considered at this point. The design models should begin by viewing systems as centralized and at some detailed model level must necessarily become distributed. Designing standard database, communications and application business logic subsystems and interfaces can help you make the migration to distributed systems easier.

Service-Level Problems

In order to adequately address user needs and expectations for the service level of the system response times, the requirements must be explicitly declared:

- Data volumes
- Response times
- Data volatility
- Data concurrency and synchronization
- Data retention
- System reliability
- System availability

Such requirements are incorporated in design and implementation when decisions are made on:

- online versus batch processing,
- redundant hardware,
- backup and recovery processes,
- distributed system structure,
- network topology,
- operating system selection,
- usage of interrupts,
- processing priorities,
- workstation/terminal to user ratios and
- maintenance plans.

Strive to assign a value to each user view of information. Each external object on a message flow diagram needs to send or retrieve system information. Try to assign values to the currency and access costs for transmitting this information and estimate what the consequences are of failure to meet these requirements. Failure to have the system meet user expectations can hamper severely attempts to maintain and increase support for development projects related to the system at hand. Meeting user service-level expectations can become a great selling tool when seeking executive support for key development projects.

User Interface Problems

The information capture from and display to users should be considered early. This is because of the need to support people's patterns of work within the limitations of the technology that is available and/or affordable for certain systems. User interfaces (discussed in the previous chapter) need to reflect a unified set of concepts such as:

- consistency in function key usage,
- menu command placement,
- help screens,
- data entry screen constructs and
- transitions from one task to another.

Good selection of physical display devices and data formats for user views of system information require knowledge of how information flows into and out of the system and the constraints of certain physical environments in which the system must operate. Consider objectives and constraints regarding hardware input/output devices:

- Size
- Weight
- Shock resistance
- Humidity
- Temperature

In addition to physical properties of user interfaces and their associated devices, pay close attention to the actual work patterns of the people who will interact with the system. Good, basic interfaces that are workable for users are likely to be much more successful than fancy, complex ones that are powerful but difficult to work with. Examine individual users and then categorize groups of them based on skills and attitudes about the system, what their limitations are, and what they are motivated to do with the system (contrasted with what they will only do if they have to). Document what the system must do to make user productivity as easy as possible. Later on build a prototype to test assumptions.

For detailed information about defining physical constraints on analysis models, see the material on derived design within the STRADIS systems development methodology or one more information engineering based, such as AD/Method. STRADIS is an older but successful development methodology, formerly owned by McDonnell Douglas and now owned by Structured Solutions, Marietta, Georgia. The company supports information engineering in their AD/Method development methodology.

12.2 MODULES

Class structures define the logical design of a system of objects, but this logical design needs to be mapped to a physical design that actually makes the system operate. Some type of module diagram can be used to depict how classes and objects are allocated to physical modules. A designer must allocate classes, class utilities, objects and any other system components to physical modules. Some programming languages support the concept of physical modules. Ada, which uses sophisticated packages, is one example. Other languages might implement modules simply as separately compiled files, such as C or C++.

Booch[2] states that the only dependency between modules is compilation dependency, represented as a straight line between modules on a module diagram. These dependencies are useful when configuring an application using a tool such as the UNIX *make* tool and also to detect cycles in compilation dependencies. Because objects in a system are loosely coupled and send messages to each other, there need not be a physical link between modules unless, perhaps, their functioning implements a cohesive class structure with more tightly coupled components. Thus the message flow diagrams from analysis can be used to depict asynchronous interactions and messaging between objects. The Booch-style module diagram (it looks much the same as a traditional structure chart) can be used to show how modules are physically packaged together to form larger modules.

12.3 SUBSYSTEMS

Large systems of many components may be decomposed into perhaps thousands of small modules. As with traditional structured design, the systems should be "chunked" into smaller pieces. Subsystems represent groups of logically related modules that represent system chunks. The object structure models help a lot with the task of determining what parts of a system should become subsystems. Each major class (or logically related group of classes) could be implemented as a separate subsystem if necessary or desirable. This is what is likely to be done in the near future as object-oriented languages and database management systems become more mature. It allows implementation of classes on dedicated servers in much the same manner as many organizations today implement subject databases on dedicated database servers.

Typically, a larger system tends to have a single module at the top of a hierarchical structure, representing the highest level of abstraction in the design. As with a program structure chart, the general physical architecture of a system can be represented concisely on a single diagram. A subsystem can represent another such module diagram, allowing representation at multiple levels in a hierarchy.

Subsystem module diagrams can be built to nearly parallel the structure of a class diagram. Classes are layered in generalization/specialization hierarchies, while subsystems are layered as aggregations. As with a process decomposition hierarchy in conventional information engineering, higher-level components in an aggregation hierarchy build (but do not inherit) upon the characteristics of the lower-level components. Several management constraints may drive designers to build subsystem hierarchies that do not mirror class structure, such as project work breakdown structure, reuse libraries or security constraints, for example.

12.4 PROCESS ARCHITECTURE

Allocating Subsystems to Processors and Tasks

Subsystems will be allocated to a processor. To do this:

- estimate the performance needs and resources needed to satisfy them,
- choose hardware and software implementations for the subsystems,
- allocate software subsystems to processors to address performance needs and reduce interprocessor communication and
- determine the connections between physical processor units.

Multiple processors may be needed if more powerful processing is required than a single processor provides. Processing power must be figured for the time required to process a single transaction multiplied by the average number of transactions per second. Then peak processing periods must be taken into account.

Subsystem processing tasks are assigned to processors because certain tasks are needed at geographic locations, because the response time or flow rate is greater than the capabilities of communications links or because processing requirements are too much for a single processor to handle. Once the types and numbers of physical processors have been determined, connections between processors can be chosen.

Network topologies are chosen. Look for associations in the object structure model as possible connections. Client/server partnerships in the message flow diagrams might also be physical connections. Then the topology of the replicated units is chosen. Consider the expected message arrival patterns and algorithms for processing them in parallel. Finally, choose the kind of connection channels and communications protocols that will be used (synchronous, asynchronous or blocking, for instance). Take into account channel bandwidths and latencies, as well as the type of channel. If connections are not physical but logical, units may be tasks in a single operating system connected by interprocess communications calls.

Edward Yourdon[3] discusses a processor model used by a systems designer when allocating processes and data stores to physical processors. The essential model of a structured analysis modeling effort is allocated to different processors than those that must communicate with each other. The processes and data stores in the essential model of structured analysis become the objects of object analysis models, but the basic idea of allocating to processors is the same. The natural boundary for allocating parts of a system to processors is the subsystem level, but the class or object levels will do, too. The various diagrams depicting interacting objects (the object message diagrams in particular) provide a nice way to identify communications between processors. The basic choices available to a designer for processor-to- processor communication are highlighted by Yourdon:

- *A direct connection between processors.* This could be implemented by connecting processors with a cable, channel or local area network. This kind of communication generally permits data to be transmitted from one processor to another at speeds of from 50,000 bps to several million bps.
- *A telecommunications link between processors.* This is common if processors are physically separated by more than a few hundred feet. Data will typically be transmitted between processors at speeds ranging from 300 bps to 50,000 bps.
- *An indirect link between processors.* Data may be written onto a storage medium and physically carried to another processor for input.

Factors to be considered when allocating processes include:

- Cost
- Efficiency
- Security
- Reliability
- Political and operational constraints

At the level of an individual task, depict processing using a conventional structure chart or Booch's module diagram. Some form of hierarchical structure is useful for implementing class behaviors, but larger sets of interacting objects might need more of a network notation for depicting interactions between tasks. However tasks and program modules are depicted, benefits from structured design guidelines include:

- Cohesion
- Coupling
- Module size
- Span of control
- Scope of effect

This is especially true if a traditional programming language is used that is not highly structured.

A module is highly cohesive if its components are necessary and sufficient to perform one single, well-defined activity. Essential processes must not be split into fragmented modules, and one module should not contain unrelated components. The best modules are functionally cohesive, in that each program statement is necessary in order to perform a single, well-defined task.

Modules that are loosely coupled are easier to build and maintain because a modification to one module requires careful study as well as any possible changes to one or more other modules. Each module needs to have simple, clean interfaces with other modules, with a minimum of shared data elements between modules (except, of course, the sharing of data via a database). One module should never modify the internal logic or data of another module except via the standard interface for that module and its parameters. In a purely object-oriented programming language, the only way to manipulate an object is through the public interface, so module coupling becomes a very minor issue.

Module size should be kept small enough that it can be easily managed, perhaps one page or screen of statements. Large, complex modules should be decomposed into smaller components, but not to the point that the resulting modules are trivial.

A top-level module in a hierarchy of modules should not manage more than just a few lower-level modules in order to avoid complexity. By keeping all modules small and responsible for only a few logical activities, modules are easier to build and manage.

Depicting Process Architecture

It can be very helpful to design and build systems that are composed of multiple programs executing in parallel, but this requires a different set of decisions than those involved with class and object modeling. Booch[4] uses process diagrams to depict how object behavior tasks are allocated to processors in the physical design of the system. One process diagram may represent all or part of the process architecture of a system. Usually, a design includes only one process diagram, but some complex systems may require several. When multiple processes must execute on a single processor, these diagrams can help depict devices or active objects that use multiple processes executing concurrently.

Which processes (programs or active objects) have been allocated to a specific processor should be depicted. Each process description should document a single thread of control. Some implementations only have one process and others may have numerous processes. Once descriptions of each process have been created, the processing load can be balanced among processors in order to avoid overloading any one processor, suboptimizing system performance.

Scheduling process executions within a processor involves some general approaches. The ones suggested by Booch[5] include those shown below:

- *Preemptive.* Higher-priority processes ready to execute may preempt lower-priority ones already executing. Processes with equal priority are given a time slice in which to execute, distributing computational resources fairly.
- *Nonpreemptive.* The current process continues to execute until it relinquishes control.
- *Cyclic.* Control passes from one process to another. Each process is given a fixed amount of processing time, which may be allocated in frames or subframes.
- *Executive.* Some algorithm controls process scheduling.
- *Manual.* Processes are scheduled by an external user.

Some system designers use timing diagrams or other specifications to depict process scheduling. These can be helpful when the dynamic behavior of programs that migrate among processors must be documented.

12.5 SOFTWARE ARCHITECTURES

There are a few architectural frameworks available for implementing a system, with each having its own advantages and disadvantages. Examining these options ahead of time can help get designs finalized more quickly. Some of these options include the following:

- Interactive interfaces
- Transaction management
- Batch transformation
- Continuous transformation
- Real-time systems
- Simulation

Interactive Interfaces

A system that uses interactive interfaces (an online system) involves heavy interactions between external objects and system objects. External objects (people, other systems, devices) cannot be controlled by the system, but system objects may request input from and respond to these external objects. The interactive interface represents the part of a system that is responsible for:

- communications protocols between the system and external objects,
- presentation of outputs,
- flow of control within the system,
- message syntax and
- ease of understanding (for user interfaces).

Such an interface might involve use of windows, a command language, a forms-based query interface or some other kind of interaction mechanism. The behavioral component of an object model with its object state diagrams can prove quite helpful in describing the interaction sequences and flow of control. The interaction model is also useful because on object message diagrams the flow of information to and from external objects is explicitly shown. These flows are implemented directly in the interactive interface. To implement an interactive interface:

- Isolate interface objects from application processing and storage objects.
- Use the object behavior model to structure programs (usually event-driven or multitasking concurrent control rather than procedural).
- Isolate physical events from logical ones.
- Fully describe application functions invoked by the interface.

Transaction Management

This kind of architecture involves storage and access of information using a database management system. Multiuser and multitasking issues must often be addressed. A transaction is viewed as a single, logical unit of work that is independent of other such units of work. Transaction management is very common and might be involved in any record-based commercial information management system.

With this type of architecture, the object structure mode is of utmost importance. The interaction model is also useful because the message responses (operations) tend to query and update information. The behavior model depicts concurrent access of distributed information, so it is very useful in modeling multiple transaction processes and for estimating transaction throughputs. Using these models, activities like the following help design and implement a transaction management architecture:

- Map object structures to database and file structures.
- Determine resources that can or cannot be shared; add new classes as needed.
- Determine the unit of work that must be accessed during a transaction.
- Design for concurrent control.

Batch Transformation

This architecture also is common in information management systems. With batch transformations, inputs are converted to outputs in a sequential fashion without interaction with external objects. The object state diagrams are of little use, and the object structure model is of some help, but it is the interaction model that specifies how input values are transformed into output values that gives the most assistance here. Batch transformations can be designed by the following activities:

- Decompose the overall transformation into stages (modeled by an object message diagram).
- Define intermediate object classes for message flows between stages.
- Restructure as needed for best performance.

See Rumbaugh et al.[6] for discussion of these types of system architectures, as well as continuous transformation, real-time systems and simulation.

General Design Considerations

When setting up plans to test the functionality of the system to be implemented, pay careful attention to boundary conditions of initialization, termination and failure. For initialization, the system must be brought from an idle state to a fully operational one. These items need to be considered:

- Tasks
- Constant data
- Global variables
- Parameters
- Class hierarchy

Initialization usually should involve only a small subset of the total system, but it can be difficult to accomplish when concurrent tasks are involved. Independent system objects must not be too far ahead or behind other objects during the initialization process.

When it comes time to bring the system down (terminate it), a task must release any external resources that it had reserved and may often need to notify other tasks of its termination. The unplanned termination of the system should result in an orderly shutdown if at all possible. Fatal errors should lead to a graceful exit, leaving behind a clean environment and an audit trail of information about the failure.

Trade-offs will usually be involved during the design process. Choices must be made between often incompatible goals such as speed and storage requirements. If the user requirements state that some goals are high-priority ones, the trade-off process can be made easier, but often a designer needs to make the decisions. Rapid prototyping of part of the system can help everyone involved understand what some of the design trade-offs are. This can reduce development time but sacrifices complete functionality, efficiency and robustness. Once a suitable prototype has been built, evaluated and improved, it can be reconstructed using different design characteristics.

END NOTES

[1] Pressman, Roger S. *Software Engineering* (New York: McGraw-Hill) 1987.

[2] Booch, Grady. *Object-Oriented Design with Applications* (Reading, MA: Addison-Wesley) 1991, p. 176.

[3] Yourdon, Edward. *Modern Structured Analysis* (Englewood Cliffs, NJ: Yourdon Press, Prentice Hall) 1989, Chapter 22.

[4] Booch, *Object-Oriented Design with Applications.*

[5] Ibid., p. 183.

[6] Rumbaugh, James, Michael Blaha, William Premerlani, Frederick Eddy and William Lorensen. *Object-Oriented Modeling and Design* (Englewood Cliffs, NJ: Prentice Hall) 1991.

13

Design for
System Distribution

Distributed systems are a reality today. Information is stored in multiple locations on rather inexpensive computers, with the trend continuing toward increasingly distributed systems. Thus, the need for good design, implementation and control of distributed systems is becoming more important each day. To avoid chaos, begin thinking early on in the design process of ways to incorporate ideas about how the systems and their components should be distributed. Question how database and application objects should be configured across a geographic network of locations. Focus first on the basic objects themselves, not on the underlying network communications and data storage issues. Determining how objects should be distributed is complex, with many reasons for distribution. Don't focus too early on network topologies and such. Focus on the analysis and design models built thus far.

13.1 REASONS TO DISTRIBUTE OR CENTRALIZE OBJECTS

The reasons for object distribution are many, but by borrowing some ideas from distributed database design, some valuable insights can be gained. For databases, it may make most sense to store data where they are used. Departmental information is often best kept at the department's location. Martin[1] lists seven properties of data that lead naturally to distribution:

1. Data are used at one peripheral location and rarely or never at other locations.
2. Data accuracy, privacy and security are a local responsibility.
3. Files are simple and used by one or a few applications.
4. Update rates are too high for a single centralized storage system.
5. Peripheral files are searched or manipulated with query systems that results in alternate search paths (inverted list or secondary key operations).
6. Fourth-generation languages that employ a database management system different than that used for the production system are used.
7. A localized decision-support system is used.

On the other hand, some types of data exhibit characteristics leading more naturally to centralization:[2]

1. Data are used by centralized applications.
2. Users in all areas need access to the same data and need the current up-to-the-minute version.
3. Users of the data travel among many separate locations, and it is less expensive to centralize data than to use a switched data network.
4. Data as a whole will be searched.
5. Mainframe database software is needed.
6. A high level of security must be maintained over the data.
7. Data are too large to be stored on peripheral storage units.
8. Details are kept of transactions that update certain data, so data are cheaper and more secure to store centrally.

When data are distributed, some integrity and synchronization problems can occur unless a good design is used. There are many advantages, though. Among them are:

- reduced transmission costs,
- improved response times,

- increased availability,
- increased survivability (from multiple copies of the same data) and
- organization of databases around the use of data.

Problems of distributing include the following:

- More difficult transaction updates
- Inconsistent views of data
- Increased opportunity for deadlocks
- Increased control overhead
- Increased recovery complexity
- Multiple data representations
- Difficulty in auditing
- Security and privacy control complexity.

Whether or not databases and other objects are to be distributed, it is a good idea to begin design by viewing an entire system as centralized. Introduce distribution issues later. This way, the focus is on the conceptual semantics of models without getting into the complexities of the physical world too soon. Also, some technology decisions may not yet be finalized as system design begins, such as:

- whether or not to distribute,
- how to distribute,
- network topology used,
- network availability,
- costs of processors and storage devices,
- communications transmissions costs,
- distributed software costs and
- actual decisions on physical locations.

When implementing an enterprise-wide architecture for systems and their networks, implementation can take a long time. Try to focus on logical, not physical mappings of system components. Collect information about probable distribution situations, but don't model these situations until the centralized versions of the system models are fairly stable.

13.2 MAPPING OBJECTS TO LOCATIONS

Often, many organization units within an organization perform the same tasks. This can be true across locations, too: Each office needs to perform some of the same tasks. The objects (initially, all data and operations) can be mapped against physical locations where the business activities that use the objects are performed. Operations can also be mapped against locations, but the object data structures themselves are most important for placing databases and their components. Instead, high-level business activities could be mapped against locations (Figure 13.1) in much the same manner that business functions are mapped to locations. These high-level activities can be decomposed into separate operations that can be mapped to objects and locations, but hopefully the mapping of operations to objects has been done already in analysis. The mapping of subject areas and functions versus locations is a good starting point for building these more detailed matrices.

Once the initial associations have been mapped between objects and the locations that access them, move on to map the basic types of object involvement (Figure 13.2) and types of accesses (Figure 13.3) as well as specific transactions required by each location (Figure 13.4) and the types of accesses (Figure 13.5). This is detail enough that distributed database components can be visualized.

To assess the need to distribute objects to a given location, build object transaction/view volumes by location matrix (Figure 13.6). This matrix shows how immediate and/or nonimmediate traffic can be projected from a central location to remote locations. Also, you construct an object volume by location matrix (Figure 13.7). A location/performance matrix can then be built to

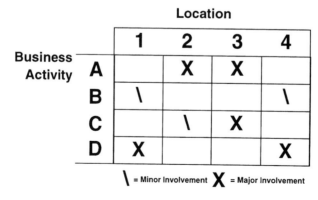

Figure 13.1   Business activities conducted at locations

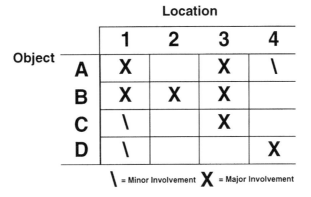

Figure 13.2   Object involvement at locations

show location/performance combinations that are achieved via a centralized solution as well as those that are not. To depict transactions or user views required at each location, build a diagram to depict the overall distributed systems architecture (Figure 13.8).

Each connection between nodes should have the following described either on the diagram or on a table for the connection:

- Distance
- Percent of processing at central site
- Immediate flow volumes
- Nonimmediate flow volumes

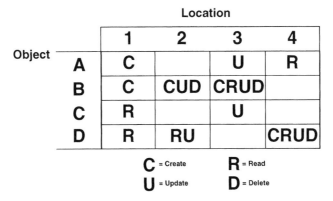

Figure 13.3   Object access types by location

	A	**B**	**C**	**D**
Objects				

Location 1
Transactions/Views

	A	B	C	D
1	\	X	\	\
2	X	X	\	
3		\		

\ = Minor involvement   X = Major Involvement

Location 2
Transactions/Views

	A	B	C	D
1	X	\	X	
2	\	\	X	
3		X		

Figure 13.4   Object transaction/view involvement at locations

Each node should have the following described for it:

- Number of users or programs
- Total data volume
- Total update volume
- Names, record sizes and instance volumes of data storage objects

Objects

Location 1
Transactions/Views

	A	B	C	D
1	R	U	R	R
2	U	U		
3		R	R	

C = Create   R = Read
U = Update   D = Delete

Location 2
Transactions/Views

	A	B	C	D
1	U	R	U	
2	R	R	U	
3		U		

Figure 13.5   Object transaction/view access types by location

Location

Transaction/View		Size (bytes)	1	2	3	Units	Volume (bytes)
	A	195	1250		3400	4650	906K
	B	68	750	235		985	67K
	C	327	1300	1300	2600	3900	1275
Total		590	3300	1535	6000	9535	2248

Figure 13.6 Transaction/view volumes by location

When this diagram has been built and details collected, begin to examine individual transaction and view volumes by individual location (Figure 13.9). At this point individual data storage objects should be placed in the network.

The physical records described via these matrices will not necessarily be stored at the same location as the procedures that use them, but this is usually what is needed to begin modeling. Client/server systems allow separation of application processing from database processing in a multitude of ways, but it begins by examining the use of data first. When the ways to separate business logic from database logic and user access logic are explored, keep in mind that a good distribution model arranges system functions into clusters such that each cluster has a high level of autonomy (is highly cohesive) and exhibits

Location

Object		1	2	3	4	Total Volume
	A					
	B					
	C					
	D					
Total Volume						

Figure 13.7 Object volumes by location

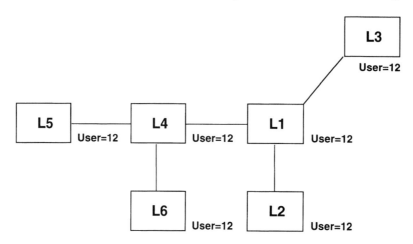

Figure 13.8   Distributed systems architecture

a low level of interdependence with other clusters (is loosely coupled to other clusters). In order to maximize flexibility without sacrificing performance, examine traffic patterns between physical locations, nodes in the communications network. Figure 13.9 shows how locations are interrelated in their sharing of object data.

13.3 ESTIMATING TRAFFIC BETWEEN LOCATIONS

When computers are very inexpensive, as are many personal computers and workstations today, it seems logical that objects be placed at the same location

Percent Data Required from Other Locations

	Location			
Location	1	2	3	4
A	–	20	15	50
B	10	–	0	20
C	10	30	–	5
D	40	10	0	–

Figure 13.9   Matrix for mapping object data sharing across locations

as the users and application programs that access those objects. Unfortunately, things are just not that simple. Replicated objects would then need to be distributed to each location each time a change to an object is made. If these objects are updated by business activities in multiple locations and the updates must all be kept current, one copy of the object is easier to maintain. Keeping multiple copies of an object is complex, increases message transmission traffic and requires more elaborate recovery protection from system failures. Maintaining one copy decreases dependencies between locations.

For purposes of calculating message traffic between locations, assume that U = uses per hour for the data and C = changes per hour of the data and that these activities are spread evenly over N locations. We can define a traffic unit as the data that are transmitted to a location and the response that is sent back. If T = the number of traffic units per hour, then for data centralized at one location the total traffic units per hour can be represented as:

$$T_c = (U + C) \frac{N - 1}{N}$$

For a totally decentralized configuration, uses of the data do not generate traffic but modifications of the data generate N – 1 traffic units. Distributing data results in less traffic if:

$$\frac{U}{C} > N - 1$$

When two locations are considered, it becomes better to distribute if:

$$\frac{U}{C} > 1$$

With 50 locations, distribute if:

$$\frac{U}{C} > 49$$

One change made for every 10 uses of data or

$$\frac{U}{C} = 10$$

results in a break-even point between centralization and decentralization at 11 locations. At more than 11 locations, it is better to centralize. When time is entered into the situation, the situation is different. Suppose that changes can be applied to data up to H hours after their origination. Every H hours a message could be transmitted to each location, given changes occurred since the last update. With centralization, this means that we have $(N-1)/D$ traffic units occurring each hour. With decentralization of data but updates relayed by the central location, $2(N-1)/D$ traffic units are needed each hour:

$$T_c = U \frac{(N-1)}{N} + \frac{N-1}{H}$$

$$T_d = \frac{2(N-1)}{H}$$

Break-even is at $U = N/D$. When $H = 1.5$ hour and 200 references are generated to data each hour in total, distribute if there are less than 300 locations (1.5×200).

Besides making these calculations, examine the following:

- Operating costs at each location
- Numbers of transactions needed to search all data in their entirety
- Costs to maintain many copies of the data
- Recovery after failures
- Failures during recovery operations
- Type of network architecture

Of course, making such calculations should be viewed as only one way of estimating what the best overall network data placement configuration should be. The best way to configure a network in the end is to describe each and every transaction transmittal and then optimize network traffic patterns, but this can be difficult. The calculations described here give a good feel for distribution effects across the entire network and in certain situations can be all that is needed. View them as only one tool for deciding upon data placement across locations.

When all locations have been identified and transaction flows analyzed, you can begin to build a distributed systems architecture (Figure 13.10).

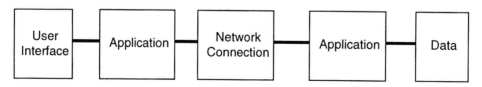

Figure 13.10   Distributed application architecture

Chapter 17 goes into detail on the technologies used to distribute parts of databases and applications.

END NOTES

[1] Martin, James. *Information Engineering*, 3 vols. (Englewood Cliffs, NJ: Prentice Hall) 1989–1990.

[2] Ibid.

14

Redesigning Existing Systems for the Future

14.1 WHAT IS REENGINEERING?

Reengineering can be described as the renovation of an existing information system to enable the development, maintenance and enhancement of systems. For this book, this process involves structured methods and associated automated tools. Reengineering is useful when it is feasible, cost effective and faster to rework an existing system than it is to build a new system. The process is most valuable when the functionality of the existing system is high but the technical quality is low, or a move to an object-oriented information systems architecture is viewed as important for strategic reasons.

The process of reengineering information systems can take many forms because systems differ in condition and the plans and goals for reworking the system may vary. Reengineering can be used to assist in:

- changing programming languages,
- restructuring code,
- modularizing programs,
- implementing data standards,
- improving documentation,

- reusing system components,
- adjusting systems architectures and
- improving system performance.

Reworking an existing system includes reverse engineering—extraction of specifications and requirements from existing system components and documentation and subsequent building of models and repositories (Figure 14.1). Another type of reengineering, business process engineering, involves restructuring of business processes to improve effectiveness and efficiency. In this book, the focus is on only reengineering systems.

14.2 WHY BOTHER REENGINEERING SYSTEMS?

The multitude of systems that have been built using older technologies cannot simply be scrapped. For perhaps decades newer, cleanly designed systems must coexist with the older, mostly successful systems in use today. The older systems are getting more and more expensive to maintain but will

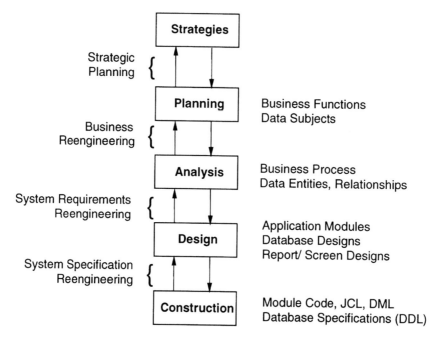

Figure 14.1   Levels of reengineering

have their maintenance greatly enhanced as CASE tools, techniques and repositories are more widely used.

Because so much investment has been made in existing information systems that do an adequate job of supporting business requirements (although at a higher maintenance cost than newer systems require), there is an economic incentive to give serious consideration to upgrading systems to new architectures. Some of the many reasons to upgrade existing systems are to:

- enhance current systems,
- implement changes quicker,
- develop new systems faster,
- improve system quality and
- migrate to new information systems architectures and tools.

It has been stated in earlier chapters that one of the greatest advantages of systems composed of objects is that development can make use of standard, reusable objects, similar to use of standard, reusable product components. Standardization in software can be achieved because the actual production of the components is fairly easy. Once object classes are defined, all instances of a class are guaranteed to be identical. Objects can be produced in quantity, are immediately available and have no production costs. The challenge of applying standardization to software system construction lies not in production but in design. System designers must define classes that are universally applicable and easily reusable. While not easy to achieve at first, the potential savings in production are immense.

To get the most out of object-oriented development, build working models of parts of an enterprise's operations, build up the models to an enterprise logical model and finally build the logical model up to the enterprise planning model. By doing this, a large inventory of reusable objects can be built. All higher-level objects can be reused in future projects. Solutions built on the enterprise planning and logical models are more flexible than solutions based directly on low-level objects. If an organization's operations change, the business models can be changed without making changes to the high-level classes that implement specific solutions. Sure, it takes a lot of time, energy and foresight to build enterprise models than it does to craft specialized solutions, but these specialized solutions are causing major problems in organizations when the solutions do not fit together.

Object-oriented development, with its emphasis on growth and adaptation to change, may allow production of far more sophisticated systems than is possible using today's conventional analysis and design techniques. It makes sense to invest the time and energy to evolve existing systems to an object architecture.

14.3 HOW TO GET STARTED ON THE PATH TO BUILDING OBJECTS

Numerous critical systems exist in business organizations around the world today (legacy systems), and it will be a very tough job to build an integrated set of information systems within an enterprise (and sometimes ones that will span enterprises). It is necessary to make sure that the new set of cleanly designed systems fits in well with the old world of legacy systems. By judicious use of object technology, an old system can sometimes be encapsulated with a "wrapper" that defines the old system as a class that has a public interface for receiving and sending object messages from/to external systems.

Today, many organizations are beginning to replace nongraphic user interfaces with graphic, object-oriented user interfaces. This is a simple example of how an old, traditional system may be wrapped with object technology. More extensive use of workstation capabilities dictates moving key parts of an application's programs and databases to the workstation in a client/server architecture, but using a newer GUI that is based on objects helps make the move to a more powerful architecture of intercommunicating objects.

Assess Impact on Systems and their Components

In order to move systems from a traditional environment to an object-oriented one, first all systems must be identified with their components that are affected by the migration:

- Databases and files
- Programs and modules
- Interfaces
- Documentation
- Manual procedures

- Hardware
- Network components

Impact analysis of this sort should be conducted from the top down, viewing the most general requirements first. Then it should move down to the strategic and detailed designs. Finally, the details of the implementation are examined. Review all information sources including repositories, technical documentation and user documentation in order to provide insights into the effects of changes on:

- inputs,
- outputs,
- processes,
- manual procedures,
- stored data,
- programs,
- other systems,
- hardware and
- personnel.

Consider following these steps when analyzing impacts of reengineering systems—determine the impact on each of the following:

- Interfaces
- Requirements
- Database/file designs
- Process designs
- Procedural code
- Documentation

The various system models discussed in this book can be used to perform a wide range of maintenance functions such as understanding and confirming change request, conducting impact analysis and planning and implementing a system enhancement. Other uses of models are to establish and test assumptions about errors, improve designs and conduct corrective maintenance. These models serve as valuable inputs into the systems enhancement process. They also provide a foundation for planning and implementing the desired changes.

Logical models of a current system provide an initial point of reference for the addition or change of processes, the storage or flow of data and data relationships, when building an initial model of the target system. Physical models represent the design into which enhancements must be built. In order to properly assess to which conceptual level a reverse engineering effort should be directed, follow these analysis and design steps:

1. Review and update the business information requirements.
2. Review and update the business system requirements.
3. Review and update the preliminary systems design.
4. Review and update the detailed systems design.

Business Process Reengineering

Michael Hammer[1] states that the usual methods for boosting business performance—process rationalization and automation—haven't yielded the dramatic improvements organizations need. Heavy investments in information technology have provided disappointing results largely because organizations tend to use technology to mechanize old ways of doing business. Simple reengineering of existing processes—leaving processes intact and using computer technology only to speed processes up—cannot address fundamental process performance deficiencies. It is important that any information system reengineering project examine closely whether the supported business processes need reengineering themselves. Reengineering existing systems can often pave the cow paths when what is needed is a total redesign of the transportation infrastructure.

Many business job designs, work flows, control mechanisms and organization structures were developed in an older business environment—even before computer automation—and emphasize efficiency and control. What is really needed today is innovation and speed, service and quality. Hammer[2] lists these principles of business reengineering that aim to avoid automation of old business rules:

• Organize around outcomes, not tasks.
• Subsume information-processing work into the real work that produces the information.

- Treat geographically dispersed resources as though they were centralized.
- Link parallel activities instead of integrating their results.
- Put the decision point where the work is performed, and build control into the process.
- Capture information once and at the source.

Once it has been determined that business processes are stable as is and are to be supported with new versions of existing systems, three basic approaches are available for addressing the systems:

Do not convert applications but build a bridge to new systems where necessary.

Restructure systems but do not rebuild them.

Reverse engineer old systems to conform to formal object models.

Reengineering an old system into a traditional information engineering environment involves a process similar to this:[3]

1. Structure the code.
2. Enter the restructured code into a CASE tool.
3. Capture the data description of the old system.
4. Convert the data elements.
5. Normalize the data structures to conform to the information engineering models.
6. Convert the file management or database management system.
7. Modify the application to conform to new process models.
8. Adopt new standards.
9. Convert system interfaces.
10. Generate modified data structures.
11. Generate data description code.
12. Convert or enhance reports.
13. Redesign the human interface.
14. Generate new program code and documentation.
15. Use a code optimizer.

14.4 IDENTIFY CANDIDATE FILE STRUCTURES FOR SUBJECT DATABASES

If the enterprise has modeled business information requirements using data subjects, it is well positioned to take advantage of object modeling of subject areas as object classes. If not, some help is available. Clustering of data subjects (or, more commonly, data entities) into groups of related data structures according to their use by business processes can be of help, as can affinity analysis.

Begin identifying data structures by examining the data dictionary or repository, but if this information is not available, several reengineering tools can be used to reverse engineer database and file structures into systems models. The same process can be performed for program module data structures (or data views) and their attributes that reference database and file structures. No matter how data structures are cataloged and modeled, a set of matrices can be built to depict data views and reference database and file structures. Then the data structures can be grouped together. See Figure 14.2 for an example of such a matrix.

The data structure grouping process can begin by grouping file structures that are accessed by module data structures or transactions. A matrix can then be built to show cells where programs create, read, update or delete file structures. The number of modules and file structures can be large, so an automated matrix modeling tool should be used. Database analysts, programmers and designers that are familiar with enterprise databases and systems should validate the matrix to ensure that it correctly depicts data/module

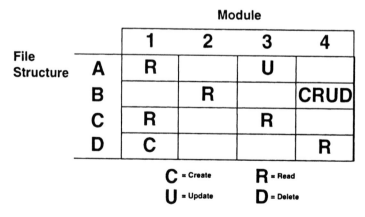

Figure 14.2   Matrix mapping modules against file structures

interactions and that no modules or file structures are missing. A data/module matrix helps highlight problems such as a data structure not created by a module or by a module that does not access any data structure. Situations can be identified that might be problems: for example, a data structure that is not updated by any module or one that is created by more than one module.

At a business planning level, an organization chart can be mapped against functions and data subjects (and/or entities). This tool can be used to check functions against organization units that perform functions. Data subjects and entities can be mapped against these organization units. Data access models (create, read, update, delete) can be built from those created using the subject/function or entity/process matrices. This helps modelers to determine how organization processes and organization units make use of data structures. (Emphasis should be placed on data structures and how they are used, not on the current or future organization structure, however. Organization structures change but organization functions and processes are more stable. Business information is even more stable.) Such analysis then helps identify key operations on data structures that can later be modeled as object operations (public) and methods (private). Techniques defined in information strategy planning, business systems planning/strategic alignment and other systems planning methodologies can be used to gather, model and validate planning information.

If analysis and design models are available in a repository-based CASE tool, these matrices can be built automatically from the models. When missing design information is discovered, this information can be either added to a design model or entered directly on the data/program matrix. Then the program and data object are added to the repository for subsequent modeling. Reengineering tools can populate the repository automatically, but often require some tweaking to get the correct results. Still, the process is often much easier than just building the models manually.

Matrix entries can be grouped in a variety of ways. During new systems development and after modeling of existing systems, an analyst or designer can use the matrix to validate models and check them for completeness. Columns and rows can be resequenced and/or hidden from the current user view. A group of programs could be selected for viewing and then sequenced in a certain order for analysis. This group can be examined in detail for completeness. The same can be done from a data structure perspective. Either way, the matrix entries can be validated against diagrams or textual models of system components. It is vital that this matrix be correct before data structures can be forward engineered into new integrated systems.

Data structures can be mapped to data entities (analysis model), which can be mapped to data subjects (planning model), but this must be done very carefully if the lower-level design model of data structures is not integrated into the views that program modules have of the data structures. On the process side of nonobject systems, modules can be mapped to programs, which in turn can be mapped to application systems, all at the design level. Design processes such as these can be mapped into business analysis model processes (actually, components of, or groups of, processes). These processes can, in turn, be mapped into business planning model functions.

Data/process matrices can be built for data structures/modules, entities/processes and data subjects/functions. Once built and validated, these sets of matrices form a solid foundation for modeling and constructing object-oriented systems. Work backward from design to analysis to planning in the reverse engineering of models, then identify data subjects and their components. These data subjects become classes and objects. Classes and objects have operations identified at the analysis level that are refined as methods in design. Forward engineering becomes object-based, whereas reverse engineering is largely nonobject-based.

In order to group similar entities together by their process usage, a process/entity or function/entity matrix can be built by clustering algorithms. One such algorithm uses a list of functions arranged in the sequence of an entity life cycle and clusters entities that are created by each function. A second algorithm uses affinities among entities as a basis for clustering. Affinities may be provided from an entity-relationship model or computed based on how many processes use both of two entities being examined. (See Martin[4] for details on these two entity clustering algorithms.)

14.5 MODEL DATABASES AND FILE STRUCTURES AS OBJECTS

Databases and file structures, once clustered into classes and objects (at least, at the modeling level), can be encapsulated with procedures. When data structures have been identified and grouped into data subjects, the data subjects become object classes. Components of these classes (entities within data subjects) are subordinate objects (at least, conceptually). The resulting sets of classes and objects (each with their own private data structures) can be modeled as described earlier in this book.

A matrix or set of matrices, along with diagrams and full repository entries, should accompany the descriptions. Mappings need to be maintained between the conventional view of databases and file structures (interacting with programs and application systems) and the newly constructed models of classes and objects interacting with each other and with other systems and subsystems (via public interfaces and formally defined operations accessed through public object interfaces and privately implemented as messages—see the next section). These mappings aid in migrating application systems that access traditional databases to ones that access object-oriented databases and on to full object-oriented application systems.

14.6 MODEL SYSTEM INTERFACES AS OBJECT INTERFACES

Encapsulation

Application systems that interact with other systems can have their interfaces defined as public object interfaces. Messages between systems are processed as operations implemented as methods. These operations are accessible only through the public message interface. In this manner of modeling and building systems, the interface can serve as an object-oriented capsule around a nonobject system. In essence, an object capsule or envelope is built around a conventional system in order to build an object-oriented system package (Figure 14.3).[5]

The interfaces between portions of an application system may be defined using object technology, too. Object-oriented designs do not require an object-oriented programming language in order to implement the designs. Object-oriented implementation requires that the world be viewed as abstract data types combined with inheritance and methods. While the object-oriented languages make implementation of object designs much easier, traditional languages such as COBOL, PL/I and FORTRAN can indeed be written in an object-oriented fashion.

Within an object model, an object type may be mapped to an abstract data type record structure, just as it is mapped to a class in an object-oriented language. An abstract data type protects data structures from improper use by outsiders by allowing only certain operations to be performed upon its data. A set of application modules within an application program can be defined in much the same way that operations are defined for classes in an object-oriented language. These languages encapsulate objects with a barrier to shield the objects from improper intervention by outside objects. This same

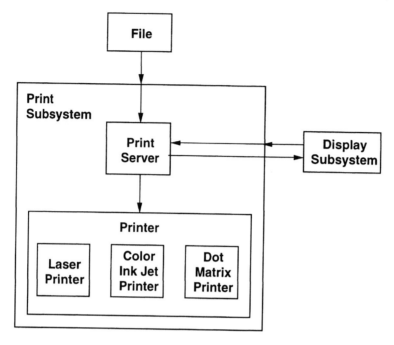

Figure 14.3   Encapsulation of subsystems

kind of encapsulation cannot be totally enforced using traditional languages, however. Strict standards for programming must be enforced in order to achieve the same clean encapsulation of objects that object-oriented programming languages support.

Inheritance

Object type inheritance allows for reuse of data and procedures through generalization hierarchies, but conventional languages do not support subtypes and supertypes at all. Thus program code is needed to get the same benefits that an object-oriented programming language provides. As with traditional code reuse, a few options are available. Martin and Odell[6] mention three basic ways to do this with conventional languages:

- *Physically copy code from supertype modules.* Copy and paste or use COPYLIB statements. Control redundant code with proper maintenance procedures.

- *Call the routine in supertype modules.* Call operations from a module to its supertype module This works as long as programs are kept up to date with what they are supposed to inherit. Proper maintenance procedures are important.

- *Build an inheritance support system.* Construct an inheritance mechanism external to the programs, and route requests to their appropriate modules based on object schema and event schema information. Modules are more stable because inheritance-related logic need not be built into programs. The system is model-driven instead of hard-coded because it is based on object and event schemata.

Methods

To build program components that only specify operations that apply to one or more objects, the system needs to choose the method for specified inputs. Conventional languages simply do not support operation requests and method selection. Two ways to achieve this using conventional languages are again from Martin and Odell:[7]

- *Hard code method selection logic within the requesting routine.* This works as long as programs are kept up to date with all requests and selection criteria.

- *Build a method selecting support system.* First enable modules to make requests for operations without knowledge of where appropriate method is located. The system is driven by a table that matches selection criteria with physical code location. The selection mechanism is integrated with an inheritance support system to take advantage of object schema and event schema information.

Object Wrapping

One shortcut to full object technology involves covering traditional application systems and their components with a veneer of object-oriented code. A very specific and well-conceived interface defines how systems and programs are to interact with wrapped applications. Wrapping old applications is only a transitional step toward full object orientation, but it can save significant development time and prevent developers from having to reinvent numerous application components. The technique is very useful when bridging the gap between mainframe architectures and client/server architectures.

Application wrapping involves defining a small piece of an application that connects to old databases and/or files or to the user interface. It should be viewed as a temporary solution, but when time and resources permit, review each application and rewrite components completely in an object-oriented fashion. As a transition step, wrapping can be a very big time saver.

According to *ComputerWorld*,[8] several large companies, including Citicorp, Deere & Co. and Boeing are leading the way to application wrapping. Citicorp in New York is considering placing wrappers around legacy systems in order to use reduced instruction set computing (RISC) machines as front-ends for legacy database servers running on mainframes. This should permit Citicorp to view legacy applications from an object-oriented viewpoint. The company plans to mix new and old programming technologies in a reengineering effort that will rebuild or discard about one half of the bank's mainframe applications inventory. This should allow business units to quickly prototype new applications, perhaps using object-oriented programming languages, and access data servers throughout the company's computer network.

Deere & Co. emphasizes tying together disparate systems on an enterprise network so that a new set of client systems can access scattered data sources. The aim is to provide a message-based front-end to existing legacy applications. Some versions of such systems have been in use for more than one year at the time of this writing.

Serious object systems will be developed only when the pieces of legacy systems are migrated to desktop workstations as parts of client/server systems. Some developers may encapsulate many parts of the existing architecture: SQL statements, data sets, programs and perhaps entire databases. However application object wrapping is approached, keep in mind that it merely covers up old systems—it does not necessarily improve them in any major way. Adrian Bowles, vice president of New Science Associates, Inc. in Westport, Connecticut, said this about object wrapping:[9] "Object wrapping is sometimes like wrapping fish. It continues to rot inside. So wrapping a system doesn't make it better. It's a lot like coating a pill to make it easier to swallow."

14.7 MODEL DISTRIBUTED SYSTEMS AS NETWORKS OF OBJECTS

The object-oriented model of object interaction (object behavior) can serve as a valuable tool for modeling distributed networks of systems and subsystems (Figures 14.4 and 14.5). One new element introduced here is the modeling of object locations.

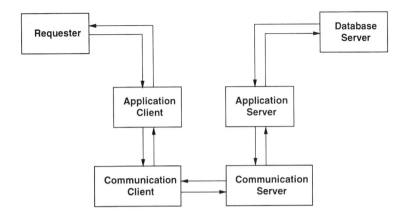

Figure 14.4   Architecture of a client/server system

Traditional information engineering incorporates techniques for modeling locations. At the planning level this might involve locations of data subjects and business functions. Analysis models refer to the location of business entities and processes. Design models describe data structure and program module locations. Construction deliverables involve the actual database definitions, program code and data structure definitions needed to implement the design models.

If object classes are viewed in an information system as setting up contracts among themselves for services to be rendered upon receipt of a message for these services, locations can be implemented simply as object classes themselves, communicating with each other as peers. Somewhere within our system there must exist a directory of locations from which to identify the physical location to send a message to. The object management group has defined an object request broker that serves as a broker or dispatcher of messages between communicating objects.

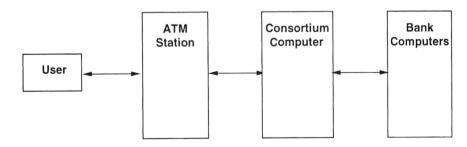

Figure 14.5   Architecture of an ATM system

14.8 PROCESS NORMALIZATION

Whereas both traditional data modeling and object structure modeling build normalized data models, information engineering does not enforce (but it does encourage to a degree) the normalization of processes in a business model. Normalization organizes data into relationships of data elements to reduce data redundancy and enhance data model usability and maintainability. Once a data structure has been properly normalized, each attribute in the model depends upon its entity's key, the whole key and nothing but the key (for a brief discussion of this technique, refer to Stephen Montgomery,[10] Clive Finkelstein,[11] C. J. Date[12] or E. F. Codd[13]).

Data normalization has no concise equivalent in process modeling. Object modeling dictates that processes be attached to the normalized data structures that the processes act upon, resulting in process normalization. Information engineering's view of separate data and process models can (and usually does) result in duplication of processes, unless great care is taken to avoid duplication. Traditional systems often were not adequately modeled in the first place, so the processes and the resulting programs are likely to be denormalized to a great degree. Structured design and programming encourage the development of procedures into modules that are highly cohesive and that have low coupling between them.

When traditional application structuring is used to model and construct information systems, the requirements for each application are analyzed, modeled and implemented separately, although the data model can be built to be consistent across all applications. Specifications for many application functions are repeated in more than one place across different applications. In a complex information systems environment, with many applications consisting of many components, it can be very difficult to identify common processing routines. If normalized processes can be achieved (as well as data structures), a very high degree of reuse can be obtained and lead to full object systems.

Gearing process modeling around data model components, instead of around application-by-application requirements studies, permits significant movement toward normalized processes and object operations and methods. William Inmon, in his book on advanced information engineering,[14] describes ways to link data and process models. His technique uses basic processes that represent the fundamental work in an information system: addition, change and deletion. These basic operations and their infrastructure must be performed for every data element in an information system. By ensuring that each basic process exists uniquely, one important condition can be satisfied for process normalization.

Inmon states that these three conditions must be met for process normalization:

- Basic processes and their supporting infrastructure exist once, and only once, throughout the process model.
- The flow of control from one module to the next is from commonalty to uniqueness.
- Each function has a high degree of cohesion.

Unique Processes

Basic processes must not exist in more than one place. Changes may exist in multiple locations as long as the change that is occurring in multiple locations is different. For instance, the ADD CUSTOMER basic process should exist in one and only one place (or only once for each geographic location in a distributed system). Within a normalized process model, each basic process must be defined only once (see Figure 14.6). When ADD CUSTOMER or any

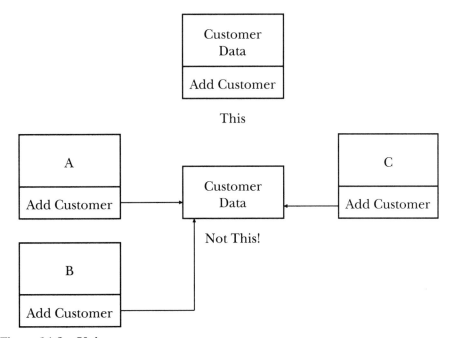

Figure 14.6   Unique processes

other basic process has duplicates, update anomalies can exist, just as is the case with unnormalized (or inadequately normalized) data models. When calls to a uniquely defined, basic process are scattered around a process model, the process infrastructure, not the basic process itself, causes the process model to be unnormalized. This is analogous to having an object operation performed by multiple objects, not the object for which the operation is uniquely defined.

Flow of Control from Common to Unique

The flow of control from one process or program to another must be in the order of common to unique. A more general process calls a more specialized process. Suppose there were a CUSTOMER process, a BUSINESS CUS-TOMER process and an INDUSTRIAL BUSINESS CUSTOMER process. The CUSTOMER process manages processing for all types of customers, the BUSINESS CUSTOMER process manages processes for business (as opposed to consumer) customers, and the INDUSTRIAL BUSINESS CUSTOMER process manages industrial (as opposed to commercial or nonprofit business) customers (see Figure 14.7). The highest level CUSTOMER process calls the

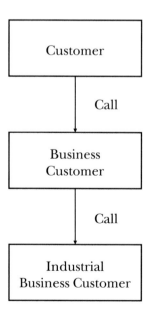

Figure 14.7   Flow of control from common to unique

BUSINESS CUSTOMER process, which in turn calls the INDUSTRIAL BUSI-NESS CUSTOMER process in order to handle processing for industrial customers.

Notice that this is conceptually the same as what happens in an object system that has the same inheritance tree defined for it (although in object-oriented environments the children have methods defined for them but no implementation, so control passes to the immediate parent). In an un-normalized system, three separate modules are defined for each type of processing, with each one operating independently of the other (a general process does not call a more specialized process). The code to manage general customer data, for instance, is defined at least twice, once in the CUSTOMER process and once in the BUSINESS CUSTOMER process. The code for managing industrial business customers is defined in all three processes: CUSTOMER, BUSINESS CUSTOMER and INDUSTRIAL BUSI-NESS CUSTOMER.

Module Cohesion

To satisfy the cohesion criterion of process normalization, processes must be packaged so that each process performs a unique function. The basic pro-cesses DELETE CUSTOMER, DELETE CUSTOMER ORDER and DELETE CUSTOMER ACCOUNT should definitely not appear in the same process but be defined separately and called when needed. The cohesion among the set of processes will then be cohesive, in contrast to the situation where all three exist in one basic process that is not cohesive (it performs all three functions, not just one).

Like the corresponding data model normalization, process normalization is useful for simplifying and structuring a process model. When a process model is normalized, procedures can be built so that flow of control is from general to specific. Additions to application requirements should have little or no impact on existing systems. Procedures should be structured for uniqueness of functions, although in practice some redundancy among processes may be necessary for performance purposes, as with data model denormalization.

The overall interaction with a database can be controlled by creation of a standard set of application modules based on a normalized process model. However, this use of input/output routines does not ensure that the overall process model is normalized. Programs that call these routines may not be normalized. The infrastructure of procedures that surrounds a basic process

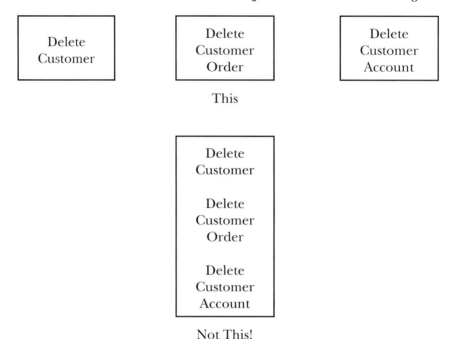

Figure 14.8   Module cohesion

must be considered when normalizing processes. If only one module calls each add and delete basic process and the procedures surrounding the call of each modify basic process is unique, the set of routines is normalized. For instance, there should exist only one application module to actually create a customer account. But the CREATE CUSTOMER module could be called independently from several application systems. Each of these applications, prior to calling the CREATE CUSTOMER module, should establish values for the new customer record independently. Figure 14.8 shows an example of module cohesion.

14.9 MIGRATING STRUCTURED ANALYSIS MODELS TO OBJECT MODELS

If you have been using information engineering or another structured analysis technique to build process and data models, you have a good starting point for migrating systems to object models. While the more traditional analysis models need significant rework to make them object-oriented, it is still much easier to manipulate analysis models than it is to work with design or construction models. When preparing to write on the subject of migrating structured analysis models to object models, I came across a paper by Mike Branson, Eric Herness and Eric Jenney of IBM.[15] Their paper does a good job of describing techniques for migrating models to object orientation. This section briefly discusses their techniques.

The process of converting analysis models involves two steps: identification of candidate objects by dissecting the analysis model and class synthesis and refinement, which takes candidate objects and refines them into a set of abstractions that can be implemented. The conversion process can be summarized as:

1. Using the analysis model as input to identify candidate objects and synthesize and refine classes.
2. Designing language-specific objects and the associated implementation.

For this book, the first phase of the conversion process is of most interest. Language-specific design depends upon the language(s) chosen for implementation, which is not discussed here due to the wide variety of available options. The following section assumes that the analysis model consists of data flow diagrams and process specifications, possibly including context data flow diagrams and event lists.

Carve Structured Analysis Models

Data flow diagrams in a traditional model are not object-oriented but do model the essence of a business solution to a problem described in system requirements. Entity-relationship diagrams are also not object-oriented but can prove very useful for object structure analysis and modeling. I do not want to enter into the controversy over whether data flow diagrams or entity-relationship diagrams are useful for object modeling, but recognize that these models exist for many systems and can prove useful for migration to object orientation.

The essential model of structured analysis can be carved up into candidate objects. Once this carving has been performed, the candidate objects can be examined to see if they will actually be classes in the final system model.

Carving does not remove duplicate objects or duplicate operations, nor does it produce classes, analyze inheritance or synthesize classes into a hierarchy. These steps must be taken, but only after the initial class identification and refinement have been completed. At that point, the analysis proceeds much as was described in earlier chapters of this book.

Carving uses a complete set of data flow diagrams and process specifications and considers the lowest level of data flow diagrams in detail. But if the objects on the available diagrams are not exploded to a low level, they are still used. The process of carving involves:

- Finding certain objects on data flow diagrams
- Dividing up operations contained in processes between all objects that the processes touch

The usual types of object on a data flow diagram are derived via carving: external entity, data store, data flow and process. The diagram is carved up by associating operations listed in process specifications with only one of these objects. Each process is carved up with its components divided among the objects. Operations should most likely be associated with one object more than others.

Examine External Entities

As discussed previously in this book, external entities (sometimes called external agents or terminators) on a data flow diagram represent objects in the real world. They might represent people, organizations or other systems, but at the interface with the system being modeled, these external agents represent devices such as printers, display terminals, tape or disk drives, sensors, control pads, etc. An object should be identified for each external entity in a data flow diagram. The objects that are identified from external entities are used to define classes that hide the messaging protocol and any hardware errors and their handling.

An external entity's class is an abstraction of the object that insulates the system from the detailed operations of the external entity. In addition to the physical devices involved with the external interface of a system, classes that many come from can be discussed—the terminal, workstation, menu or control buttons of the interface. These classes also hide underlying interface details and present the rest of the system with classes such as window, select list, radio button or menu bar.

Examine Data Stores

Usually, a data store represents one or more data entities. Initially, each entity within a data store, as well as the store itself, can be viewed as a potential object. Start by identifying a potential object from each data store in a data flow diagram. Draw a line around the store and part of each process that touches it via a data flow (some CASE tools allow you to select all neighbors for a store or other data flow diagram component, so this step is fairly automatic).

Objects identified from data stores are used to define data classes that encapsulate sets of data and the associated operations to manipulate the data. Data classes might include:

- Customer order
- Product
- Employee
- Supplier

Operations for data stores are obtained from the specifications for the processes that touch the data stores. Any operation that manipulates an instance of data in the data store should be included in the list of data store operations. Each statement in a process specification that manipulates data must be associated with one data object.

Examine Data Flows

When the data modeled by a data flow is significant to the system, it might become an object. If the flow's data structures are complex, it may be a good candidate for an object. Three types of data flows should be considered:

- Flows from an external entity to a process (system inputs)
- Flows from a process to an external entity (system outputs)
- Flows between processes

Input and output flows are more likely to contain objects than flows between processes. Output flows should be examined to see if they should be objects. If such a flow represents a complex data flow that has a set of operations that must be performed on it, carve it out as a candidate object.

Input flows may also represent objects. Examine them to see if they have complex data structures and a set of operations that act on that data. Carve out any such flows as candidate objects. Occasionally, flows between processes can be considered as candidate objects. Examine them to see if they have complex data structures and sets of operations performed on them. Carve out these flows, too.

Classes carved out from data flows tend to be transient data (not persistent, needing to be stored), so may not become database objects. Examples include:

- Lists of objects passed to a terminal for display, with sorting and merging operations
- Time stamps passed between processes, with formatting and conversion operations
- Control blocks and associated manipulation objects
- Commands issued at terminals and operations to validate parameters and instantiate objects needed to perform functions
- String input from a display passed to the system for manipulation.

Examine Processes

Once all other data flow diagram objects have been carved up, some process fragments may remain. These must be dealt with to see if the operations contained within them can be associated with any of the objects already identified. When leftover operations still exist, identify process objects. These tend to be functional objects:

- Essential managers
- Shells
- Sequencers
- Controllers

Process objects tend to use other classes and instantiate and manipulate other system objects. Identify an object for each set of operations not already associated with a class. Draw a line on the data flow diagram to depict carving for these objects. Process objects that are identified are really manipulators of other classes, so later on will likely become operations of these classes.

Results after Carving

Once carving has been completed, every process in a data flow diagram should be accounted for in candidate objects. Process specifications should have been completely partitioned into components associated with candidate objects. The candidate objects and associated objects that result include things such as:

Terminal object (read string, write string)

Customer (validate, update, create, delete)

Synthesize Classes

After carving data flow diagrams, an initial set of objects has been produced. Class synthesis is where object modeling begins. During this process, objects are placed into classes and these classes placed into a class hierarchy. It is assumed that the class hierarchies already exist. Thus, class synthesis is a bottom-up activity that works upward from objects to mid-level and high-level classes.

Identify Classes

Candidate objects must be examined to see if they can be put into the same class as other objects identified to be of the same type and to see if they really represent a class. Object classification is performed by associating objects with other objects of the same type. An object represents a single entity but a class represents many such entities. Two objects can be members of the same class if their operations are similar. Objects that belong in the same class may have operations identified that do not appear similar. Look for similar operations not only from their names but also how they act on objects.

Refine Classes

Once classes have been identified, they can be refined. This involves these steps:

1. Split a class into two classes.
2. Combine classes.
3. Refine class operations.

All methods for a class must be defined for the class to be considered complete. New classes may need to be identified when developing user interfaces. In order to narrow the scope of the interface functions presented to the user, one or more application classes may need to be defined to bridge between existing classes and the abstraction needed to present an understandable set of operations to users. (The chapter in this book on user interface design covers some of this topic.) Sources for application classes include:

- entity models,
- context models,
- data classes and
- process objects left over from carving.

Relationships between classes in a hierarchy must be defined. Operations on existing and candidate classes must be examined. Look at the class interfaces within class hierarchies, similar operations between candidates, and look for utility classes (based on abstract data types such as lists, queues and so forth). Finally, classes should abstract single entities, methods should perform a single action, classes should only have a few methods (say, 20—or classes should be combined) and method implementations should be short (perhaps 25 to 50 lines of code).

Classes should be associated with each event on a business event list. Doing this allows for tracing of requirements down to the class level. Each event needs to be mapped to the class that implements the event, and this fact should be documented on the event list. Each event may have one or more classes that implement it.

14.10 DESIGN AN OBJECT-ORIENTED SYSTEMS ARCHITECTURE

After a set of object-oriented analysis and design models has been built, an overall sytems architecture can be constructed. John Zachman[16] created a framework for an information systems architecture. This architecture is discussed in Chapter 18.

Figure 14.9 shows graphically how components of the systems architecture are interrelated. By building such an architecture, you can position your organization to make full use of reusable components (Figure 14.10). Such

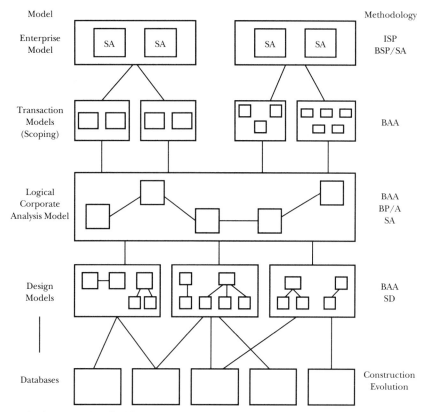

Figure 14.9 Levels of object models

1. Clear purpose
2. Minimal size
3. Simple
4. General
5. Adaptable
6. Portable
7. Sensibly packaged
8. Coordinated
9. Robust
10. Handles errors gracefully

Figure 14.10 Properties of reusable system components

What components are available?
What are their capabilities?
Where can they be deployed?
Where are they now deployed?
How are they built?
How are they impacted by change?
Who supports them?

Figure 14.11   Questions a reuse repository should answer

objects must be designed for reuse, however, and must be promoted to and made available to developers across the enterprise. Otherwise, enterprise-wide reuse is difficult, if not impossible, to achieve. Use of a repository to manage and report on reusable components can be a big help in moving toward full model and system component reuse (see Figure 14.11). It is very important to do good planning and analysis work to ensure effective reuse. *Waiting until design and construction to consider reuse is a big mistake.*

END NOTES

[1] Hammer, Michael. "Reengineering Work: Don't Automate, Obliterate." *Harvard Business Review* (July/August 1990), pp. 104–112.

[2] Ibid.

[3] Martin, James. *Information Engineering*, 3 vols. (Englewood Cliffs, NJ: Prentice Hall) 1989–1990.

[4] Ibid.

[5] Adapted from Wirfs-Brock, Rebecca, Brian Wilderson and Lauren Wiener. *Designing Object-Oriented Software* (Englewood Cliffs, NJ: Prentice Hall) 1990, p. 146.

[6] Martin, James, and James Odell. *Object-Oriented Analysis and Design* (Englewood Cliffs, NJ: Prentice Hall) 1992, p. 434.

[7] Ibid.

[8] *Computerworld*, (November 30, 1992) p. 73.

[9] Ibid.

[10] Montgomery, Stephen L. *Relational Database Design and Implementation Using DB2* (New York: Van Nostrand Reinhold) 1990.

[11] Finkelstein, Clive. *Introduction to Information Engineering* (Reading, MA: Addison-Wesley) 1989.

[12] Date, C. J. *An Introduction to Database Systems*, 5th ed. (Reading, MA: Addison-Wesley) 1990.

[13] Codd, E. F. *The Relational Model for Database Management* (Reading, MA: Addison-Wesley) 1990.

[14] Inmon, William. *Advanced Topics in Information Engineering* (Wellesley, MA: QED) 1989, pp. 103–130.

[15] Branson, Michael, Eric Herness and Eric Jenney. "Moving Structured Projects to Object Orientation." In *AD/Cycle International Users Group Second Annual Conference*, October 1991, pp. 151–170.

[16] Zachman, John. "A Framework for Information Systems Architecture." *IBM Systems Journal*, vol. 26, no. 3.

15

Programming Languages

15.1 OBJECT-ORIENTED LANGUAGES

There exist many good books on object-oriented languages, so the syntax and use of any of them are not discussed here. Instead, some key languages and how they can contribute to development of systems of objects are covered briefly.

Smalltalk

This language was created at Xerox's Palo Alto Research Center and now represents one of the most important object-oriented languages available. It is both a language and software development environment for building systems of objects. This language is a pure object-oriented programming language because it views everything as an object—even integers and classes.

The Smalltalk language is simple and built around the ideas that everything should be treated as an object and that objects communicate by passing messages among themselves. Variables and attributes are untyped. Classes can be added, extended, tested and debugged interactively, and memory management is handled by a garbage collector. Normally, the language supports only single inheritance, but multiple inheritance is possible by redefining certain primitive methods.

Smalltalk uses an online interpreter and class browser. This allows for a highly interactive development environment, avoiding the edit, compile and

213

link required with traditional compiler-based programming. The class library is designed to be extended and adapted by adding subclasses to address application-specific needs. The untyped feature of the language allows library components to be combined for rapid application prototyping. Smalltalk is a pure object-oriented language with extensive metadata available and modifiable at run time.

Object Pascal

This language was developed by Apple Computer, along with Pascal's designer, Niklaus Wirth. Object Pascal has been available to the public since 1986. It influenced the development of Microsoft's Quick Pascal and Borland's Turbo Pascal and their descendants.

Object Pascal does not provide class methods, class variables, multiple inheritance or metaclasses. It supports separate compilation of unit interfaces and implementations, so the outside and inside views of classes are often placed in separate files. All fields are unencapsulated in the language, but it is common to treat them as private and accessible only via method calls.

C++

This language was developed at AT&T Bell Laboratories by Bjarne Stroustrup. Mostly, C++ is a superset of the more familiar C language that provides type checking, overloaded functions and other enhancements. Object-oriented programming features added to C language include single inheritance, polymorphism, type checking and overloading. Multiple inheritance has been added recently. Future versions may include support for generic units and exception handling.

C++ is a strongly typed language that corrects many shortcomings of C language, adding support for classes, type checking, overloading, free store management, constant types, references, inline functions, derived classes and virtual functions. Programming style often has the outside view of each class placed in header files. The definition of the languages does not include a class library, but AT&T and others offer libraries for I/O, coroutine tasking and complex arithmetic.

This language does support inheritance and run-time method resolution, but C++ data structures are not automatically object-oriented. Method resolution and operation overriding in a subclass are available only if an operation is declared virtual in the superclass. Method overriding must be anticipated and written into the original class definition. Because authors of classes might not anticipate the need to define specialized subclasses or know what operations will need to be redefined by a subclass, the superclass often must be modified when a subclass is defined. This makes it difficult to reuse library classes by creation of subclasses.

Eiffel

This language is a strongly typed one developed by Bertrand Meyer. Its programs are composed of collections of class declarations, including methods. Eiffel supports multiple inheritance, parameterized classes (generics), memory management and assertions. It provides a class library that includes lists, trees, stacks, queues, files, strings, hash tables and binary trees. The Eiffel compiler translates source programs into C. The language includes facilities for encapsulation, access control, renaming and scope.

Eiffel class declarations list attributes and operations, providing uniform access to these by an abstraction called a feature. Class declarations may include lists of exported features, ancestor classes and feature declarations.

This language manages memory via a coroutine that detects objects no longer referenced and releases their allocated memory. The run-time system executes the coroutine when available memory gets low. The language supports preconditions, postconditions, invariants and exceptions. The compiler provides switches for various levels of error checking.

See Figure 15.1 for a summary of the features of several popular object-oriented languages.

15.2 TRADITIONAL LANGUAGES

Abstract Data Types

The interfaces between portions of an application system may be defined using object technology, too. Object-oriented designs do not require an object-oriented programming language in order to implement the designs. Object-oriented implementation requires that the world be viewed as abstract data types combined with inheritance and methods. Object-oriented languages make implementation of object designs much easier. Traditional languages such as COBOL, PL/I and FORTRAN can indeed be used to implement designs in an object-oriented fashion, but it is more difficult than with object-oriented languages.

	Small Talk	Object Pascal	C++	Ada
Abstraction				
Instance Variables	Yes	Yes	Yes	Yes
Instance Methods	Yes	Yes	Yes	Yes
Class Variables	Yes	No	Yes	No
Class Methods	Yes	No	Yes	No
Encapsulation				
of Variables	Private	Public	Public, Protected, Private	Public, Private
of Methods	Public	Public	Public, Protected, Private	Public, Private
Modulations				
Kinds of Modules	None	Unit	File	Package
Hierarchy				
Inheritance	Single	Single	Multiple	No
Generic Units	No	No	No	Yes
Meta Classes	Yes	No	No	No
Typing				
Strongly Typed	No	Yes	Yes	Yes
Polymorphism	Yes (single)	Yes (single)	Yes (single)	No
Concurrency				
Multitasking	Yes	No	Yes	Yes
Persistence				
Persistent objects	No	No	No	No

Figure 15.1   Booch/Schmucker genealogy of object-oriented languages

Within an object model, an object type may be mapped to an abstract data type record structure, just as it is mapped to a class in an object-oriented language. An abstract data type protects its data structures from improper use by outsiders by allowing only certain operations to be performed upon its data. A set of application modules within an application program can be defined in much the same way that operations are defined for classes in an object-oriented language. These languages encapsulate objects with a barrier to shield the objects from improper intervention by outside objects. This same kind of encapsulation cannot be totally enforced using traditional languages, however. Strict standards for programming must be enforced in order to achieve the same clean encapsulation of objects that object-oriented programming languages support.

Translation of classes into data structures usually involves implementation of each class as a record structure wherein each class attribute is a record element. Attributes have a declared type (primitive, such as the data type of integer, real or character) or a structured value such as embedded structures or fixed length arrays. Each object has an identity and states and is subject to side effects in implementation. Identifier variables must be implemented as sharable references, not by copying values of attributes. References can be built as memory addresses or array indexes, but need to permit sharing of a single object in memory from multiple references.

In C, each class becomes a structure, with each attribute defined in a field of the structure. In Ada, a class is implemented using a record type with an object reference represented by an access type. These access types are required for dynamic allocation and for association between objects. FORTRAN has no user-defined data structures except arrays so classes must be represented as an implicit group of arrays (one for each class attribute). Arrays for a single class may be grouped into a common block. A counter must maintain the number of objects of a given class that have been allocated for assignment of new object identifiers. An object can be represented by indexes into an array of attributes for its class, with attributes accessed by index into the appropriate array. The class of an object must be known.

Encapsulation

Object-oriented languages provide formal constructs for implementing encapsulation. C does allow encapsulation, but this requires discipline. To improve encapsulation in C language, follow these steps:[1]

1. Avoid use of global variables.
2. Package methods for each class into a separate file.
3. Treat objects of other classes as type "void."

Ada allows strong encapsulation enforcement. It does this by distinguishing between external views of packages and the internal views of the implementations, which are compilable separately. Private types can also be used. A type declared in the package specification is visible outside. Ada hides the implementation mechanisms for private type declarations. External packages of a private type must access objects only through operations defined by the package, and the type implementation and its operations can be changed without impacting clients of the package.

In Ada a class can be implemented for exporting a private type. This class package encapsulates the type implementation and any operations that can be performed on the type. Class instances can have attributes if the type is a record type; class operations are implemented as invisible subprograms. Class variables are implemented as variables declared in the package specification or within its body.

FORTRAN does not support pointers, resulting in inadequate encapsulation capabilities. FORTRAN common blocks containing class attributes need to be encapsulated and visible only to methods for that class. External classes need to access an object by its index value; all access to class attributes must be via an access procedure defined internally in the class. When a distinct data manager is written in a language other than FORTRAN, encapsulation can be improved.

Inheritance

Object type inheritance allows for reuse of data and procedures through generalization hierarchies, but conventional languages do not support subtypes and supertypes at all. Thus some program code is needed to get the same benefits that an object-oriented programming languages provides. As with traditional code reuse, a few options are available. Martin and Odell[2] mention three basic ways to do this with conventional languages:

1. *Physically copy code from supertype modules.* Copy and paste or use COPYLIB statements. Control redundant code with proper maintenance procedures.

2. *Call the routine in supertype modules.* Call operations from a module to its supertype module. This works as long as programs are kept up to date with what they are supposed to inherit. Proper maintenance procedures are important.

3. *Build an inheritance support system.* Construct an inheritance mechanism external to the programs. Route requests to their appropriate modules based on object schema and event schema information. Modules are more stable because no inheritance-related logic needs to be built into programs. The system is model-driven instead of hard-coded because it is based on object and event schemata.

Rumbaugh et al.[3] lists some ways to implement data structures for inheritance in a traditional language:

- Avoid it.
- Flatten the class hierarchy.
- Break out separate objects.

These techniques avoid inheritance implementation, but when inheritance is required, the actual implementation depends upon the language and application. To implement single inheritance in C, embed the superclass declaration in the first part of a subclass declaration. The first field of each structure serves as a pointer to a class descriptor object shared by direct instances of a class. The descriptor object structure contains class attributes that describe the class name and methods.

In Ada, variant records can implement single inheritance. Such a record contains a discriminant that identifies the alternate forms of the record. One variant record is defined for the root of each class hierarchy and one for each subclass. A single method may operate on all variants of a root class. FORTRAN does not support user-defined records, so variant records cannot be used. An alternative is to build a class hierarchy as a universal record, containing an attribute for each attribute in any subordinate class. Unneeded attributes are ignored. This method is useful when variant portions of a record are small. Another approach (also useful in other languages) is to separate a class into subclasses implemented as separate classes with their own arrays and object indexes. An array contains a code for the subclass and another contains the index of an object within its subclass array. This requires that a unique code be assigned to each class in the system.

Methods

To build program components so that an operation to apply to one or more objects is the only thing to be specified, the system needs to choose the required method for specified inputs. Conventional languages simply do not support operation requests and method selection. Two ways to achieve this, using conventional languages, are (again from Martin and Odell[4]):

1. *Use hard-code method selection logic within the requesting routine.* This works as long as programs are kept up to date with all requests and selection criteria.

2. *Build a method selecting support system.* First enable modules to make requests for operations without knowledge of where the appropriate method is located. The system is driven by a table that matches selection criteria with physical code location. The selection mechanism is integrated with inheritance support system (see above) to take advantage of object schema and event schema information.

Each method must have at least one argument—the implied self-argument. In traditional languages, an argument must be made explicit and methods may have additional objects as arguments. Arguments may be data values rather than objects. A reference to an object must be passed if the values of an object may be updated within a method in order to pass objects as arguments to methods. Object queries can use a call-by-value technique if the programming language allows this, but passing arguments by reference is more consistent.

C allows an object to be passed by pointer or by value. Passing by pointer is typically more efficient and provides consistent access for queries and updates. With Ada, an object may be passed as an access type. For concurrent access, encapsulate objects entirely within a task and allow access only from within that task. An object may be passed in FORTRAN as an index into the class arrays. An object queried but not modified can be passed as a list of attribute values but an index may be easier to use.

When polymorphism is used (a single operation is implemented by many methods), method resolution may be implemented in several ways:[5]

- Avoid it.
- Resolve methods at compile time.
- Resolve methods at run time.

Methods to be resolved at compile time may be built in C as ordinary function calls. This works well for methods that are never overridden and therefore do not require run-time resolution. More generally, though, a class descriptor object needs to be defined for each class that contains a pointer to the function for each operation visible from the class.

Method resolution in Ada can be done by overloading method names based on types of subprogram arguments, but this must be resolved at compile time. Dynamic method resolution can be achieved using a single procedure shared by all operations called whenever run-time resolution of the method is needed. This method of dispatching a method uses a case statement to check for the actual class of the object and calls the appropriate method implementation directly. Adding methods involves adding statements to the case in the dispatch method.

Methods for objects whose class is determined at compile time may be resolved using direct procedure calls. Other objects require class identifiers stored within them. A dispatch method may be built for each operation using class numbers and object indexes for each object as parameters. This dispatch method uses a computed GOTO or a conditional check for each possible class value in order to call the appropriate method.

Languages

The C language provides enough flexibility via loose type checking to allow implementation of some key object concepts. Pointers and run-time memory allocation prove helpful. Implementation of classes, instances, single inheritance and run-time method resolution is relatively simple with little performance degradation. Indeed, several languages and application generators produce C as output.

Pascal with its strong, rigid type checking and lack of function pointer variables is more limiting than C. A language similar to Pascal in its limitations, Ada supports data abstraction and discrete objects, but does not support object inheritance and therefore cannot be considered truly object-oriented. Ada uses rigid typing and lacks procedure pointers. Object-oriented designs can, however, be implemented in Ada but less easily than in C. Ada provides good encapsulation facilities that prove useful when developing large systems. COBOL and FORTRAN require that the programmer manually translate many object constructs that may be supported directly in Ada or C. The solution to building object-oriented systems using traditional languages may involve coding some parts in one language and other parts in an object-oriented language.

15.3 SELECTING A PROGRAMMING LANGUAGE

When using a traditional language, any object construct can be translated into the language. Any universal language will do. The problem with traditional languages is the ease with which the translation is made to objects. Implementing object concepts with a truly object-oriented programming language is easier and more reliable. This is because many constructs are automatically provided, and the developer does not need to spend time on the details of translating object designs to object programs. Rumbaugh and his colleagues[6] list these issues to consider:

- *Expressiveness.* Programmers need to map object operations such as method calling or subclass declaration into explicit operations.

- *Convenience.* Developers must manually navigate a class hierarchy when calling methods or passing arguments. When the hierarchy is modified, another manual navigation review must be conducted.

- *Error protection.* Developers need to ensure that all methods are included in a dispatch method or structure. Any new object must be initialized with its class and accessing internal attributes of other classes prevented.

- *Maintainability.* When changes to an object declaration are made, a developer must determine effects on code and implement the required changes. Object languages provide support for class modularity that prevents object changes from propagating throughout a system. Traditional languages require manual discipline to achieve this.

The overriding factor to consider when selecting a programming language to implement object designs is the cost to build and maintain the system being considered. Traditional languages have numerous tools available, and many developers are already trained and experienced using these languages. Object-oriented languages definitely have advantages in new construction and subsequent maintenance, so should be considered for their long-run advantages. In the short run, the cost may be high if a team of developers needs to learn not only object modeling but object programming as well.

One key benefit of full object-oriented languages (and database management systems) is the productivity gain to be realized through extensive reuse of designs, code and database definitions. The best way to build new systems and modify existing ones is to have analysis models, design specifications and construction components already built and tested for reliable reuse. Object analysis, design and construction together provide a solid framework for organizing reuse of models, specifications and actual system construction components.

Many object-oriented programming languages and database management systems provide a solid development environment today. Many also have a wealth of reusable class libraries available from a variety of sources. The development environments supply powerful editors, compilers and interpreters, browsers and debuggers. Class libraries provide help with support for multiple GUIs, database management systems, language interfaces and so on. Support for multiple computing platforms is a reality for those development environments that provide easy-to-use class libraries, customized to the particular target platforms that the new systems will run on. Finally, consider other aspects of object-oriented development environments versus traditional development environments:[7]

- Availability of developer training
- Availability of team-based development tools and utilities
- Human interaction tools
- Development platform support
- Operational platform support
- Performance
- Memory requirements
- Ease of integration with existing systems

END NOTES

[1] Rumbaugh, James, Michael Blaha, William Premerlani, Frederick Eddy and William Lorensen. *Object-Oriented Modeling and Design* (Englewood Cliffs, NJ: Prentice Hall) 1991, p. 359.

[2] Martin, James, and James Odell. *Object-Oriented Analysis and Design* (Englewood Cliffs, NJ: Prentice Hall) 1992, p. 434.

[3] Rumbaugh et al., *Object-Oriented Modeling and Design*, pp. 347–348.

[4] Martin and Odell, *Object-Oriented Analysis and Design*.

[5] Rumbaugh et al., *Object-Oriented Modeling and Design*, p. 266.

[6] Ibid.

[7] Coad, Peter, and Edward Yourdon. *Object-Oriented Design* (Englewood Cliffs, NJ: Yourdon Press, Prentice Hall) 1991, p. 125.

16

Database Environments

16.1 PERSISTENT DATA

When a program needs only a few data elements to work, these elements can be provided to all the modules that compose the main program. This method works well because the shared data can be exchanged whenever the need arises for cross-module communication. When the number of data elements within a system grows large, data communications between program modules can lead to strange errors and erratic behavior. Data sharing of this type violates modular programming principles that require modules be as independent as possible (exhibit low data coupling).

When data are shared directly between modules, the behavior of one module can depend heavily upon other modules. Object-oriented systems model and implement procedures alongside the appropriate data structures. This information hiding tends to minimize the undesired interactions between program modules and allows these modules to be modeled and built more independently. Database management systems extend this concept to the database itself, where data can be stored over a long period of time for use by many program modules. Object databases encapsulate data structures with procedures specifically designed to manipulate those data structures.

16.2 DATABASE MODELS

Hierarchical

This is the earliest form of database management. In this type of database model, data items called records are represented as tree structures (Figure 16.1a). A department could include records for positions contained and the equipment allocated to it. Each position could in turn be associated with a list of responsibilities and a list of employees within the department holding such a position.

Network

This is a more recent type of database that allows data to be interconnected freely with no requirement that they fit into a tree structure such as a hierarchical model would dictate. Figure 16.1b depicts a network database model. In this model, each piece of equipment could be associated with a department and a list of employees authorized to use it. This association type would not be allowed in the hierarchical model.

Relational

Hierarchical and network databases make it easy to represent complex relationships among data elements, but at a cost. Accessing data in a way other than the one dictated by the predefined relationships is slow and inefficient. Data structures are difficult to modify, requiring system administrators to shut down the database manager and rebuild the structures. The newer relational model addresses such problems by removing information about complex relationships from the database entirely. All data are stored in simple tables, with basic relationships among data items expressed as references to values in other tables using attributes called foreign keys. Each entry in an equipment table would contain a value indicating which department owns it. Figure 16.1c depicts a relational database model.

The relational model is more flexible than the older database models but has its own drawbacks. Information about complex relationships not appearing in the database itself must be built into procedures in every program that accesses the database, violating module independence concepts. Performance can also suffer when original data structures must be rebuilt each time data are accessed.

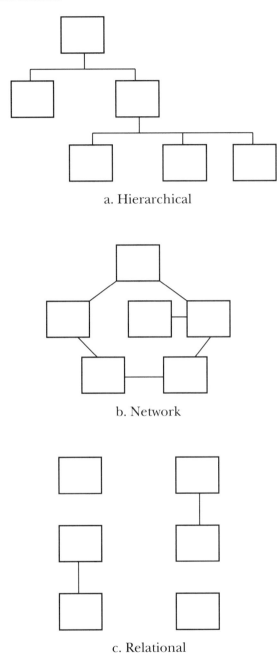

a. Hierarchical

b. Network

c. Relational

Figure 16.1   Database models

Object

Object-oriented database management systems (OODBMS) allow each real-world entity, regardless of complexity, to be represented by a single data model object. Object identity, abstraction and operator encapsulation build on this basic principle.

Obviously, object-oriented databases support object-oriented data models, but some additional considerations must be given to database system services:

- recovery
- security
- transaction management
- concurrency control

The systems covered in the next section address each of these considerations in order to support real-world applications.

Complex Objects

One important feature of OODBMS is that they support complex objects. Many applications require the modeling of objects that have an internal structure that consists of smaller subobjects and their respective relationships. Many types of complex objects exist in current systems.

Object Identity

In conventional database systems, entities are often accessed by reference to certain attributes of an entity. There are problems with this approach of allowing objects to be identified only via their properties. What happens to an object when attribute values change? Maintaining consistency of associations results in significant overhead when identifier attribute values are modified. When the identity of an object is used, changes to object properties are allowed with no adverse effects. Identifiers can be unique, system-generated values that are never reused, staying with an object for a complete lifetime.

User-Defined Operators

Operations on complex objects may require users to collect all component parts of an object before an operation can be performed. To delete a complex object, all parts of that object must be explicitly referenced before the parent object can be deleted. This requires programmers to know data structures in detail and reduces modularity and information hiding in the data model.

Object-oriented systems often include mechanisms that allow operators to be defined over complex objects. Such operators are specific to object classes—a set of operators can be defined that are appropriate to a particular class of objects. When the structural definition of an object class changes, a database administrator needs to ensure that all operators perform the correct actions. Users and programmers should be unaffected by changes to these operators.

Encapsulation

A specific set of operators needs to be defined for each complex object type. Some database management systems allow the definition of new object types to give not only the structure of an object class but also the definition of a set of operators a user or program can access and manipulate complex objects. These operators are encapsulated with the structural definition of objects upon which they are designed to operate.

Using defined operators (methods) as the only way to access objects, an interface is provided to each object that is user defined and specific to each object class and that hides the actual implementation of the object from users of the object. Both structure and operations are defined.

Class and Inheritance

Some OODBMS are based around a class hierarchy, with structural and behavioral inheritance between classes. This is similar to the way that Smalltalk deals with persistent objects. Several other approaches are also used, each of which can be considered object-oriented. POSTGRES (discussed in a later section) adds programming language procedures to a relational database. Other systems use nonfirst normal form data models.[1]

16.3 OBJECT-ORIENTED DBMS

International Data Corporation has estimated that object-oriented DBMS will generate $500 million in revenue by 1996, up from almost nothing at the beginning of the 1990s. This is probably due to the fact that an object model can be made much more semantically rich than other database models.

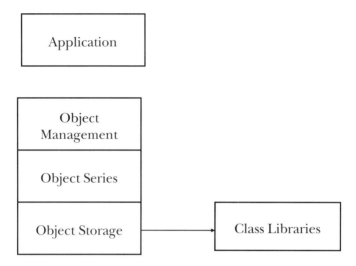

Figure 16.2   Object-oriented DBMS architecture

High-performance, highly flexible database management systems are at least feasible in the object DBMS arena. However, they are very difficult to achieve with other database models.

Object-oriented databases differ in significant ways from traditional databases. In an object-oriented environment, database management systems must be able to store objects (messages, methods, attributes and instance variables), their relationships (subclass-of or superclass-of) and the class hierarchy. An object-oriented database system must be able to retrieve objects, relationships and hierarchy at a later time. This ability to store object information is sometimes referred to as management of persistent objects. Figure 16.2[2] shows one way to view object-oriented database architectures.

The database schema in an object-oriented database management system consists of class definitions and inheritance structure. Changes in the class structure are actually schema changes, so users must be able to make many more schema changes in an object-oriented system than is allowed in more traditional systems. Changes to the class structure fall into three different categories, classified by Banerjee,[3] as follows:

1. Changes to the contents of a node:
    a. Changes to an instance variable:
        — Add a new instance variable to a class.
        — Drop an instance variable from a class.

— Change the name of an instance variable.

— Change the domain of an instance variable.

— Change the inheritance (parent) of an instance variable (inherit another instance variable with the same name).

  b. Changes to a method:

— Add a new method to a class.

— Drop an existing method from a class.

— Change the name of a method of a class.

— Change the code of a method of a class.

— Change the inheritance (parent) of a method.

2. Changes to an edge:

  a. Make a class a superclass of another class.

  b. Remove a class from the superclass list of another class.

  c. Change the order of the superclass list of a class.

3. Changes to a node:

  a. Add a new class.

  b. Drop an existing class.

  c. Change the name of a class.

Class Invariants

Several rules must be obeyed by the database management system through schema evolution. Banerjee[4] notes that these invariants are extracted directly from the data model. Other researchers and practitioners of information engineering refer to a similar concept as *entity life cycle analysis.* The class invariants in an object-oriented database can be described this way:

Class Lattice Invariant

A class structure is a rooted and connected directed acyclic graph (DAG) with labeled edges. The graph has exactly one root, the class object. There are no isolated nodes. The labels associated with edges are used to resolve conflicts.

Distinct Name Invariant

All instance variables and methods of a class must have distinct names defined and inherited.

Distinct Identity Invariant

All instance variables and methods of a class have a distinct origin (applicable only with multiple inheritance).

Full Inheritance Invariant

A class must inherit all instance variables and methods from each of its superclasses. The only selective inheritance situation occurs when full inheritance would lead to a violation of the distinct name and distinct identity invariants.

Domain Compatibility Invariant

If an instance variable of a class is inherited from an instance variable of a superclass, the domain of the second instance variable must be either the same or a subclass of the domain of the first instance variable.

Schema Changes

Many times a schema change can be interpreted in different ways, all leaving the class structure consistent. Rules are needed to govern which interpretation is most semantically meaningful. Following are examples of such rules:[5]

Default Conflict Resolution Rules

Select a single inheritance option when a name or identity conflict exists. This ensures that distinct name and identity invariants are satisfied. Rules can be overridden to resolve conflicts differently.

If an instance variable is defined in a class and its name is the same as that of one of its superclasses, the newly defined instance variable is used.

If more than one of the superclasses of a class has instance variables with the same name but distinct origin, the instance variable selected for inheritance is from the first superclass in the superclass definition list.

If two or more superclasses of a class have instance variables with the same origin, the instance variable with the most specialized domain is selected for inheritance (if the domains are the same, the above rule is applied).

Property Propagation Rules

When instance variable or method properties in a class are changed, changes are propagated to all subclasses of that class that had inherited them (unless these properties were previously redefined within the subclass).

When the properties of a class's variables or methods are changed, changes are propagated to all subclasses that had inherited them (unless these properties were previously redefined with the subclass).

Name changes of newly added instance variables or methods are propagated to only subclasses that encounter no new name conflicts as consequence of this schema modification.

Directed Acyclic Graph Manipulation Rules

Edge addition If a class is made superclass of another class, the first class becomes the last superclass of the second.

Edge removal If a class is the only superclass of a second class, and the first is removed from the superclass list of the second, then the second class is made an immediate subclass of each of the first's superclasses.

Node addition If no superclasses are specified for a newly added class (the root class), object is the default superclass of the new class.

GemStone

The GemStone system architecture consists of the Gem server and the Stone monitor. Gem runs object behavior routines specified in C or Smalltalk/GS, GemStone's data manipulation language, as well as evaluates queries. Stone allocates new objects in blocks to avoid having the monitor become a bottleneck. Stone coordinates commit activity. Gem performs all actions to commit transactions. Stone coordinates activities of multiple Gems. Application programs can link directly to Gem servers. A client application does not need to know whether it is linked to its Gem server.

GemStone supports distributed environments, providing high availability to large amounts of data. Referential integrity is fully supported based on object identifiers. Concurrency control is optimistic (transactions may operate without getting locks, assuming the probability of a conflict is small) with optional locking. This type of concurrency control provides four advantages:

1. Neither objects nor pages need to be locked.

2. Deadlocks cannot occur.

3. Each transaction has a consistent view of the database.

4. Shadowing provides protection against process, processor and media failures.

GemStone also provides pessimistic concurrency control with user-selectable locking levels.

GemStone provides a mechanism (not a policy) for versioning, supporting linear versioning and parallel versions. Other versioning policies (such as a hierarchy of versions) are also supported. GemStone supports indexing, queries, clustering and managing large objects.

Smalltalk/GS is a language that supports:

message passing,

encapsulation of behavior,

a class hierarchy,

inheritance and

object identity.

Definition of classes, class hierarchy and code to define behaviors are stored within the database. Such information is available at runtime and forms an active data dictionary. The Smalltalk/GS data manipulation language is a complete programming language, unlike SQL, which lacks iterators and recursion. This language provides a strong basis for object-oriented application development through the ability to store, manage and execute behaviors within the database itself. C code can be encapsulated with Smalltalk/GS and invoked from the data manipulation language.

GemStone supports multiple languages and tools through interfaces directly to C, C++ and Smalltalk. Also provided for use with the product are relational gateways and a gateway tool kit to integrate proprietary and legacy systems.

The GemStone C++ interface provides both persistent storage for C++ programs and access to persistent objects stored in the database by other languages. Stored C++ objects are unique and exist independently of the programs that create them. Other database applications can use these objects.

The GemStone Smalltalk interface consists of a set of classes installed in a Smalltalk image allowing access and modification of objects in the database. Classes and methods control connections to GemStone databases, transactions and cooperative session management. Data access is initiated either via proxy objects stored in the Smalltalk image or by name. A Smalltalk program gets access to named GemStone objects via messages sent to return a proxy for the database object. Smalltalk objects use these proxies to send messages to database objects, replicate the state of database objects in the Smalltalk environment and obtain structural access to database objects.

The GemStone Object Development Environment (GeODE) provides tools for visual programming. The GeODE Forms Designer allows building sophisticated graphical forms connected automatically to objects in the database. GeODE's Visual Program Designer supports the creation of complex applications without writing code via a design canvas that visually represents processing logic or behavior. The GeODE Application Designer assists in the assembly of classes, instances and forms for an application. Other tools support the publishing of applications to system users. GeODE is completely integrated with the database and takes advantage of GemStone's ability to store database behavior within the database itself. This integration provides several unique features:

- Developers can build default forms from existing objects or classes.
- GeODE can show live database objects in the forms while they are being developed.
- At any point during development of an application, any portion can be tested against live data.
- When forms are running, they have direct connections to the database, avoiding expensive input or output database transactions.
- Developers need not port their applications built against a portable, environment-independent layer of classes.

ONTOS DB

The ONTOS DB system is a distributed object database management system that uses object-oriented programming languages for description and application development. This system supports flexibility, extendibility and accessibility at the data model, the transaction and storage management level and the tool and application level. Object-oriented languages and object techniques can be used to customize and extend the ONTOS system for higher performance and higher-function applications.

ONTOS DB incorporates an active data dictionary that describes the schema and permits applications to access this information online. The dictionary is a class library with individual objects representing schema information. Developers can use ONTOS tools or write programs using C++ and Smalltalk to access and manipulate the dictionary. This provides the ability to create schema-driven tools as well as the ability to support dynamic integration of third-party systems.

ONTOS DB Designer is a GUI browser/editor that uses the active data dictionary to read the schema definition from the ONTOS database. It creates a graphical display of the class hierarchy. Users can view all parts of a class definition—including the member functions—and can create new classes or modify existing classes directly from the user interface. Functions can be dynamically invoked by the dictionary.

ONTOS Object SQL allows sending of messages from within a query. Developers can combine object-oriented programming with query techniques, even for C++, which does not provide online type information about objects or classes. ONTOS Studio is a GUI builder that uses the active data dictionary to automatically generate intelligent forms. The tool reads class definitions from the dictionary and uses this information about the classes of various fields to generate a complete interface automatically. Developers can customize the interface, and the dictionary allows testing of the interface without leaving the developer environment. Finished applications can be developed against the database quickly via iteration rather than a rigid compile-edit-link cycle.

The ONTOS DB Extensible Storage Management (ESM) subsystem allows developers to extend and adapt the various subsystem layers in a database management system: the data model, the integrity (transaction) layer and the storage management layer. Most database systems do not support access to the description or calls of any layer beyond the data model. At the lowest level, ONTOS DB uses the same object techniques as at the logical interface to provide a class library representing the physical interface (or ESM). This allows the creation of high-performance applications in a wider range of environments and the ability to incorporate new disk and memory management mechanisms transparently.

The ESM subsystem of ONTOS DB allows different storage management classes within a single application. Both an object-based representation and a page-based representation can be used simultaneously, with the result that applications developed with ONTOS DB provide high performance across a variety of application domains. The ESM subsystem allows two different storage approaches to be used within a single application.

ONTOS DB not only supports a client/server model but allows more of the client application processing be executed in the client workstation. The resulting systems can deliver much higher performance to the user. Off-loading processing from the server allows a given server on a network to support a larger number of client workstations.

This database system allows the use of multiple server machines, further distributing database processing. With other database systems, this is accomplished by allowing the application to connect to multiple databases, with one database associated with each server in the network. This forces programmers to be aware of the actual databases and servers in the network and to know which objects are in which database. ONTOS DB adds a layer known as a logical database to encapsulate multiple physical servers and physical databases into a single logical interface for developers. An application need not be aware of the servers or locations of objects in physical databases in the network.

This approach helps developers by insulating applications from the physical configuration of a network. Servers and databases may be moved, reconfigured or added without effect on applications. Application performance may be increased by adding servers to a network. This scalability helps increase the amount of objects in a database and the number of users supported without modifying application code.

ITASCA

The ITASCA distributed object database management system incorporates the object concepts of unique object identifiers, states and behaviors. Attributes represent object states and methods define object behaviors. The system has class objects and instance objects, and supports both class and instance attributes and methods. Class objects can receive messages similar to instance objects. Messages return attribute names, lists of subclasses or superclasses and other class information. Subclasses derive from existing classes. Each subclass inherits all attributes and methods of its superclasses. ITASCA supports multiple inheritance, so a subclass can derive from multiple superclasses.

In ITASCA, traditional transactions are short transactions. Sessions encapsulate a series of transactions and can be shared or nested. Locking is fine-grained on object levels and locks change dynamically based on operations performed on objects. Concurrency control is pessimistic, guaranteeing that once an object lock is obtained the commit will succeed. Optimistic concurrency control does not guarantee a commit after obtaining locks.

Support is provided for applications written in C++, C and Common LISP. Objects can be stored using one language and accessed or updated using other languages. Programs written in different languages can invoke the same database methods and can have specific nondatabase methods or member functions.

A high degree of data independence is provided for supported languages, and changes made to the structure of data or schema stored in the database do not always require changing or recompiling of existing programs. The ITASCA query language is interactive, but queries can be embedded in programs.

The ITASCA database is active: The system stores and activates methods directly in the database, allowing:

- database methods to be changed without recompiling or relinking applications,
- database methods to be reused by multiple programming languages and
- objects to be reused by multiple programming languages.

Shared and private databases can exist in a distributed environment using ITASCA. Partitions of the shared database are placed at multiple sites in a network. An ITASCA server controls the database partition at each site and clients provide transparent access to the various shared database partitions. Multiple private databases are allowed at each distributed database site. Database schema are stored redundantly at each network site for improved performance. This includes storage of database methods. Schema update management is automatic across a network. ITASCA also supports dynamic schema modification for added flexibility and reduced maintenance costs.

Long duration transactions are allowed for checking out objects from shared, distributed databases into private databases. Objects in private databases may be changed without effect upon shared databases. Long duration transactions persist after system crash and recovery.

Version control of objects is supported by ITASCA. New versions of objects promote the originals or parent objects to restrict further changes to the parents. Alternate versions are also supported so that multiple versions can have the same parent. Generic versions are used to dynamically reference most recent or default versions of objects without user or application intervention.

ITASCA supports both linear and spatial data. Linear data objects are sequential, such as text or audio. Spatial objects could be bit-mapped images. Version control allows reduction in data storage space.

New classes and methods can be defined or existing ones changed at any time or at any level of an inheritance structure. Class and attribute names can be changed at any time. Kernel-level methods (add, change, delete) can be refined at a class level to customize behavior. Methods are included for checking in and out, making versions and promoting versions of objects.

The ITASCA Dynamic Schema Editor allows direct creation and modification of a schema without generation and unloading of data definition language. The ITASCA Active Data Editor provides an interface into the database management system. No programming is necessary to use the tool. Objects are displayed dynamically with contents determining the actual display. Schema changes automatically reflect on screens. This database administration tool supports:

- setting up authorizations,
- examining and changing object locks,
- examining database communications, storage statistics and buffer sizes and
- compressing physical databases.

ObjectStore

ObjectStore is a database management system designed for use in applications that perform complex manipulations on large databases of objects with intricate structure. The system supports a C library interface, a C++ library interface and an extended C++ interface. The library interfaces are accessible via C or C++ compilers. Persistence is not part of the type of an object in ObjectStore. Objects of any C++ data type may be allocated transiently on the heap or in a database. There is no need to inherit from a special persistent object base class. Different objects of one type may be persistent or transient within a program.

The ObjectStore system supports access of persistent data inside transactions, a library of collection types, bidirectional relationships, an optimizing query facility and a version facility. Also provided are tools for:

- Database schema design
- Database browsing
- Database administration
- Application compilation and debugging

The ObjectStore server provides a long-term repository for persistent data, storing and retrieving objects in response to client requests. A collection facility is provided in the form of an object class library. Such collections provide a variety of behaviors, including lists and collections with or without duplicates. In addition, collections provide a variety of representation for each set of abstract behavior. Different representations are tuned for differing collection sizes and access patterns. Users may either select a desired representation or describe an intended usage pattern.

A relationship facility assists in the modeling of complex objects such as parts hierarchies, designs, documents and multimedia information. ObjectStore supports one-to-one, one-to-many and many-to-many relationships. Relationships are accessed just as data members in C++, but updating relationship values causes update of reverse relationships. ObjectStore guarantees consistent update of both sides of a relationship.

Queries in ObjectStore are closely integrated with the host language. This is in contrast to SQL, which has its own variables and expressions distinct from those in the host programming language. Query expressions in ObjectStore are handled differently from other kinds of expressions. The query optimizer can index paths through objects and collections, not just through fields contained directly in objects.

ObjectStore supports versioning. Users can check out versions of objects or groups of objects, make changes and check changes back into the main database. Other users can continue to use previous versions without concurrency conflicts on shared data. Versions may be merged back together at a later time to reconcile differences from concurrent changes. Private workspaces can be set up to control object versioning. Workspaces may inherit from other workspaces. Persistence and versioning of objects are independent of type.

VERSANT

VERSANT is a database management system that supports persistent storage of application objects implemented in C++, C or Smalltalk. The system provides a class library application programming interface for C++ and

Smalltalk. Application programs can work with persistent and transient objects consistently using host programming language syntax. Object references are handled just like C++ or Smalltalk references, even across database or platform boundaries.

Extended functionality is provided through dynamic access to the database schema allowing run-time type checking, subclass and superclass information location and class attribute identification. This is important for development of tools and extensible applications. Dynamic class definition capabilities of Smalltalk are supported. Also supported are inheritance (multiple for C++, single for Smalltalk) and interobject references, as well as management of bidirectional references and collections of objects. Schema evolution allows creation and modification of class attributes at runtime and evolution of associated instances. Schema evolution also includes creation, naming and dropping classes, attributes and methods, automatic incremental upgrade of instances and automatic version history maintenance. Utilities are provided for managing authorizations, installation and backup and system configuration.

VERSANT supports heterogeneous multiple client and multiple server environments. There can be any number of servers in a network and any machine can be both server and client. This provides distribution, reliability and database availability with no single point of failure in a network. Transactions may span databases and machines.

Full support is provided for group and personal databases. Included is the capability to check objects out of a group database into a personal database using long transactions, even if a server fails. Persistent object locks are stored in server databases. When objects are checked out, a database maintains a persistent local copy and allows for optional preservation of object identifiers. Also supported are:

- flexible specification of check-out selection criteria,
- flexible check-out scope across multiple sites,
- detection of redundant check-outs,
- automatic check-out of pertinent schema information and
- automatic check-out on long transaction commit.

VERSANT versioning works closely with the check-out, check-in and long transaction capabilities. Versioned objects are always available for check-out, regardless of locks. After object modification in a private database, check-in to a group database results in a shared version. A derivation history of objects is maintained, even if objects move across different databases over time. Applications that access such an object dynamically bind to the most current version. Other versioning features include:

- Object-level versioning
- Version branching and merging
- Explicit or implicit creation
- Access to multiple object versions in a program
- Program access to version history
- Status enforcement of working, transient and released versions
- Status downgrade and upgrade
- Automatic linking resolution
- Static and dynamic binding

16.4 EXTENDED RELATIONAL DBMS

Much research is being conducted to develop database management systems that support object-oriented designs and data structures. This section discusses just a small sample of the many types of systems on the market in the near future.

One goal of these systems is to make as few changes as possible to the relational model. The idea is to extend the relational model with new data types, operators and access methods. Data types might include complex numbers, graphics, images or recorded sound. New operations might include checks of decision tables for completeness (and consolidation of rows in cases where a decision criterion is irrelevant) or special derivation procedures for user-defined data.

Since no single database model will suffice for all kinds of data and situations (at least, in today's world), advanced relational DBMS must provide support for addition of custom features. Rumbaugh et al.[6] discuss some advantages of the advanced relational DBMS approach:

- *Definitely adds to existing RDBMS functionality.* It preserves traditional strengths of relational systems: many simultaneous users, large quantities of data, reliability, distributed data management and programming support tools.
- *Integrates well with existing relational databases.* It provides smooth flow of data between engineering and business applications.

- *Data Sharing.* A database is truly a central repository and not wedded to any particular programming language or application.

The authors go on to state some disadvantages of this approach:

- *Performance.* Even augmented relational systems may not be capable of performing efficient operations on individual objects.
- *Functionality.* The relational paradigm might interfere with the ability to deliver needed capabilities. These limitations may cause problems for real applications.
- *Security.* Open architectures might make it more difficult to protect data against unauthorized reading and writing.

POSTGRES

POSTGRES is an example of an advanced relational DBMS. It is a prototype at the University of California at Berkeley and is a successor to the INGRES relational system. POSTGRES adopts a one database approach, whereby one database can be extended to serve a variety of applications. It supports data types that include variable length data, QUEL (a query language that is similar to SQL), queries and procedures. POSTGRES has facilities for active databases such as triggers and inferencing with forward and backward chaining.

Informix

In recent years, Informix announced plans to release a new version of its DBMS that would include object-oriented features. The new database will support binary large objects (BLObs), allowing Informix to store data that it could not previously store, such as spreadsheet components, images and word processing files. These new data types can be manipulated in the same way that ordinary database files are manipulated.

EXODUS

This system is a prototype developed at the University of Wisconsin. The system adopts the database generator approach, whereby a host of custom DBMSs each serve an application niche. EXODUS provides kernel facilities for use by all applications and a set of tools to assist database administrators with generation of custom portions of each database.

16.5 TRADITIONAL DBMS WITH OBJECT-ORIENTED DESIGNS

Relational database management systems are popular target environments for information engineering CASE tools and methods. When object-oriented models are used to generate relational databases, some issues must be addressed in the areas of database design and interfaces to application programs. Relational database designs can be generated directly from object models. While the resulting databases will conform to object model specifications, they may not perform very efficiently. Performance tuning will be required to optimize the designs.

Object Identifiers

Database designs are driven by object models and each object data structure can be implemented as a table. Attributes are either references to other tables or to internally stored data values. Ordinarily, a pointer in relational databases is implemented as a foreign key, an attribute or set of attributes containing the unique identifier of the table to which the foreign key points. For this to work, a unique identifier must be defined for each table in a relational database design.

An alternate approach to choosing a primary key from a table's attributes is to assign a single unique identifying attribute to each table. This unique attribute becomes the object identifier, whose value for each table record is system generated and unchangeable. If a record is deleted, the object identifier can never be reissued to any other record. While some relational database management systems support the assignment of surrogate keys that correspond in concept to object identifiers, these surrogate keys cannot be made accessible to programming languages. Object identifiers can be used to avoid the significant problem of maintaining referential integrity in relational databases.

Classes

An object class will map to one or more relational tables and a table may correspond to more than one class. Class objects may be split horizontally or vertically or both ways. Horizontal partitioning can improve efficiency by placing frequently accessed objects in one table and the remaining objects in a second table (Figure 16.3a). This works well for classes that have many

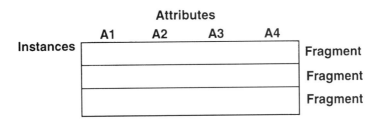

Figure 16.3a   Horizontal object partitioning

instances, a few of which are often accessed. This requires that each application or query have knowledge of how to find required data. Vertical positioning can be used to partition objects in a class that has attributes with different access patterns (Figure 16.3b).

Associations

Associations between objects might map to tables or they may not, depending on the association cardinality, performance trade-offs and other factors. Many-to-many associations always map to distinct tables. Two options for mapping a one-to-many association to tables are creating a distinct table for the association or burying a foreign key in the table for the many side of the association. Rumbaugh et al.[7] state the advantages of merging an association into a class:

Fewer tables.

Faster performance due to fewer tables to navigate.

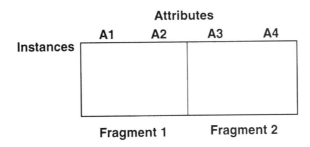

Figure 16.3b   Vertical object partitioning

The disadvantages of merging an association into a class:

Less design rigor. Associations are between independent objects of equal syntactic weight. This is related to the argument in favor of encapsulation for object-oriented languages.

Reduced extendibility. It is difficult to get cardinality correct on the first few design passes. One-to-one and one-to-many associations may be externalized. Many-to-many associations must be externalized.

More complexity. An asymmetrical representation of the association complicates search and update procedures.

The actual decision of whether to collapse associations into related classes depends on the situation. One-to-one associations may be collapsed into object tables or merged even further and both objects and the association stored together in the same table (but watch out for cyclical associations). Merging into a single table increases performance and reduces storage requirements but causes loss of extendibility and possible violation of third normal form of the table. One-to-many associations may allow for collapse of both classes and the association into one table but this may be undesirable and may violate second normal form. See Rumbaugh et al. for details on this and on the mapping of ternary associations to tables. The authors[8] list some rules for modeling objects to tables:

Mapping object classes to tables. Each class maps to one or more tables.

Mapping associations to tables.

Each many-to-many association maps to a distinct table.

Each one-to-many association maps to a distinct table or may be buried as a foreign key in the table for the many class.

For one-to-many and one-to-one associations, if there are no cycles, the association and both related objects may be stored in one table (but with possible redundancy and normal form violations).

Role names are incorporated as part of the foreign key attribute name.

N-ary (n>2) associations map to a distinct table (an n-ary association may be promoted to a class).

A qualified association maps to a distinct table with at least three attributes—primary key of each related class and the qualifier.

Aggregation follows the same rules as association.

Mapping single inheritance generalizations to tables.

The superclass and each subclass map to a table.

There are no superclass tables—superclass attributes are replicated for each subclass.

There are no subclass tables—bring all subclass attributes up to the superclass level.

Mapping disjoint multiple inheritance to tables. The superclass and each subclass map to a table.

Mapping overlapping multiple inheritance to tables. The superclass and each subclass map to a table, and the generalization relationship also maps to a table.

Relational database design requires that special attention be given to the higher overhead involved with joins. As the number of tables increase, you incur more overhead in traversing through relationships between the tables. It becomes more desirable from a performance standpoint to collapse tables than to separate classes into separate tables. Performance tuning is important in any database and should be tested early in the database design process.[9]

Operations

Because relational databases store data and not the operations that access the data, implementations of operations must be carefully controlled. If possible, operations should be placed directly into the databases so that when an application or query needs to access data, only the correct operations can be used. Relational database management systems (to my knowledge) do not support embedded procedures, so application programs must ensure integrity of data when process models are implemented separately from data models. Object models dictate that data access logic be placed in the data structures (in the database itself), not in application programs.

Consider implementing operations as separate database server classes (implemented in conventional programming languages as separate programs) that access databases. Separate classes can then be insulated from possible changes in database structure changes. This gives the database class designer the flexibility to optimize the database calls without affecting application programs or user queries. Object model classes should change only when the conceptual object model changes, not when the implementation of the model changes (see Booch[10] for a discussion of the effects of change on an object-based system). Another advantage of this approach is that when database requests are made from one database access class directly to another class in order to fulfill a complex request, the call is hidden from the original requester application or user.

16.6 DISADVANTAGES OF OBJECT-ORIENTED DBMS

Object-oriented DBMS have great potential but have not yet caught on in a big way with businesses. Some reasons why this is so include:

- Object-oriented techniques have not proven themselves in business.
- Object-oriented programming languages often do not generate highly efficient code.
- Reliability has not yet been proven in major applications.
- Not enough development tools have been made available.
- Retraining costs for developers of traditional systems will be high.
- The potential benefits are not understood by many developers and business people.

See Figures 16.4 and 16.5 for a summary of database technology today.

When should an OODBMS be used? Consider it if applications contain complex data structures. Doug Barry[11] suggests that data are complex data if you make one or more of the following statements when designing a relational system and using the proper design techniques for relational technology:

- "I'll need to 'denormalize' if I want to get any performance."
- "The number of relational joins I'm going to need for most users will kill the system."
- "I'm going to need different relational views for each type of data so I do not show all the null fields."
- "Different types of data have the same field or attribute name. The names have different meaning depending on the type of data."

Today OODBMSs lack:

Links to standard relational DBMSs
Standard query languages
Short program learning curves
Numerous preprogrammed
 libraries
Widespread standards
Low up-front entry costs
Storage memory/network
 bandwidth adequate for full
 OO advantages

Today OODBMSs offer:

Unique object identification
Class reusability
Quick application development
Good performance between
 handling complex objects
Hardware/software independence
Compatibility with OOPLs such as
 C++ and Smalltalk

Figure 16.4   The state of object-oriented DBMS today

- "My program needs to use graph data structures such as binary trees. I'll need to transform trees to relational tables and vice versa to provide graphic support."

Complex data can be found all around. A personnel database might contain exempt employees and nonexempt employees. These two types of employees may be treated differently or the same depending upon the particular view an application or query takes. With an object database, different methods could be created to handle different cases. The name "pay" could be used for each method, one to calculate pay appropriate for each

OO DBMS

Support inheritance
Good for BOM, BLOb
Lack of tools
Objects represented by data
 plus appropriate procedures
 (not just relations)
Objects stored in class library
Instance retrievals may be
 insufficient
The validation routine is a method
Written once, stored once,
 revisions made once

RDBS

Do not support inheritance
Not good for BOM
Plentiful tools
Objects represented as data-
 only relations
Objects stored in data
 dictionary/catalog
Instance retrievals very efficient
 (except where joins are required)
Each program has its own record
 validation routine
Any change in data structure
 requires each program to be
 revised

Figure 16.5   OODBMS versus RDBMS technologies

object class and another one to handle employees in general. This multiple use of a single method name (polymorphism) works because the object DBMS knows how to handle different method implementations for different object classes, and the application does not need to know how to handle the method implementations differently.

Relational joins may disappear because of the use of an object data model or may be replaced with data references. Traversing a data reference is a lot faster than building a join. Object databases can often be made more efficient than relational systems, but only when the data model has been properly constructed and the strengths and weaknesses of each DBMS model and implementation have been carefully considered. Object-oriented DBMSs will probably not replace relational technology but will handle complex data processing situations that require graphics, hypertext or multimedia capabilities.

END NOTES

[1] Kuspert, K., P. Dadam and J. Gunauer. "Cooperative Object Buffer Management in the Advances Information Management Prototype." In *Proceedings of the 13th International Conference on Very Large Databases*, 1987.

[2] Adapted from Bozman, Jean S. *Computerworld* (October 26, 1992), p. 28.

[3] Banerjee, J., and H. Chou. "Data Model Issues for Object-Oriented Applications." *ACM Transactions on Office Information Systems* (January 1987).

[4] Ibid.

[5] Ibid.

[6] Rumbaugh, James, Michael Blaha, William Premerlani, Frederick Eddy and William Lorensen. *Object-Oriented Modeling and Design* (Englewood Cliffs, NJ: Prentice Hall) 1991, pp. 387–388.

[7] Ibid., p. 377.

[8] Ibid., p. 386.

[9] Montgomery, Stephen L. *Relational Database Design and Implementation Using DB2* (New York: Van Nostrand Reinhold) 1990.

[10] Booch, Grady. *Object-Oriented Design with Applications* (Redwood City, CA: Benjamin/Cummings) 1991, pp. 359–362.

[11] Barry, Doug. "When to Use Object DBMSs." *Computerworld* (October 26, 1992), p. 122.

17

Client/Server and Cooperative Processing

As information systems become more sophisticated and the need for distributing part or all of an application and/or database becomes necessary, building and maintaining these systems becomes more difficult. Object modeling will simplify this to a great degree, allowing networks of intercommunicating objects to be modeled via simply constructed yet semantically powerful messages.

17.1 DISTRIBUTED DATABASES

Environments

There are several ways that distributed data stored can be represented in information systems:[1]

- On heterogeneous hardware platforms
- On different operating systems
- Under control of different database management systems
- As used by different application software

251

A distributed database is a collection of independent storage locations, perhaps a large distance from each other, connected with a communications network. Data access should be transparent to users and application programs and synchronized across all locations as required. A data access is transparent when a user or application program does not need to know where data are stored, in what format and how they are accessed. Intelligent objects or use of an object request broker (see Chapter 18 for a discussion of object request broker) can make this transparency easier to achieve.

In practice, data synchronization can be difficult because data sometimes need to be replicated across a network for better performance and better reliability. Better performance can be achieved when data can be made accessible locally instead of transferring transactions from various locations. Better reliability can be realized if the same data reside at multiple network nodes, preventing total network downtime if some nodes become inoperable. Guidelines defining where data are replicated and when maintenance is performed must be established and adhered to. Data may be distributed (some data stored at one site and other data stored at another site), partitioned (logically related data physically split between several sites) or replicated (multiple copies of data stored at many sites).

As with any information engineering–modeled system, a distributed database needs to support the business system architecture, data architecture and network architecture. Object models make this easier by integrating data and process views, and encapsulation and information hiding allow for building in the network architecture under the covers. The Object Request Broker component of Object Management Groups' Object Management Architecture (see Chapter 18) is designed to route requests for services to the appropriate object. This message routing can include messages sent over a distributed network of objects.

Requirements

In order to provide for a robust, effective and efficient distributed data environment, a distributed DBMS needs to fulfill some important requirements. First, it needs to provide a way of locating files and data sets. Application program objects should not need to know where data are located, but this information needs to be provided somewhere within the database management or communications network subsystem. One way to provide this is via a directory facility that is used by the system to determine how to access data across networks. The directory facility needs to provide cross-references to where data are and how they can be accessed.

Another important requirement that a distributed DBMS must address is security and authorization. Data residing on workstations around the network must be made secure. In an object-oriented environment, each object can be made responsible for administering its own security, possibly in concert with a network object request broker.

Maintaining consistent states of data in a distributed data environment will be a challenge due to greater probability of processor and network failures. Data consistency, integrity and access performance must be maintained. A transaction is a sequence of tasks that executes a business task or activity. It might specify a query or an action that changes the state of database information. With a transaction processing environment, a transaction executing at any network node could fail or any other point along a network communication line could malfunction. A distributed DBMS must provide for restoration of part or all of a database to a consistent state.

Providing consistent data and reasonable performance dictates that a distributed DBMS must provide ways to optimize overall network database performance. Shaku Atre[2] lists some items that such a system must determine in order to select a site for constructing a database join:

- How to select the appropriate site
- How to create an order to the joins of relations
- Which method to use to join them
- Which synchronization method to use to update redundantly stored data
- In case of transaction failure, which backout procedure to use

This list gives some idea of how complicated performance optimization can be. An OODBMS will do an excellent job of hiding implementation details via encapsulation and information hiding. Some of the same benefits can be achieved by using object design concepts with traditional database management systems, but this requires a good deal of discipline.

Features

It is beyond the scope of this book to discuss distributed database management systems in detail, but it seems appropriate to mention briefly the key features that such a system should provide. First, the system should support a variety of hardware platforms: mainframes, minicomputers, microcomputers and workstations. Network support should include serial and parallel ports and synchronous and asynchronous transmission. The hardware support should include any and all vendor hardware that an organization has or wishes to use.

Distributed database technology can be useful in a variety of business situations. One scenario might include homogeneous hardware, perhaps from the same vendor. Another scenario might be a heterogeneous utilization of hardware from a variety of vendors. Finally, a network might consist of a heterogeneous mix of operating systems. Ideally, applications and databases work equally well in any of these environments. Again, object technology can make it easier to support one set of system designs with a variety of implementations. Strict encapsulation and information hiding inherent in object modeling make support of mixed computing platforms go much more smoothly.

Network support must include local area networks (LANs) and wide area networks (WANs) and various combinations of these. Network support is extremely important in distributed data systems. Network status must be transparent so that an application program or query does not need to know which links in a network are available at any one time. A single system image can make a distributed database seem to be totally centralized at one network node. Selection of optimal or available network routes should be left to the DBMS and network system, not applications. A message sent to a network broker should be routed with no prior knowledge of a requesting application or user query. Object technology should insulate such details from users of a database and network system.

Data distribution support should include:

- Horizontal fragmentation
- Vertical fragmentation
- Replication
- Data dictionary/directory
- Naming conventions

Processing support should provide a single system image: query, update, view and performance transparency. When transactions occur at more than one network site, the transaction termination must be uniform: A transaction must either commit or abort; all sites commit or all sites abort. Two-phase commit protocol should be used to ensure consistent transaction commits or aborts. The first phase reaches a common decision and the second implements the decision. A database coordinator object could perform this function.

Site autonomy allows different database sites to act independently and to have individual nodes operate when others fail. Each node must be responsible for its data and the association processing. If each node is a distinct object, this becomes a natural extension of object behavior modeling. Each database node object will then be responsible for its own locking, logging, recovery and restarts.

In a traditional distributed DBMS, change management tends to be a problem. Most attention is given to data creation and little to maintenance. A designer needs to consider the effects of change upon multiple locations. Applications and users must be insulated from change in programs, views or dictionary/directory entries.

Implementers of distributed databases should consider whether data should be distributed, or just the access to those data. Database administration may need to be more sophisticated than with a centralized database. Authorities for data definition and access must be considered locally and globally. Data availability and data integrity issues must be balanced.

Reasons for Using Distributed Databases

One reason that an organization may choose to distribute databases is that data can be stored and accessed in a way that is more closely aligned with the organization's structure. Another reason is that distributed data helps provide overall system resilience—when one node fails, data access is limited or prevented. Distributed databases may be able to manage much larger volumes of data. Partitioning into individual, smaller databases (actually, database objects and their component objects) helps make database management and control easier.

Distributed database can also allow incremental growth in data volume because components of a database tend to grow at different rates. Placing database objects on their own dedicated servers (or at least on their own storage partitions) allows for flexible system scalability. Often, this may mean using less expensive workstations or network servers instead of midrange or mainframe systems.

Cost considerations may significantly affect how data are centralized or distributed. Perhaps costs can best be minimized by keeping data close to the applications or users that access those data. Communication costs may be high enough to result in a need to minimize the amount of communications required for transactions and queries. Also consider the complexity of applications, operational procedures required and the performance requirements and capabilities.

The advantages of distributing databases (especially when objects are distributed, not just tables or database segments) include support for heterogeneous computing platforms, better response time via locally available data and system resiliency via matching database structure locations with organization structure locations and usage patterns.

Disadvantages of distributing databases include difficulty in achieving true location transparency, site autonomy, partition independence and replication independence.

17.2 COOPERATIVE PROCESSING

Even though many large organizations still process the bulk of their information on large mainframe computers, the trend is that this processing is migrating down to smaller, more cost-effective computers such as microcomputers and LAN servers. Cooperative processing environments provide the capability for parts of an application to execute on different computers, with data at various networked sites.

One common architecture used to implement cooperative processing is client/server architecture (discussed later in this chapter). More generally, though, cooperative processing architectures have two or more computers sharing application and/or database processing. This allows distribution of programs, files and databases across a network of interconnected computers. Cooperative processing provides transparent access to computing resources in a network so that application programs and users do not need to know where resources are located.

Cooperative processing can provide a single user interface to a wide variety of remote computing resources. Typically, this user interface is a graphical one such as Microsoft Windows, IBM OS/2 Presentation Manager, Hewlett-Packard New Wave, Apple Macintosh or the Open Look and Motif interfaces available on various UNIX systems. These GUIs make computer applications easier to use (once the user learns the interface, all applications appear consistent) and should reduce user errors when interacting with the interface.

Cooperative processing can also reduce the processing load on host computers or network server computers. Application work can be distributed among a variety of clients and servers, with server computers being larger and more powerful. The cost of processing work on a server computer is higher than on a client, so some work may be performed on the client machines as required and feasible.

Types of Cooperative Processing

Host-Based Processing

Front-end processing involves host applications sending user interface information to client workstations as if these workstations were simple host terminals. A workstation application reads host computer transmissions by calling an application program interface resident on the workstation (Figure 17.1a). Host user interface data are mapped to fields on the workstation user interface screens. Then the workstation application may proceed to edit and process the input from the user. Once a transaction has been completed, the workstation application must move data from the workstation user interface back into host transaction fields and send the data back to the host using host terminal emulation. This type of processing is more advanced than simple dumb terminal processing. Not much is gained from this type of processing, since most of the work is still done on the host. Still, the workstation user interface can be tailored to the user in ways that the host terminal interface cannot be.

Peer-to-Peer Processing

With this type of processing, two computers share the work load as if the two were equivalent computers (even though one could be a workstation computer and another a powerful mainframe computer). One computer typically handles the user interface processing while the other computer handles database processing. The two may share parts of the application processing. This type of processing can be modeled as objects communicating with messages (Figure 17.1b).

Workstation-Based Processing

With this type of cooperative processing, a workstation program captures all user interface information, processes the information much the same as any other application program would and then translates some or all of the database or file information into a format that can be used on a host computer. This transaction or query can then be shipped to one or more host computers using ordinary communications lines but acting as if the host computers are the local database and file managers (Figure 17.1c). The workstation environment can then act as a control center to process data from multiple host computers. This approach loads most of the application pro-

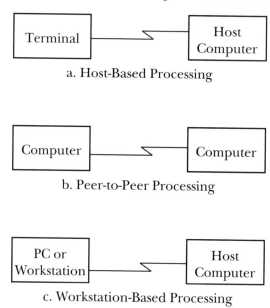

a. Host-Based Processing

b. Peer-to-Peer Processing

c. Workstation-Based Processing

Figure 17.1   Types of cooperative processing

cessing on the client workstations, so it can save processing costs avoided on the host. It typically requires a more powerful workstation if multiple complex applications are to operate simultaneously. If only one application is used by the workstation user at a time, then a less costly workstation may be used.

Downsizing

Many organizations implement cooperative processing solutions in order to take advantage of smaller, more cost-effective computers. This is often referred to as *downsizing*, or euphemistically, *rightsizing*. Rightsizing can also refer to migration from smaller computers to larger ones as an organization's information processing needs grow, but most often the trend is from large to small computers. The more powerful small computers are often used on LANs as servers and the less powerful workstations are used as clients. Together, these systems may be implemented in a formal client/server architecture.

Downsizing may involve the migration of complete applications or just some parts of these applications from large, centralized host computers to networks of smaller decentralized computer systems. The smaller computers offer not only reduced costs but improved user interfaces and multitasking flexibility. The main limitation to downsizing seems to be the large investment most large organizations have in host-based applications and the necessary training, hardware and software costs of moving to smaller networked computers.

The costs to break up large, centralized applications and databases into smaller, distributed ones can be significant. If object models are used to analyze, design and implement client/server architectures, the partitioning of functions among distributed processes becomes somewhat easier—each major class could be implemented on a different logical server, and this architecture can be extended to one or more physical servers.

Workstation hardware and software are significantly less expensive than mainframe technology in many cases. However, distributed computer systems of any size may require more support due to the multiple sites involved. As network management systems become more sophisticated, this support issue will become moot. Development costs on the workstations tend to be much less expensive today.

As mentioned earlier in the section of this chapter on distributed databases, distributed network systems tend to reflect more accurately organizational structure and functioning than do centralized systems. A business enterprise is a collection of separate operating units. Downsized distributed systems can often fit the individual needs of organization units better than the large host-based systems. Microcomputer-based systems can be scaled to reflect the size and scope of organization units. This works best with smaller organization units, of course, so coordination between many individual nodes in a network can become a problem. This is not a problem with applications that only address a small organization unit and not the enterprise as a whole.

Large host-based systems are best for application systems that require very large databases and/or around-the-clock communications. Reliability of mainframe computers is largely unsurpassed. Extremely large communications networks and data storage requirements will still be served best by mainframes for the future. Checkpoint/restart and other reliability features of mainframe operating systems and databases must be available on smaller computers in order to justify moving mission-critical systems to LANs of microcomputers. Performance of mainframes cannot be matched for many types of applications.

Downsizing has evolved from centralized batch processing on host computers to centralized online host processing with data manager and video displays. Then it moved into distributed dialog management by transferring requests and data from hosts to terminals. File servers provide connection to a server (the back-end), perhaps a host-based system and transfer data files to a client (the front-end). Both the back-end and front-end have the application and database management system running. Database server architecture provides a DBMS operating on a host server computer to provide data for client applications. Many downsized systems today are implemented using client/server architecture, where parts of the application execute on different computers. Various types of servers are available in such an architecture, providing services to applications in the form of data services, communications services, printing services and computation services.

To be successful at downsizing, model the proposed system as a network of application, database and communications objects. (Actually, this is a good idea even if the system is to remain centralized for the future.) This will position you to easily identify areas where physical partitioning can take place. Object modeling provides a natural, logical partitioning before physical partitioning is performed.

First, identify applications that are well suited for easy and quick implementation in the new environment. Then, just as with any other new and important technology, obtain management commitment. This is crucial. Then evaluate the existing and future technology bases. Existing development staff will need to be moved away from traditional development and maintenance and into the new world of workstations and LANs. This transition can be difficult for individuals and organizations, so be prepared with adequate planning and education.

Finally, be realistic. As with object orientation in general, don't try to do too much too soon. Focus on providing real business benefits first and learning the new technologies second (unless given a specific mission to build pilot systems for the sake of examining the possibilities of the new technologies).

17.3 NETWORKING

Connectivity

Communication between computers is defined by connectivity, which defines specific protocols to be used to send and receive messages. Cooperative processing needs transparent connectivity between computing platforms.

Various types of networks are used to implement connectivity concepts. These networks include, among others, local and wide area networks. Network architectures include IBM Systems Network Architecture (SNA), Integrated Services Digital Network (ISDN), X.25 and Open Systems Interconnection (OSI).

LANs are used to connect together workstations in one building or group of buildings. The distances between nodes in the network are limited (hence the "local" part of the name). WANs are often used to support communications between widely separated computers, even worldwide, and usually with larger computers. WAN technology has been in use for a long time and so is more mature and reliable than LAN technology.

LAN technology includes several different architectures (see the next section), the most common being star, ring or bus. An LAN is a group of microcomputers connected by cables and networking software. In a typical LAN configuration, one computer acts as a server, the center of the network (or that part of the network). Other (usually less powerful) computers are used as nodes that store and execute programs.

There are two main types of WANs: packet-switched and T-1 multiplexing. Packet-switched networks are used a lot with value-added networks, wherein extra information is added to packets of data passing through the network. T-1 uses time division multiplexing.

SNA is IBM's data communications architecture that defines protocol levels for communications between terminals or workstations and application programs. ISDN is a standard for constructing global digital communications networks. It uses digital signals to achieve a very large bandwidth. Data are still sent over a telephone network, so no new cabling need be installed. X.25 is an international standard for connecting to packet-switched networks. OSI is a set of international standard protocols and services that are represented as a seven-layer communications model. It was developed by the International Standards Organization (ISO). This model works from application software down to hardware and includes layers for application, presentation, session, transport, network data link and physical links. Each layer represents a distinct communications function.

Network Topologies

Basic network topologies are star, ring and bus (see Figure 17.2). Other topologies can be created from these basic ones as needed. The star topology uses cables connected to a central server node out to each client node, like

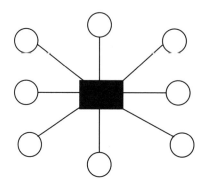

a. Star Topology

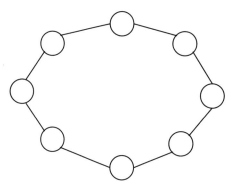

b. Ring Topology

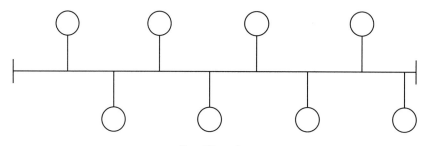

c. Bus Topology

Figure 17.2   Network topologies

the spokes of a wheel. The server sends a message to each client node, asking that node if it has any data to transmit. If yes, the data are transmitted immediately. If there are no data to send for that node, the server continues polling around the points of the star, asking each client node for data to transmit.

The benefits of using a star topology are that it is easy to add nodes to the network and to identify wiring problems, and it is cost-effective for a small network with short spans of cable. Weaknesses of this topology include that the central server is the single point of failure—if a server fails, client nodes will not be polled for data—and that in some configurations, adding client nodes is expensive because a new cable must be run from the client all the way to the central server.

A ring topology uses a single cable running through each network node, linking these nodes sequentially to the main server. A software token is passed from node to node, carrying a single packet of data at one time. As this packet passes by a client node, the client checks the packet to see if any data are addressed to that node. If the packet is empty, the node can attach some data to be transmitted to another node. Each client node needs to wait for an empty token in order to transmit data.

The advantages of a ring topology are that it is deterministic—rules establish the time period that each node can control the token—and that it can be made more reliable—multiple nodes can be connected to a node used as a multistation access unit to bypass a failed node.

The disadvantage of a ring topology is that network response time degrades as the number of nodes increases (only one packet of data is on the ring at a time when a token-passing protocol is used).

A bus topology is implemented using a single cable shared by all devices on the network. This cable is not connected at the ends but rather closed with bus terminators. This architecture uses a contention protocol called carrier sense multiple access (CSMA) to detect traffic on the network. Data are not sent if traffic is detected, but rather only when there is no traffic. Two nodes may detect no traffic and begin to transmit simultaneously, causing a collision of data. When this occurs, a node will stop transmitting and wait a random time period before retransmitting.

An advantage of the bus topology is wiring simplicity—only one wire is used with two terminators. Disadvantages of the bus topology include a single point of failure—if the bus fails, nodes past the failure point cannot communicate—and response time degrades with increases in traffic due to increased collisions.

Advantages of LANs

An LAN allows microcomputers to share printers, plotters, network gateways and other peripheral devices. Services the network supplies are selected beyond simple device sharing to electronic mail, corporate database access and shared applications. Sharing applications and databases means that users of client machines do not need to swap diskettes in order to share information. Networked versions of microcomputer software often cost much less per user than stand-alone packages. Backup and restore operations on shared databases are much easier to manage with a shared server on a network. Also, the memory requirements of client workstations may be much less if a power server can handle intensive data management functions.

Network Management

Because of the trend to downsize large information systems to networks of interconnected smaller computers, management of network hardware and software will become much more important in the future. Network management needs to be planned in order to be most effective. Potential problems need to be detected and resolved, and recurring problems need to be addressed. Network modification and repair requests need to be tracked. Performance needs must be tracked and adjusted. Reports need to be generated and distributed. Setting up network devices and software utilities as objects can provide a network manager with a powerful means to manage "smart" network objects that send and receive messages to and from the operator.

17.4 CLIENT/SERVER ARCHITECTURE

Client/server computing involves servicing requests from one computer (the client) via a second computer (the server). This type of computing allocates certain computing functions to clients, usually on an LAN, and other functions to one or more servers, either on an LAN or on a larger network. A client may process application programs and the user interface and the server might be a terminal server, file server, database server, disk server, mail server, communications server or even a display server (for sophisticated graphics functions). Figure 17.3 depicts a client/server contract. Figure 17.4 lists client/server partnership characteristics.

Figure 17.3   A client/server contract

The Client/Server Model

With a more traditional file server system, a client workstation has a database management system and user interface function resident in it. The file server contains file management software and certain files to be stored and managed. A client requests a file or files from the file server, which sends the contents of a file. The client database management software processes the file. The file server allows clients to share and manage files centrally and needs very fast disk drives and file access methods to be efficient. Figure 17.5 lists characteristcs.

A client/server system, on the other hand, has the user interface in the client and only database requests are sent to a database server. All database processing is performed on the server machine, with only the necessary data records sent to the client (not entire files unless so requested).

Services
- A server is a provider of services
- A client is a consumer of services
- The client/server model provides a clean separation of function based on service

Shared resources
- A server can service many clients at the same time and regulate access to shared resources

Asymmetric protocols
- A many-to-one relationship exists between clients and a server
- Clients always initiate a dialog by requesting a service
- Servers passively wait for requests from clients

Figure 17.4   Client/server partnerships—characteristics of client/server architectures

Transparency of location
  • A server is a process that can reside on the same machine as the client or on a different machine across a network
  • Client/server software usually masks the location of the server from clients by redirecting service calls when needed

Hardware and operating system independence
  • Ideally, client/server software is independent of hardware or operating systems
  • There should exist the capability to mix and match client and server platforms

Message-based coupling
  • Clients and servers are loosely coupled systems that interact through a message-passing mechanism
  • A message is the way that service requests and replies are delivered

Encapsulation of services
  • A server is a specialist
  • A message tells a server what service is being requested; the server decides how to get the job done
  • Services may be upgraded without affecting clients as long as the published message interface remains unchanged

Scalability
  • Client/server systems may be scaled horizontally or vertically
  • Horizontal scaling refers to the addition or removal of client workstations with only a slight performance impact
  • Vertical scaling refers to the migration to a larger and faster server machine or multiple servers

Integrity of code and data
  • Server code and data are centrally maintained
  • Maintenance is less costly
  • Shared data integrity is maintained more easily

Figure 17.4 (continued)   Client/server partnerships—characteristics   of   client/server architectures

Services
Shared resources
Asymmetric protocols
Transparency of location
Hardware and operating system independence
Message-based coupling
Encapsulationg of services
Scalability
Integrity of code and data

Figure 17.5   Client/server architectures—characteristics

Today, an implementation of the client/server model needs to have a user-friendly GUI as well as most or all of the application logic on the client. The client usually initiates actions. The client and a server must be distinct from each other yet they need to interact seamlessly. They need to be able to operate on different computing platforms but can reside on the same computer. A server needs to be capable of serving multiple clients simultaneously. A database server should provide functions such as security, backup, recovery, database query and data integrity protection. Finally, the system needs to be able to communicate over an LAN, WAN and other networks.

In order to write transparent, portable client/server applications, developers must be able to isolate application development from any one computing platform. Object-oriented development provides this platform independence via encapsulation and information hiding, and client/server development requires it. Three components are essential to any client/server application: data access, processing and interfaces. Data access includes the user interface and stored data access. Processing includes business processing logic. Interfaces link services with other applications. The separation of these components leads to a development of one component that is isolated from the other technology layers. Each layer isolates technology characteristics of that layer from the other layers.

Types of Client/Server Processes

Client/server architecture defines that each application is implemented in two parts: a client task (any task communicating with the user) and a server task (any other task that communicates with client tasks and/or other server tasks). Such an architecture has several components. Major services include

Typical clients:
   • User window process
   • Workstation application
   • Host application

Types of servers:
   • Application server
   • Database server
   • Transaction server
   • File server

Typical servers:
   • Print server
   • Graphics server
   • Mail server
   • Communications server
   • Network server

Figure 17.6   Typical client/servers

presentation, client, distribution, server and database functions. Figure 17.6 lists typical clients and servers. Figures 17.7 through 17.10 discuss the characteristics of some servers.

Presentation services include user interaction, memory management and user dialog control.

   • A server may itself be a client for some system functions.
   • An application may consist of numerous "contracts" involving many clients and many servers.
   • A "contract" between objects consists of one or more "collaborations." The contract between two objects is defined by the set of requests that a client can make of a server.
   • A "collaboration" between objects consists of a stimulus (request) and a response (action).
   • Collaborations and contracts can be modeled using state-transition models.

Figure 17.7   Client/server architectures—characteristics

- A client passes a request for file records over a network to a file server.
- This is a very primitive form of data service requiring many message exchanges over the network.

Figure 17.8   File servers—characteristics

- A client passes database requests as messages to a database server.
- Only the final results are returned to the client over the network.
- Database request code and data reside on the same machine.
- This allows the server to use its own processing power to find the requested data (no need to pass all records back to client, as with a file server).
- Server code is packaged by the DBMS vendor but code must often be written for client applications.

Figure 17.9   Database servers—characteristics

- A client invokes remote procedures that reside on a server, which also contains a database engine.
- Remote procedures on the server execute database calls as units of work (transactions).
- Applications are created by writing code for both client and server components.
- This is also referred to as on-line transaction processing (OLTP).
- Used for mission-critical applications requiring 1–3 second response all of the time.
- This requires tight controls over database security and integrity.
- Communication overhead is kept to a minimum—an exchange is a single request/reply pair (not multiple database calls).
- This requires a peer-to-peer protocol to issue calls to remote procedures and obtain results.

Figure 17.10   Transaction servers—characteristics

- Developers supply code for client and server.
- An application server is not necessarily database centered, unlike transaction servers.
- This is a general-purpose, customizable network application using the client/server model.

Figure 17.11   Application servers

Client services include:

Data capture
Client front-end functions (user interface event handling and error handling)
Shared data management
Session management
Security

Distribution services include:

Program-to-program communication
Message management
Protocol enforcement
Location of network resources

Server functions include:

Multiuser processing
Server front-end functions (messaging, recovery, error handling)
Security
Database isolation

Database services include:

Data integrity and recovery
Security
Accounting and chargeback
Performance tuning

Application isolation
Multiuser locking

Client tasks work with GUIs and need to format screen presentations and user actions in response, manage dialogs between systems and users and determine capabilities of servers. Clients also need to determine which server to send a task to. Different types of servers might be print servers, facsimile servers, database and file servers, computational servers, communications servers and application servers.

To gain the greatest benefit from client/server architectures, the environment should include such major technologies as:

Distributed databases that support synchronized multiuser updates
Application development tools for applications that work synchronously and dynamically as well as perform on heterogeneous process architectures
Communications processes that operate independent of underlying network topologies

17.5 CLIENT CHARACTERISTICS

The Client's Role

As stated earlier, a client is primarily a user of services provided by one or more server tasks. The client/server model clearly separates functions based on client and server roles. A client (or server) may act as a client at one moment in time and then as a server at another moment in time. A client always will provide presentation services to users, probably in the form of a GUI. A GUI supports windows and allows a client user to conduct several simultaneous tasks in multiple sessions.

At present, Microsoft Windows and Macintosh system software do not support true multitasking—they only execute one task at a time in a communications session. OS/2 and the various versions of UNIX are preemptive multitasking operating systems and support any number of active communications sessions (limited only by physical memory constraints).

Client system software provides such facilities as Dynamic Data Exchange (DDE) and Object Level Embedding (OLE) that support cut-and-paste operations for spreadsheets, graphics and text between user windows. A client workstation can act as both a client and server when all needed information and processing logic for a request are resident and operable within the client workstation. Software that supports user interface functions of field editing, context-sensitive help, navigation, local data storage and manipulation are usually executed on the client workstation using GUI functionality if available. Business processing logic can also reside in the client workstation.

A client workstation needs to have its own operating system, which can be the same or different from that of one or more servers. For full client/server functionality, this client operating system needs to be more powerful than simple personal computer operating systems have been in the past. Typically, the operating systems suitable for supporting powerful client functions include OS/2 and UNIX. X-terminals (or their equivalent functions running in OS/2 or UNIX environments) also can be considered as client workstation operating systems due to their powerful windowing and session management capabilities.

Client Services

Traditional host applications that use a client for presentation services only send and receive character data streams to and from a server. All logic for the application resides on the server. The host processor is used to handle functions that probably should be placed on the workstation.

Some client/server applications today allow input and output data streams to be reformatted at the client with no change to the host applications. These use an application programming interface that defines the data stream formats. GUIs may add additional functionality that does not require changes to host applications. The added functions might include allowing for selection of input items from a list, selective use of color or merging of other data into the presentation. GUIs allow users to be more productive with less training on the application (but initial training on the interface system itself) because the interface is more intuitive.

Client functionality can be further enhanced by adding logic not implemented in host server applications. This logic might handle local editing, automatic data entry, help and other processes. When errors are detected at the client, or help functions off-loaded to the client, host server workloads decrease and client functions become more powerful.

17.6 SERVER CHARACTERISTICS

The Server's Role

Servers provide services in the form of applications, file and database access, printing, fax and image processing, communications, security and systems and network management. Application services can be provided for part or all of a business process invoked through a remote procedure call. Groups of application servers may work together to provide an entire business process. As mentioned earlier, different servers may be running different operating systems on different hardware and may use different database software. A client may request the services of these servers without knowing what the underlying server technologies are.

A file server provides record-level data to nondatabase applications. Storage space is allocated and free space managed by the server. Catalog functions are provided to support file naming and directory structures. Stored programs are often loaded from a file server for execution on a client or host server.

Database servers are management by a database management system. A file server provides initial space and the database management software allocates space for database components within the space provided by the file server. Database services provide automatic backup and recovery, space management within files, database reorganization, record locking, deadlock detection and database management.

Print servers support the receiving, queueing, prioritizing and printer driver execution for documents sent from clients. Print servers must be able to support different types of printers, including printer control and error recovery. Facsimile servers work like print servers but also support queueing for delayed distribution of documents. These servers must support compression and decompression for client facsimile document distribution, printing and display.

Communications servers support WAN communications. This includes support for a wide range of synchronous and asynchronous protocols. Security must be provided on the communications server to restrict access to programs and data stored on the server. Systems and network management services for WANs must be provided from a central location.

Server Functions

Functions provided by servers in a client/server environment include:

- File services
- Fax/print/image services
- Database services
- Communications services
- Security services

File services handle data accesses to virtual directories and files placed on a client workstation and on permanent servers. All file requests are mapped into a virtual pool of resources and redirected as necessary to an appropriate local or remote server. File services provide this support at the remote server. Software, shared data, databases and backup data are usually stored on storage devices managed by the file server.

Application software should be loaded from the file server for execution on clients. New versions are placed on the server and immediately made available to all clients using that server. Backups of programs and data at the server can be managed by dedicated support staff, and client workstations can also be backed up from the server.

Fax/print/image services involve centralized, shared use of high-quality printers, workstation generated facsimile images and other graphics generating devices. A server accepts requests from many clients, queues these requests according to their priority and handles their assignments to available devices. Facsimile requests can be queued at the server and transmitted to clients immediately or upon requests. The work queues are maintained by a supervisor at the server that can determine how best to distribute the work. Paper mail or other documents can be converted to electronic images and then routed to clients through a network rather than through the ordinary mail. Images can be captured once and then made available for multiple users immediately.

Database servers evolved from file servers. The database management software initially executed on the clients and used file services to gain access to records and free space. Concurrent access control is managed by application programs and by the database server. File access is at the record level, so all records satisfying a search criterion are returned to the client workstation. Database management requires significant programming support for back-out and recovery after a system failure.

More powerful database systems can execute database requests issued from client workstations. File services are used for space allocation and basic directory services but all other services are managed by the database server itself. These more powerful database server systems rival those found on large mainframe systems.

Communications services support communications on LANs and WANs. LAN services are built into the network operating systems; WAN services are implemented in communications server software. Security services require users to log into the network with user ID and password. These may be encrypted, and users may be required to change their passwords routinely.

END NOTES

[1] Atre, Shaku. *Distributed Databases, Cooperative Processing and Networking* (New York: McGraw-Hill) 1992, p. 25.

[2] Ibid., p. 33.

18

Object-Oriented Systems Architecture

18.1 DESIGN AN OBJECT-ORIENTED SYSTEMS ARCHITECTURE

After a set of object-oriented analysis and design models has been built, an overall systems architecture can be constructed. All models need to fit together so that the systems built are reasonably well integrated. An overall information system architecture can provide this kind of integration, but it requires planning before and during development of business and systems models. The information system development profession can gain valuable insights from other, more mature disciplines. John Zachman, formerly of IBM and now an independent consultant, wrote a pivotal paper on information systems architecture. This section of this chapter highlights the key points from Zachman's paper. Please refer to the original paper for details.[1]

When searching for ways to develop a framework for information systems architecture, start by examining classical architecture. The first model that an architect develops is a simple conceptual representation of a building (Zachman calls this a "bubble chart"), which depicts in very simple terms the size, shape, spatial relationships and basic intent of the structure to be built. This conceptual model begins with the initial conversions between the architect and the prospective owner of the building.

A very simple model is built first because the owner must express what he or she wants the building to be used for, and second because the architect needs to convince the owner that the owner's wants are understood enough that the owner will pay for the modeling to follow. This process serves to initiate the building project. Once the owner has a basic understanding of the building, the architect proceeds to the next set of deliverables, the architect's drawings.

Architect's drawings transcribe the owner's perceptions into drawings for floor plans, cutaways and pictures. These drawings help the owner to agree or disagree on what was in mind for the building. Sometimes, these drawings are very detailed, but are developed only in enough detail that the prospective owner can understand and approve or disapprove the designs so far. When the owner agrees that the drawings represent the desired result, the architect can develop the next set of deliverables, the architect's plans.

Architect's plans translate the owner's perceptions into a modeled product. They represent a designer's view of the final product. The plans represent the owner's view. Designer plans specify explicitly the material composition of the building. The plans describe various material relationships as diagrams and include lists of materials to be used. Architect's plans represent the final deliverables constructed by the architect. They form the basis for owner negotiation with a general building contractor. During these negotiations, the plans may need modifications due to cost and other issues, but serve to depict what is committed to be constructed.

Contractor's plans redraw the architect's plans to generate a builder's perspective of the project. They are developed in order to help manage the development of the complex product. Some phased development is required over time and technology constraints may exist. For one home, for example, the site needed to be specially prepared for a walk-out basement. The plans depicted the elevations required for the foundation, which had to be constructed in stages. Contractor's plans are used to depict various categories of development so that the work may be divided among subcontractors.

The subcontractors are presented with shop plans and drawings of parts or subsections represented out of the context of what will be actually fabricated or assembled. Drawings and architect's and contractor's plans are in context because they deal with the entire project; subcontractor's plans deal only with parts of the project structure.

The final product, of course, is the physical building itself. Figure 18.1 lists the deliverables generated during the process of constructing a building.

Zachman points out that the basic ideas of such a framework are:

Bubble charts	Basic concepts for a building
	Gross sizing, shape and spatial
	  relationships
	Mutual understanding between
	  architect and owner
	Initiate a construction project

Architect's drawings	Building as viewed by the owner Floor plans, cutaways, pictures Agreement between the architect and owner Establish a contract

Contractor's plans	The final product as viewed by the
	  designer
	Translation of the owner's view into
	  a product
	Detailed drawings in 16 categories
	Forms the basis for general contractor
	  negotiation

Contractor's plans	The final product as viewed by the
	  builder
	Architect's plans constrained by nature
	  and technology
	Describes how to build
	Directs construction activities

Shop plans	A subcontractor's view of a part or section Detailed stand-alone model Specification of what is to be built Forms a pattern
Building	The final product

Figure 18.1   Architectural deliverables for constructing a building

- There is a set of architectural representations produced over the process of building a complex engineering product representing the different perspectives of the different participants.

	Data Description	Process Description	Network Description
Scope Description (Ballpark View)	List of entities important to the business	List of processes the business performs	List of locations in which the business operates
Model of the Business (Owner's View)	E.G., Entity/Relationship Diagram	E.G., Functional Flow Diagram	E.G., Logistic Network
Model of the Information System (Designer's View)	E.G., Data Model	E.G., Data Flow Diagram	E.G., Distributed Systems Architecture
Technology Model (Builder's View)	E.G., Data Design	E.G., Structure Chart	E.G., System Architecture
Detailed Description (Out-of-Context View)	E.G., Database Description	E.G., Program	E.G., Network Architecture
Actual System	Data	Function	Communications

Figure 18.2   An information systems architecture

- The same product can be described, for different purposes, in different ways, resulting in different types of description.

For each type of description, there are different perspectives (and different representations) for each of the different participants in the project. For materials, functions and locations, there are owner, designer and builder perspectives. Zachman's framework for an information systems architecture (Figure 18.2) describes the same kinds of processes and deliverables for information systems. At the higher levels are the simpler, broader models and at the bottom are the more detailed, narrower models.

	Structure (Data)	Function (Process)	Behavior (Process)	Network
Objectives/ Scope	Class	Class of Process	Business Event	Business Locations
Model of the Business	Class Model -Object Types -Object Subtypes	Function Model -Class Protocols -Message Connections	Business Event Model -Event Type -Business Cycle	-Business Units -Business Relationships/Flaws
Model of the Info. System	Class Structure Model -Classes -Associations	Object Function -Methods -Messages	Event Model -Events -Class Life Cycle	-I/S Functions -Line Characteristics
Technology Model	Class Design -Class Structures -Object Identifiers (Keys)	Method Design -Models -Integrity rules	Event Designer -State Transaction -Life cycle rules	Hardware System Software -Line Specifications
Detailed Representation	Class Structure Specs. -Attributes -Addresses	Method Specs -Language statements -Message parameters	Event Specification -Trigger -Clock cycle	-Address -Protocols
Functioning System	Classes	Methods	Events	

Figure 18.3   An object-oriented information systems architecture

This framework is important because each element on either axis of the matrix is explicitly distinguishable from all other elements on that axis. The participant views are different from each other, but so are the descriptions of materials (data), functions (processes) and locations. What models belong in each cell of the matrix can be defined precisely. Zachman's framework can be extended further to support the models discussed in this book and in other object-oriented modeling methodologies. This extended framework represents object structures, processes, behavior and locations. An example of such a framework is shown in Figure 18.3.

Even without building an object-oriented information systems architecture in the near future, there are a few things that can be done to move existing systems in that direction:

- Minimize data redundancy—in the data definitions if not the actual instances.

- Develop sharable data building blocks—build subject databases encapsulated with essential data management logic.

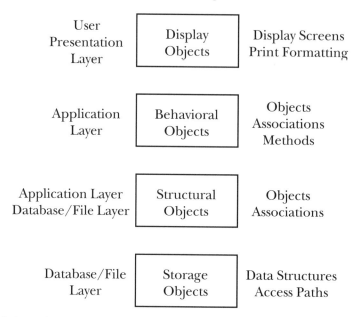

Figure 18.4   Information systems architecture layers

- Separate data access and integrity management logic from business application processing logic.
- Establish standard documentation for all databases, applications, user presentations, communications, etc.—focus on data definitions first.

Any information systems architecture should strive to separate systems components into distinct processing categories, if not explicit object classes. Information systems can then be viewed as assemblies of components from the various systems architecture layers:

- Database/file layer
- User presentation layer
- Application layer
- Communications layer

Figure 18.4 shows how the first three of these layers fit together conceptually. The communications layer would connect objects together across multiple locations in a network. Separating just these basic systems components from each other using standard interfaces can greatly improve systems quality, especially in the maintenance of the systems. Definitions of model components and systems architecture layer components should be placed in an enterprise repository or dictionary so that systems integration across the enterprise is at least feasible.

Achieving true systems integration is proving to be very difficult while managing very old legacy systems. Systems must fit together better. This author feels very strongly that organizations need to evolve systems toward a formal information systems architecture. An object-oriented architecture seems to provide great benefits, if only in the organization of problem and solution domains. Actual systems that are constructed need not be fully object-oriented but only conceived of, analyzed and designed with object orientation in mind.

18.2 THE OBJECT MANAGEMENT GROUP

In order to make full use of object models, specifications and system components, industry standards are needed that allow classes in one system to interact with those in other systems. Support for multiple computing platforms, database management systems, networking interfaces, user interfaces and programming languages is also needed. Development tools must be consistent in the way that models are built and systems generated. One organization, the Object Management Group (OMG) is, at the time of this writing, developing industry standards for just this need.

OMG is a nonprofit, international trade organization funded by close to 200 computer hardware and software suppliers. It is dedicated to maximizing the interoperability, portability and reusability of software components. To date, OMG is the leader in producing an object framework and specifications for commercially available object environments. This organization provides a reference architecture with terms and definitions upon which all specifications are based. OMG creates industry standards for commercially available object systems, focusing on remote object network access, encapsulating existing applications and object database interfaces. It provides an open forum for industry and education and for promotion of endorsed object technologies. Systems built should use a methodology that supports modular software creation, reuse, integration across groups of developers, computing platforms and enhanced system maintenance.

18.3 OBJECT MANAGEMENT ARCHITECTURE

OMG has developed a reference model for an object management architecture, the goal of which is to enable heterogeneous software to interoperate. This model should influence design only to achieve interoperability and encompasses:

- How objects send and receive requests and responses,
- Basic operations needed for each object and
- Object interfaces for common facilities.

The object management architecture is composed of four parts:

- Application objects
- Common facilities
- Object services
- Object request broker

Figure 18.5 shows a graph of these object management architecture components.

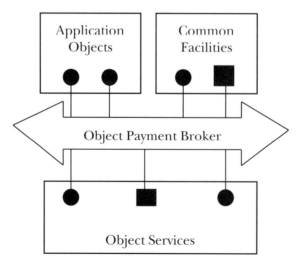

Figure 18.5   Object management architecture

Application objects are applications designed for end use and may originate from a variety of sources. Common facilities consist of objects and classes that supply general-purpose functions in other applications:

- Class and object cataloging and browsing
- Link management
- User interfaces
- Printing
- Error reporting
- Help
- Electronic mail
- Training
- Remote information repository access
- Agent facilities
- External system interfaces
- Object querying
- User preferences/profiles

Object services is composed of services that provide basic object maintenance:

- Class management for class definitions, class interfaces and relationships between class definitions (create, modify, delete, copy, distribute, describe, control)
- Management of class instances and their relationships (create, modify, delete, copy, move, invoke, control)
- Storage of objects and their state and methods (permanent storage, transient storage)
- Integrity of objects and groups of objects
- Security access definition and enforcement
- Query of classes and objects
- Version control (store, correlate, manage)

The object request broker allows for object intercommunication, independent of computing platform and techniques. Its purpose is to guarantee object interoperation, whether on the same node in a network, working as clients or servers or on heterogeneous computers. An object generates request messages using a standard format and the object request broker induces some method invocation and conveys results to the message requester. Below are listed the functions of the object request broker:

- *Name services* maps object names from requester domain to/from method execution domain. It does not require unique or universal object names, and it uses request object names to locate the method to perform. The location may involve simple attribute lookups. Usually, different object systems or domains will contain local object naming schemes.

- *Request dispatch* determines which method to invoke. It does not require a request to be delivered to a specific destination. A request may go to a method that operates on object state variables as parameters or to an object in the parameter list.

- *Parameter encoding* conveys local representation of requester parameter values to equivalent for recipient. It may employ standards or de facto standards.

- *Delivery* uses standard transport protocols to deliver requests and results. The location may be characterized by a node, address space, thread or entry point.

- *Synchronization* handles object parallelism in request generation and processing. Synchronization may be asynchronous, synchronous or deferred synchronous.

- *Activation* performs housekeeping before method invocation. It activates and deactivates persistent objects in order to obtain object state for object access. For nonobject facilities, explicit requests can be made to objects to activate and deactivate themselves.

- *Exception handling* reports to requester/recipient any failures of object location. Actions include session resource recovery and resynchronization of requester and recipient.

- *Security mechanisms* ensure secure movement of requests among objects, as well as the identities of requesting and receiving objects, threads, address spaces, nodes and communication routes. They assure the integrity of data being moved and enforce access and licensing policies.

18.4 STANDARDIZED MESSAGING

For smooth interaction between objects, objects must send and receive messages in a standard way. The OMB object management architecture provides definitions for message request and response formats. Each request must name an operation and include necessary parameter values and identify specific objects as needed. Requests may be sent to the object request broker for processing and conveyance to the requester. The object request broker may need to interface with object services to locate a class and method requested. Object services, in turn, might utilize a class dictionary service or search run-time method libraries.

18.5 INTERFACING TO TRADITIONAL SYSTEMS

Most organizations today have a large stockpile of existing systems and components that must be integrated with any new object systems. The existing software to be integrated with objects might be database management systems, applications, communications subsystems and the like. Object Management Architecture's object services and application objects support nonobject systems.

Object interfaces must be provided to process object requests in standard format (see Chapter 14 for a discussion of object interfaces and object wrapping). When such interfaces are built around nonobject software components, existing components can utilize the object management architecture. This architecture does not define a specific user interface for end users, so a variety of user interfaces can be used. OMG does not address this type of standardization yet. User interfaces need to interact with the object request broker with standard message formats.

END NOTES

[1] Zachman, John A. "A Framework for Information Systems Architecture." *IBM Systems Journal*, vol. 26, no. 3.

Glossary

Abstract Class. A class that contains no attribute types. Usually this class is a high-level representation of a generic concept that has no information stored about it but which acts as a superclass of several concrete classes.

Aggregation Hierarchy. A hierarchy of classes that depicts how components are assembled into a higher-level object. An aggregation hierarchy describes "part of" relationships, whereas the higher-level objects are completely described by all of their components. Contrast with a **generalization hierarchy**, which depicts "type of" relationships and inheritance.

Analysis Phase. Within an information engineering methodology, a detailed analysis of components of a business that is conducted within a defined business area prior to the design of systems that support this part of the business.

Association. A link between two objects used to capture information about the relationship between those objects. In planning, associations may be built among such objects as goals, processes, entities, critical success factors, functions, etc.

Attribute Type. Attributes are the components of an **object** that describe that object. Examples include name, address, phone.

Behavioral Requirements. System requirements that specify inputs (system stimuli), outputs (system responses) and behavioral relationships between inputs and outputs. Behavioral requirements are sometimes referred to as functional or operational requirements.

Business Area. A portion of an entire business enterprise that is modeled as a set of highly processes and entity types. A business area can form the scope of an analysis project during the **analysis phase** of information engineering.

Business Area Analysis. A set of development activities conducted to analyze a specific area of a business to model business information requirements. Ideally, this analysis effort begins with the output of a planning study such as that conducted during an **information strategy planning** study.

Business Event. An occurrence of something significant, initiated by an entity external to an information system, which triggers a business process (in a business analysis model) or system process (in a system design model) to form a response. See also **system event**.

Business Function. A set of business activities (processes) that act together to support completely one aspect of furthering an enterprise's mission.

Business Process. A set of one or more business activities that has a specific beginning point and end point (as opposed to a **business function**, which is ongoing without specific beginning and end points). Functions are composed of processes and higher-level processes are composed of lower-level processes. The lowest level processes (variously referred to as fundamental, atomic or sequential) implement a basic business task such as calculating sales tax for a customer order. Order processing (a low-level function) consists of a set of processes beginning with processing an individual order (a high-level process) down to processes such as calculating order sales tax and order totals.

Business Process Redesign. A set of analysis techniques for examining business processes for ways to improve those processes. Also referred to as business process reengineering.

Business Systems Design. A set of activities conducted during the **design phase** of development to transform business system requirements into designs for a computer system that will support those requirements.

Cardinality. Contrast with **optionality**, which defines the minimum number of **instances** (occurrences) of one **object** (entity) that can exist for one **instance** (occurrence) of another object (entity).

Class. A class is an **object** into which similar objects can be grouped together. Each object in the group of objects shares both **instance variables** and **methods** with other objects in the group.

Class Hierarchy. A class hierarchy defines a parent-child relationship between **subclasses** and one or more **superclasses**.

Class Method. A method that belongs to a **class** itself. Such a method is typically used to allocate new instances of the class or to report on the number of instances of the class that currently exist. A class method is accessible by all instances of the class and is defined only once—in the class definition.

Class Variable. A variable (attribute) that belongs to a class. This variable can be referenced by either a **class method** or an **instance method**. It is global to the class and all of its subclasses.

Client. An **object** or **subsystem** that requests system services from another object or subsystem. A client may sometimes act as a **server** for other clients. In a client/server system, the client may represent a combination of hardware and software components that request particular services to be performed on its behalf from another system entity.

Cohesion. A measure of how closely related tasks performed by a module or process are. Systems should exhibit high cohesion within modules or processes and low **coupling** between modules or **processes**.

Collaboration. Cooperation between **classes** to achieve some goal. Often, classes collaborate by delegating work to the most appropriate classes in order to perform a requested service for a **client**. Collaboration is a form of **reuse** and is often used more than **inheritance**.

Concrete Class. A class that contains **attribute types** and which therefore has information recorded about it. A concrete class will have specific instances of the class that exist in a system that implements the class. Contrast with an **abstract class**, which will not have any actual **instances** created from it. Concrete classes can derive characteristics from an abstract class, so abstract classes can be useful during system modeling and development.

Contract. A client/server agreement between two object classes, one being the **client** (requester of services) and the other being the **server**. In an object-oriented model, a contract represents an abstract of a group of related public responsibilities that are to be provided by **subsystems** and **classes** to their clients. These class responsibilities can be implemented as methods.

Corporate Logical Data Model. A complete set of analysis models that describes an entire enterprise (or significant subset of the enterprise). This would include all **entities**, **attributes** and **relationships**.

Coupling. A measure of the strength of interrelatedness of two modules (design) or processes (analysis). Systems should exhibit low coupling between components and high **cohesion** within components.

Data Dictionary. Often referred to as a repository or encyclopedia, a data dictionary represents a place to store all information about model components defined during planning, analysis, design and construction phases of systems development.

Data Flow Diagram. A graphical depiction of the flow of data into, out of and within an information system. Such a diagram consists of **data stores**, external **entities** (also called external agents or terminators), **processes** and data flows.

Data Hiding. See **encapsulation**.

Data Store. An object on a **data flow diagram** that indicates where data come to rest between **processes**. A data store model is independent of its implementation—it may refer to a file, database, manual file or other place to store data.

Decision Table. A chart that shows logic relating various combinations of processing conditions to a set of actions (decisions). Similar in function to a **decision tree**.

Decision Tree. A graphical chart that shows branching logic relating various combinations of processing conditions to a set of actions (decisions). Similar in function to a **decision table**.

Design Phase. The phase of James Martin's information engineering framework that begins by translating system requirements into system designs and ends by defining in detail how a system should actually be constructed. The method used to conduct work in the design phase is often called **business systems design**. In practice, the **design phase** consists of two separate activities: modeling of the architecture of a system (sometimes called the strategic, high-level, architectural or preliminary design) and modeling of the algorithms for software modules (sometimes called the tactical, low-level, procedural or detailed design).

Domain. In data modeling, the definition of the universe of values that an **attribute type** may contain (the values that any attribute may take on). The domain of an attribute type defines the range or list of possible values and the data types (and possibly output formats) of attribute values.

Elemental Process. The most fundamental process in an analysis model, appearing at the lowest level in a **process decomposition diagram** and at the lowest level in a **data flow diagram**. The elemental process (also referred to as a fundamental or sequential process) should always perform one basic task, and it contains a detailed, step-by-step specification (a mini-specification) of what algorithms and data the process uses to perform its work. In an object-oriented model, an elemental process will likely be an operation, implemented as a method within a class.

Encapsulation. The hiding of data structures behind a wall (a "capsule") of program code. Pure object-oriented programming languages and database management systems prevent data from being accessed except through methods that are defined along with data in object classes.

Enterprise Model. A business model that spans an entire business organization. It is usually defined within the **planning phase** of information engineering and defines the business directions (mission, goals, strategies, critical success factors, critical assumptions), information requirements (subject areas, high-level **classes**, **entity types**, more fundamental classes, relationship types, associations between classes, and **attribute types**) and business activities (functions and processes).

Entity. A fundamental data structure that models a real-world person, place, thing, concept or event. The model of a category of entities is usually called an entity type, while an instance of this type is called an entity occurrence. In an object model, an entity would represent the object data structure, to which procedures called **methods** would be added to form an **object**. (These procedures might be called **operations** in analysis and methods in design and construction.) Entity types are related to each other, and the relationships between entity types (the relationship types) are modeled on an entity-relationship diagram during the data modeling portion of an analysis study.

Event. Some significant occurrence outside a business system that must be responded to by the system. In analysis, a business event may trigger a business process; in design, a system event may trigger execution of a **class method**.

Event Model (Event Schema). A diagram and accompanying text that describes how a business or system event is responded to by a system. Typically, an event triggers more than one process or method, which in turn triggers other processes or methods. The event model maps the route that an event response takes through a system.

Evolutionary Prototype. A mock-up of all or part of a system built to learn more about the problem or its solution. An evolutionary prototype mock-up can then be built on or expanded to become the final system. Also referred to as an evolvable prototype. Contrast with a **throwaway prototype**.

Finite-State Machine. A virtual machine or processor that can be in any one of a set of finite states and whose next states and outputs are functions of input and current states only. A finite state machine is helpful for describing the behavior of a complex system as if it were a single processor.

Functional Decomposition. The breakdown of business functions and activities within an enterprise into progressively increasing detail and decreasing scope. Functions are composed of other functions or processes, and processes are only composed of other processes. See also **process decomposition diagram**.

Generalization Hierarchy. A hierarchy of object classes that depicts hierarchical "type of" relationships between parent and child classes. Contrast with an **aggregation hierarchy**, which models hierarchical "part of" relationships between a parent class and its child components.

Horizontal Object Partitioning. Within a system of distributed objects, it can be helpful to split object data structures along instance lines. By including certain instances of an object in one object fragment and other instances in one or more other object fragments, an object data structure can be split horizontally for distribution purposes.

Implementation Phase. A synonym for the **construction phase** of system development.

Information Hiding. See **encapsulation**.

Information Strategy Planning. The set of methods used to conduct modeling work within the **planning phase** of information engineering. An analyst interacts with business executives and managers to define the enterprise model for a business organization during an information strategy planning study. This enterprise model is then used for building various **business area analysis** models during the **analysis phase**.

Inheritance. The process of obtaining object class characteristics from a **superclass** (supertype) class in a **generalization hierarchy**. In an object-oriented programming language or database management system, the characteristics of a superclass that can be inherited by **subclasses** include **instance variables** (attributes), **instance methods**, **class variables** (attributes) and **class methods**.

Instance. An instance is one of a set of objects that belong to a **class**. Sometimes referred to as an occurrence of a type. In traditional systems, an instance of a file object would be referred to as a record within a file of records.

Instance Method. A **method** in a **class** that is executed when a message is sent to an instance of that class. Contrast with a **class method**, which is executed when a message is sent to the class itself.

Instance Variable. Data within a class instance, listed and named within the class definition, which define a list of instance variables (the attributes of that class instance). Contrast with **class variables**, which belong to the class itself and which are global to the class and its subclasses (if any).

Integration Testing. The stage of the system development life cycle, immediately following unit testing, during which previously unit-tested system components are integrated together to evaluate their functioning. Also referred to as string testing.

Message. A message is a request made to an **object** to perform one of its defined operations in order to transform the object or retrieve information from it. Messages specify what operations are to be performed, not how those operations are to be performed. The receiver of a message determines how an operation is to be performed.

Message Connection. A connection between two **objects** that involves one message. It appears as a message flow on a message flow diagram (in a manner similar to data flows appearing on a **data flow diagram**).

Message Diagram. In this book, a message diagram depicts information flowing between objects in the form of object messages. Such a diagram is similar to a **data flow diagram** used in structured analysis in that each diagram includes external agents (external objects) and flows of information. A message flow diagram depicts information (object messages) flowing between active objects rather than processes. It usually displays data stores (if at all) only within the context of a class that encapsulates the data structure depicted by the **data store**. Rumbaugh's object-oriented methodology uses data stores on **data flow diagrams**.

Method. A method contains the control and procedural information required to perform transformations on **objects** or to retrieve information from objects. Methods are also called **operations**.

Method Implementation. The actual definition of a **method** and how it works. In C++, a method is declared within a class definition, but the implementation may either appear after the method definition or later on in a program file.

Methodology. A set of activities that describe the steps to take, information required and project deliverables required to facilitate the orderly production of information systems.

Model. A system documentation component can said to be a model of a system if it can be used to answer a well-defined set of questions about the system to a degree useful for a stated purpose. For instance, an analysis model can answer questions about what a system must do for users of the system in functional terms; a design model describes how analysis model functions are to be implemented using a particular technology.

Multiple Inheritance. This is the term that describes a situation when there is more than one **superclass** from which a **class** can inherit some of its properties. Modeling systems using multiple inheritance can more closely reflect class associations in the real world, but implementing such models can be difficult.

Object. An object is a conceptual representation of a real-world thing, concept or event about which information must be stored. Each object has sets of attributes that describe the object, a set of defined operations that cause transformations to be performed on the object or to have information retrieved from it and a private data structure that represents the organization of information stored about the object. An object type (category of objects) is usually referred to as a **class**, while an instance of an object type (an object itself) is usually referred to as an **instance** of a class.

Object Behavior. A set of actions (**operations**) that an object can perform on its attributes and in collaboration with other objects.

Object Interaction Model. A model that describes how objects interact with each other via messages. An object message diagram, similar to a data flow diagram, is used to graphically depict the interactions between objects.

Object-Oriented Database Management System. A database management system that implements objects directly, in contrast to relational, network or hierarchical database management systems. An object-oriented database contains not only data structures but also procedures that act upon those structures. Some relational database management systems do implement some procedures in a database via rules and triggers, but an object database contains methods—complete, perhaps very complex, procedures along with data structures. In pure object-oriented database management systems, the only way to access database data structures is through methods.

Object-Oriented Development. An approach to systems development in which each component represents an object in the real world. These objects are encapsulated with attributes that describe the objects, plus the possible actions that can be taken upon the object and its attributes. Objects may be grouped together into classes (see **object** and **class**). Object-oriented development refers to the overall system development process. See **object-oriented programming** for a discussion of the actual building of such systems from design specifications.

Object-Oriented Programming. A type of programming that involves four characteristics of objects: **encapsulation**, hierarchical object structures, **polymorphism** and messaging between **objects**.

Object Structure. The way that object data structures are connected to each other. Described in an **object structure model** and depicted on an **object structure diagram,** these data structures can be composed of other structures and can depict generalization/specialization, aggregation and other types of structural associations between object data structures. Each class's object data structure contains **attributes** (unless the object class is an **abstract class**).

Object Structure Diagram. A diagram that graphically depicts the structural connections between object classes. Similar to an entity-relationship diagram, an object structure diagram may show object hierarchies: generalization/specialization (classification) and aggregation (composition or whole/part).

Object Structure Model. A data model that defines data components of classes and their subclasses and/or component classes. Classes may be connected to each other on an object structure diagram using association lines. Each object data structure contains **attributes**.

Object Type. An object class, a group of similar objects. Object type (class) customer could represent such objects as AT&T, IBM, DEC, etc. The objects are instances of an object type (class).

Operation. A business or system activity or task that will be implemented by one or more object classes. Each operation may consist of other operations. In design models, operations are specified as object methods, each of which is built using a **method implementation**.

Optionality. Defines the minimum number of **instances** (occurrences) of one **object** (entity) that can exist for one instance (occurrence) of another object (entity). Contrast with **cardinality**, which defines a constraint on an association between objects (a relationship between entities) that limits the maximum number of instances (occurrences) of one object (entity) that can exist for one instance (occurrence) of another object (entity).

Partitioning. The process of subdividing a problem or system into constituent components. This often involves combining things into larger things as well as dividing larger things into smaller things.

Planning Phase. The first phase of James Martin's information engineering methodology. This phase consists of high-level study of an enterprise, or significant part of one, to define organization structure, mission, goals, strategies, critical success factors, critical assumptions, functions, processes, subject areas, data collections, entities and relationships between entities. With an object-oriented approach, subject areas become high-level classes and entities become lower-level classes. Lower-level processes become operations on **objects**.

Polymorphism. The ability of an **object** to send the same generic message to many other objects. Each target object implements the generic message in a different way. An example might be a print message sent from an application to many different target file objects, each of which implements the print message differently depending on the physical characteristics of the data contained within the target object.

Primitive Object. A primitive object is one that has no instance variables, only a value. Integer or character or string constants are primitive objects in object-oriented programming languages.

Process. A business activity that appears on data flow diagrams to indicate some transformation of data flowing through a system.

Process Decomposition Diagram. A chart that depicts the breakdown structure of a high-level process into its component parts. The parent process is more general and is completely described by all of its components, which are smaller in scope but much more detailed.

Prototype. A partial implementation of a system (often just an abstract mock-up), built to facilitate a greater understanding of a problem or its solution. Typically, a prototype of an information system simulates the main user interfaces such as menus, screens and reports. See also **evolutionary prototype** and **throwaway prototype**.

Reengineering. The process of extracting data and business processing rules from a system (reverse engineering), redefining data and processing rules (redesign) and implementing the changes in a new version of the system (forward engineering). In this sense, we speak of systems reengineering. In actuality, reengineering can be conducted on **objects** across a system life cycle, from enterprise planning models to analysis business models to business system design models to technical systems design models to the systems objects themselves. At the business planning and analysis levels, we often refer to reengineering as business process reengineering or **business process redesign**.

Relationship. An **association** between **entities** in a business data model. For instance, customer places an order. Customer and order are the entities and "places" is the relationship. **Optionality** and **cardinality** constraints may exist on the relationship to define how many occurrences of one entity exist for each occurrence of another entity. An entity-relationship diagram is used to graphically depict such associations between entities.

Responsibility. In a **model** of interacting objects, a responsibility defines a message that an **object** will respond to and act upon (using a method and its implementation). In a client/server relationship, the **client** object requests a service from the **server** object. The requested service is the responsibility of the server object.

Reuse Library. A store of tested components that can be reused across multiple information systems. With an object-oriented environment, the reuse library will contain classes, so the library is often called a class library.

Server. An object that fulfills a request for service from a client object. When a **client** sends a message to the server requesting the service, the server object interprets the message to see if the server object has defined for it any methods that support the responsibility defined in the request message. If yes, the server object (perhaps in collaboration with some of its own server objects) searches for the implementation of the method defined in the request message and proceeds to service that request.

State. A particular value that an object's attributes can be in (status values). A customer order is first created, then perhaps modified in some way, is filled, is shipped and finally is closed and archived. Each of these steps represents a state that the customer order can be in at any point in time. The changes from one state to another are referred to as **transitions**, implemented by object operations and their associated methods.

State Transition Diagram. A diagram that depicts object states and the transitions between states. As a customer order goes through various states from creation to modification to termination, it goes through various transitions. This set of states and transitions may be drawn using a set of parallel lines (a fence diagram) or using a set of bubbles or boxes connected by curves or lines (a network diagram).

Structure Chart. A diagram used in systems design for the design and architecture of executable modules of an information system, including modules and the calling sequences and parameters passed between modules.

Subclass. This refers to the child in a parent-child relationship in a **class hierarchy**. The subclass represents a type of the parent and depicts the more specialized characteristics. The **superclass** represents the more general characteristics of the overall class. The relationship between the superclass and its subclasses is called a generalization/specialization relationship.

Subject Area. A collection of related **classes** (or entities) representing a higher-level class. Person might be a subject area that contains employee (and its various types), supplier (and its types), customer and so on.

Subsystem. A collection of system objects that are packaged together for implementing part of a system. Usually, the objects within a subsystem have some logical connection to each other, so that the components of a subsystem are cohesive, but different subsystems are not. Subsystems should be loosely coupled to other subsystems.

Superclass. This refers to the parent in a parent-child relationship in a **class hierarchy**. The superclass contains more general information, while the **subclass** contains the specialized characteristics. The relationship between the superclass and its subclasses is called a generalization/specialization relationship.

System Development Life Cycle. A series of states of activity from the concept of a system through development, deployment, maintenance and evolution and ending when the system is permanently taken out of service. The information engineering approach to the system development life cycle begins before an actual system is conceived but rather models of the business enterprise itself are constructed. This **planning phase** proceeds on to detailed business modeling and systems requirements documentation in the **analysis phase**. The **design phase** specifies how analysis functional requirements are to be generally implemented in an information system, while the **construction phase** defines specifically how the designs are to be actually implemented in a particular technology. Construction is followed by **evolution** of the system into newer version of the original system.

System Event. Something of significance that occurs, requiring some response on the part of a system. Contrast with a **business event**, which is a similar but higher-level concept that is modeled in analysis.

System Testing. The stage of system development that immediately follows integration testing. During system testing, fully integrated system components are checked to see if they meet all system requirements.

Test Case. In an object-oriented system, a series of messages to send, along with the expected results. Execution of a test case often involves the logging of execution results.

Testing. The point in system development that includes at least three distinct states: unit testing, integration testing, and system testing. When systems are extremely complex, testing may also include system integration testing.

Throwaway Prototype. A mock-up of a system or part of a system that is built to discover more about a problem or solution. A throwaway prototype is intended to be discarded after the discovery process has been completed. Contrast with an **evolutionary prototype**.

Transition. A change from one object state to another, implemented by an operation and its associated methods. States and transitions between them are depicted on a **state transition diagram**.

Trigger. An **association** between a cause and effect whereby a system responds to events and determines which operations to perform in the response. See also **business event** and **system event**.

Unit Testing. The stage of system development immediately after coding, during which system components are checked in isolation from other system components to see if these components meet the specifications defined in design.

Validation. The process of checking the results at each stage of system development to ensure that the results correctly follow the previous stage.

Verification. The process of checking system development deliverables (especially in design and construction), to ensure that the final product matches system plans, requirements and specifications.

Vertical Object Partitioning. Within a system of distributed objects, it can be helpful to split object data structures along attribute lines. By including attribute types in one object fragment and other attribute types in one or more other object fragments, an object data structure can be split vertically for distribution purposes.

Bibliography

Andrews, Timothy A. "ONTOS DB: An ODBMS for Distributed AIX Applications." *AIXpert* (May 1992), pp. 59–62.

Atre, Shaku. *Distributed Databases, Cooperative Processing and Networking.* New York: McGraw-Hill, 1992.

Banerjee, J., and H. Chou. "Data Model Issues for Object-Oriented Applications." *ACM Transactions on Office Information Systems* (January 1987).

Barry, Douglas. "When to Use Object DBMSs." *Computerworld* (October 26, 1992), p. 122.

———"ITASCA Distributed ODBMS." *AIXpert* (May 1992), pp. 63–67.

Blaha, Michael R., William J. Permerlani and James E. Rumbaugh. "Relational Database Design Using an Object-Oriented Methodology." *Communications of the ACM* (April 1988), pp. 414–427.

Boar, Bernard H. *Implementing Client/Server Computing: A Strategic Perspective.* New York: McGraw-Hill, 1993.

Booch, Grady. *Object-Oriented Design with Applications.* Redwood City, CA: Benjamin/Cummings, 1991.

Bozman, Jean S. "A New Approach to Data Management Catches on." *Computerworld* (October 26, 1992), p. 28.

——— "Wrapping Code Can Save Time." *Computerworld* (November 30, 1992), p. 73.

Branson, Michael, Eric Herness and Eric Jenney. "Moving Structured Projects to Object Orientation." In *AD/Cycle International Users Group Second Annual Conference*, October 1991, pp. 151–170.

Brodie, Michael L. "On the Design and Specification of Database Transactions." In *On Conceptual Modeling: Perspectives from Artificial Intelligence, Databases and Programming Languages*, edited by Michael L. Brodie, John Mylopoulos and Joachim W. Schmidt. New York: Springer-Verlag, 1984, pp. 277–306.

Brown, Alan W. *Object-Oriented Databases: Applications in Software Engineering.* London: McGraw-Hill, 1991.

——"From Semantic Data Models to Object Orientation in Design Databases." *Information and Software Technology* (January/ February-1989).

Coad, Peter, and Edward Yourdon. *Object-Oriented Analysis,* 2nd ed. Englewood Cliffs, NJ: Yourdon Press, Prentice Hall, 1991.

—— *Object-Oriented Design.* Englewood Cliffs, NJ: Yourdon Press, Prentice Hall, 1991.

Codd, E. F. *The Relational Model for Database Management.* Reading, MA: Addison-Wesley, 1990.

Date, C. J. *An Introduction to Database Systems,* 5th ed. Reading, MA: Addison Wesley, 1990.

Dittrich, Klaus R. "Object-Oriented Database Systems: The Notion and the Issues (Extended Extract)." In *International Workshop on Object-Oriented Database Systems*, September 1986, edited by Klaus R. Dittrich and Umeshwar Dayal. New York: IEEE Computer Society Press.

Embley, David W., Barry D. Kurtz and Scott N. Woodfield, *Object-Oriented Systems Analysis: A Model-Driven Approach.* Englewood Cliffs, New Jersey: Yourdon Press, Prentice Hall, 1992.

Finkelstein, Clive. *An Introduction to Information Engineering: from Strategic Planning to Information Systems.* Reading, MA: Addison-Wesley, 1989.

Fleming, Candace C., and Barbara von Halle. *Handbook of Relational Database Design.* Reading, MA: Addison-Wesley, 1989.

Freytag, Johann Christoph, Rainer Manthey and Mark Wallace. "Mapping Object-Oriented Concepts into Relational Concepts by Meta-Compilation in a Logic Programming Environment." In *Advances in Object-Oriented Database Systems.* New York: Springer-Verlag, 1988, pp. 204–208.

Hammer, Michael. "Reengineering Work: Don't Automate, Obliterate." *Harvard Business Review* (July/August 1990), pp. 104–112.

Herness, Eric N. "Object-Oriented Analysis and Design." *AIXpert* (May 1992), pp. 40–44.

IBM Corporation. *Cooperative Processing in an Object-Oriented Environment.* Research Triangle Park, NC: IBM Corporation, 1991.

Inmon, William H. *Advanced Topics in Information Engineering.* Wellesley, MA: QED, 1989.

King, R. "My Cat Is Object-Oriented." In *Object-Oriented Concepts, Databases and Applications,* edited by W. Kim and F. H. Lochovsky. New York: ACM Press, 1989.

Klein, H. K., and R. A. Hirschheim. "A Comparative Framework of Data Modeling Paradigms and Approaches." *The Computer Journal,* vol. 30, no. 1 (1987), pp. 8–15.

Korth, Henry F. "Extending the Scope of Relational Languages." *IEEE Software* (January 1986), pp. 19–28.

Kuspert, K., P. Dadam and J. Gunauer. "Cooperative Object Buffer Management in the Advanced Information Management Prototype." In *Proceedings of the 13th International Conference on Very Large Databases,* edited by P. M. Stocker, W. Kent and P. Hammersley, 1987.

Laenens, Els, and Dirk Vermeir. "A Language for Object-Oriented Database Programming." *Journal of Object-Oriented Programming* (January/February 1989), pp. 18–27.

Landis, Gordon. "Overview of the ObjectStore ODBMS." *AIXpert* (May 1992), pp. 68–72.

Loomis, Mary E. S. "The VERSANT ODBMS." *AIXpert* (May 1992), pp. 73–76.

Lorenz, Mark. *Object-Oriented Software Development: A Practical Guide.* Englewood Cliffs, NJ: Prentice Hall, 1993.

March, Steven G. *An Object-Oriented Analysis Method for Ada and Embedded Systems.* Wright-Patterson Air Force Base, OH: Air Force Institute of Technology, 1989.

Martin, James. *Information Engineering,* 3 vols. Englewood Cliffs, NJ: Prentice Hall, 1990.

———*Strategic Information Planning Methodologies.* Englewood Cliffs, NJ: Prentice Hall, 1989.

Martin, James, and Carma McClure. *Structured Techniques: The Basis for CASE.* Englewood Cliffs, NJ: Prentice Hall, 1988.

Martin, James, and James J. Odell. *Object-Oriented Analysis and Design.* Englewood Cliffs, NJ: Prentice Hall, 1992.

McLeod, Dennis. "A Learning-Based Approach to Meta-Data Evolution in an Object-Oriented Database." In *Advances in Object-Oriented Database Systems.* New York: Springer-Verlag, 1988, pp. 219–224.

Meyer, Bertrand. *Object-Oriented Software Construction.* Hertfordshire, England: Prentice-Hall International, 1988.

Montgomery, Stephen L. *AD/Cycle: IBM's Framework for Application Development and CASE.* New York: Van Nostrand Reinhold, 1991.

———— "Object Orientation and AD/Cycle Tools." In *AD/Cycle International Users Group Second Annual Conference,* October 1991.

———— "Object-Oriented Modeling of Client-Server Systems." In *AD/Cycle International Users Group Third Annual Conference,* October 1992.

———— *Relational Database Design and Implementation Using DB2.* New York: Van Nostrand Reinhold, 1990.

———— "Relational Database Design Using Object-Oriented Methodologies." In *International DB2 User Group Annual Conference,* August 1989.

Mylopoulos, John, and Hector J. Levesque. "An Overview of Knowledge Representation." In *On Conceptual Modeling: Perspectives from Artificial Intelligence, Databases and Programming Languages,* edited by Michael L. Brodie, John Mylopoulos and Joachim W. Schmidt. New York: Springer-Verlag, 1984, pp. 3–17.

Orfali, Robert, and Dan Harkey. *Client-Server Programming with OS/2, Extended Edition.* New York: Van Nostrand Reinhold, 1991.

Otis, Allen, and Jacob Stein. "The GemStone Object Database Management System." *AIXpert* (May 1992), pp. 54–58.

Pace, Brenda. "Object-Oriented Programming Begins to Move." *Business Software Review* (May 1988), pp. 20–23.

Parsave, Kamran, Mark Chignell, Setrag Khoshafian and Harry Wong. *Intelligent Databases: Object-Oriented, Deductive Hypermedia Technologies.* New York: John Wiley & Sons, 1989.

Pressman, Roger S. *Software Engineering.* New York: McGraw-Hill, 1987.

Rumbaugh, James, Michael Blaha, William Premerlani, Frederick Eddy and William Lorensen. *Object-Oriented Modeling and Design.* Englewood Cliffs, NJ: Prentice Hall, 1991.

Schlaer, Sally, and Stephen J. Mellor. *Object-Oriented Systems Analysis: Modeling the World in Data.* Englewood Cliffs, NJ: Yourdon Press, Prentice Hall, 1988.

Seidewitz, E. and Stark, M. *General Object-Oriented Software Development,* Report SEL-86-002. Greenbelt, MD: NASA Goddard Space Flight Center, 1986.

Smith, Patrick. *Client/Server Computing.* Carmel, IN: Sams Publishing, 1992.

STRADIS Systems Development Methodology. Marietta, GA: Structured Solutions, Inc.

Taylor, David. *Object-Oriented Technology: A Manager's Guide.* Reading, MA: Addison-Wesley, 1992.

Teorey, Toby J., Dongqing Yang and James P. Fry. "A Logical Design Methodology for Relational Databases Using the Extended Entity-Relationship Model." *Computing Surveys* (June 1986), pp. 197–222.

Vardi, Moshe Y. "The Universal-Relation Data Model for Logical Independence." *IEEE Software* (March 1988), pp. 80–85.

Vianu, Victor. "A Dynamic Framework for Object Projection Views." *ACM Transactions on Database Systems* (March 1988), pp. 1–22.

Ward, Paul T., and Stephen J. Mellor. *Structred Development for Real-Time Systems,* 3 vols. Englewood Cliffs, NJ: Yourdon Press, Prentice Hall, 1985.

Wirfs-Brock, Rebecca, Brian Wilkerson and Lauren Wiener. *Designing Object-Oriented Software.* Englewood Cliffs, NJ: Prentice Hall, 1990.

Yourdon, Edward. *Decline and Fall of the American Programmer.* Englewood Cliffs, NJ: Yourdon Press, Prentice Hall, 1992.

——— *Modern Structured Analysis.* Englewood Cliffs, NJ: Yourdon Press, Prentice Hall, 1989.

Zachman, John A. "A Framework for Information Systems Architecture" *IBM Systems Journal,* vol. 26, no. 3.

Index